EDUCATIONAL PSYCHOLOGY

the text of this book is printed on 100% recycled paper

The Authors

Dr. Rudolf Pintner was a pioneer in the field of intelligence testing. He served for many years as Professor of Educational Psychology at Columbia University. He was the author of notable works, including *Intelligence Testing, Educational Psychology,* and *Psychology of the Physically Handicapped.*

Dr. John J. Ryan was formerly Associate Professor of Education at Hunter College.

Dr. Paul V. West is Professor of Education, Emeritus, at New York University. He is the author of numerous books and articles relating to educational psychology.

Dr. Lester D. Crow is Professor of Education, Emeritus, at Brooklyn College. He is the author of many books on education, psychology, and guidance.

Dr. Adolph W. Aleck was formerly Professor of Psychology at Mississippi State University.

Dr. Samuel Smith was formerly Editor-in-Chief of Barnes & Noble, Inc. He is the author of *Best Methods of Study* and *Read It Right* and co-author of numerous tests and educational textbooks.

College Outline Series

EDUCATIONAL PSYCHOLOGY

SIXTH EDITION

Rudolf Pintner
John J. Ryan
Paul V. West
Adolph W. Aleck
Lester D. Crow
Samuel Smith

BARNES & NOBLE BOOKS
A DIVISION OF HARPER & ROW, PUBLISHERS
New York, Evanston, San Francisco, London

©

Copyright 1934, 1935, 1938, 1941, 1951, 1956, 1970
by BARNES & NOBLE, INC.
Copyright Renewed, 1962, 1963, 1966, 1969
Sixth Edition, 1970

All rights reserved. No part of this book may be reproduced or utilized in any form or by any means, electronic or mechanical, including photocopying or recording, or by any information storage and retrieval system, without permission in writing from the publisher.

L. C. catalogue card number: 73-101209

SBN 389 00102 3

MANUFACTURED IN THE UNITED STATES OF AMERICA

Preface to the Sixth Edition

This outline presents the essentials of educational psychology from the diversified views of various schools of thought. It summarizes the main points elaborated in numerous leading textbooks. In this edition, the several contributors have brought their sections up to date in accordance with recent developments in the field. The editor is grateful to the heirs of the late Dr. Rudolf Pintner for permission to make minor revisions in his chapters.

This edition of the outline thus comprises a bird's eye view of contemporary psychological knowledge applicable to teaching and learning situations. A bibliography of selected references for each chapter is included at the end of the book to enable the reader to consult recent literature on each of the topics.

The following companion books published by Barnes & Noble, Inc. are recommended as valuable aids for students of educational psychology.

Abnormal Psychology
Child Psychology
General Psychology
Readings in General Psychology
Best Methods of Study
Biology
History of Western Education
How to Improve Your Memory
Principles of Sociology

The authors and editor are indebted especially to Joan Smyth of the Editorial Department of Barnes & Noble, Inc., for her expert guidance and assistance in the preparation of this edition.

Samuel Smith

Contents

PAGE

INTRODUCTION: THE SCIENCE OF EDUCATIONAL PSYCHOLOGY   1
by Samuel Smith

PART ONE: HUMAN EQUIPMENT AND BEHAVIOR
by Rudolf Pintner

1. Heredity and Environment 21
2. Physical Structure 31
3. Human Growth and Development 45
4. Behavior Processes 57

PART TWO: THE LEARNING PROCESS
by John J. Ryan

5. Nature and Scope of the Learning Process 71
6. Factors that Condition Learning 83
7. Laws and Theories of Learning 101
8. Transfer of Training: Subject Matter 117

PART THREE: TESTS AND MEASUREMENTS
by Paul V. West

9. Measurement—Basic Definitions and Principles 141
10. Applications of Measurement 162
11. Elements of Statistical Techniques 181

PART FOUR: MENTAL HEALTH AND CHARACTER EDUCATION
by Adolph W. Aleck

12. Mental Health 227
13. Psychology of Character 235

PART FIVE: THE PSYCHOLOGY OF SCHOOL SUBJECTS

by Lester D. Crow

14	Psychology of Elementary School Subjects	243
15	Psychology of Subject Areas in the Secondary School	268
	Bibliography	291
	Index	303

INTRODUCTION
The Science of Educational Psychology
by Samuel Smith

Introduction
The Science of Educational Psychology

Educational psychology is the modern science which applies the findings of psychology to the learning and growth of human beings. The problems with which this science is concerned have a very long history in Western cultures, for even the most ancient societies were confronted with the necessity for educating the young. The earliest communities adhered to their own philosophy of life which inevitably influenced methods of education, and some of their ideas about children and learning have persisted through the centuries down to our time. Education, as an integral part of the culture of each society, has always been shaped by existing social institutions, traditions, and customs which it has, in turn, helped to preserve and transmit to our own civilization. Some of the most potent ideas which have been inherited from the past are still reflected in educational practices today. It is therefore imperative for the teacher to bear in mind the cultural backgrounds of modern education as he endeavors to stimulate the interests and guide the efforts of children.

The cultural foundations of the Western world can be traced back to ancient Babylonian, Egyptian, Hebrew, Persian, Greek, and Roman origins. In the earliest primitive societies, man's thinking about nature was restricted to uncritical traditions and superstitions. Animism attributed natural events to spirits, or souls, presumed to exist within both inanimate objects and living things. The worship of fertility gods prevailed for thousands of years. Next came the polytheistic beliefs of the Babylonians and Egyptians, the ethical monotheism of the Hebrew prophets, and, in the sixth century B.C., Persian Zoroastrianism. The latter religion, which divided the universe into good and evil elements, had considerable influence on the tenets of Judaism and Christianity. The Greeks and Romans, however, maintained their polytheistic interpretations of nature until the triumph of Christianity in the fourth century of the Christian era.

The Greek sages of ancient times, beginning with Thales of Miletus (640–546 B.C.), rejected the animistic beliefs of primitive man in supernatural forces and developed systematic philosophy as a nonreligious type of orderly reasoning or speculation. Thales believed that the entire universe consists of water in its different states of liquid, solid, and gas. Empedocles (495–435 B.C.) held that the world consists of four elements: fire, air, water, and earth. Other Greek philosophers speculated about man's nature and his relationship to the universe. Hippocrates (460?–?377 B.C.), Father of Medicine, incorrectly postulated four humors of the body to explain the temperament of the individual. Socrates (470–399 B.C.) held that knowledge acquired through discussion would discipline the mind and reveal universal truths. Leucippus (5th century B.C.) and Democritus (460–370 B.C.), both of Abdera, outlined rudimentary theories of atomic structure and biological evolution. Plato (427–347 B.C.) formulated a dualistic theory which separated the body (material things) from the mind (ideas) and stated that education transmitting knowledge of ideas would prepare every individual for his proper role in society.

Development of Scientific Method

Although the earliest Greek philosophers developed educational theories consistent with their philosophical views, there could be no systematic science of educational psychology until new, scientific methods of inquiry came into being. A great philosopher, such as Plato, could advocate educational procedures based on logical metaphysical theories, but a new approach to the discovery of truth was necessary before psychology or any of the other sciences could be developed. Educational psychology did not emerge full-blown in the nineteenth century; its roots are to be found in the application of a new point of view during the fourth century B.C. which eventually captured the loyalty and transformed the intellectual, cultural, and social life of mankind.

A definitely scientific point of view may be traced back as far as Aristotle (384–322 B.C.), who utilized both the deductive method characteristic of his system of logic and the inductive method applied in his biological observations, experiments, and hypotheses. Unfortunately, for centuries afterward his conclusions were accepted as final, authoritative, and irrefutable; the fact was ignored that Aristotle himself believed in and to some extent practiced the scientific procedures of observation and experimentation.

Although Aristotle's deductive ideas were adopted universally in the Christian world, very few scholars attempted to revive his advocacy of the inductive method. Saint Augustine (A.D. 354–430) used introspection to report the facts of his own mental experiences and espoused the theory of mental faculties. Saint Thomas Aquinas (1225–1274) made a sharp distinction between religious truths (based on divine authority) and scientific truths (based on research and experimentation). Early in the sixteenth century, Juan Luis Vives (1492–1540) insisted on inductive methods in philosophy and psychology, outlining plans for educational experiments and the observation of child behavior. Nevertheless, throughout the Middle Ages and in early modern times, the main emphasis in education and literature remained theological and theoretical.

Scientists and philosophers who built the foundations of modern science included Copernicus (1473–1543), Francis Bacon (1561–1626), Galileo (1564–1642), Descartes (1596–1650), Locke (1632–1704), Newton (1642–1727), Comte (1798–1857), and Darwin (1809–1882). These men reverted to Aristotle's inductive method, demanded experimental proofs, and insisted on empirical evidence to justify generalizations about man and nature. Observation and experimentation disclosed facts contradicting

Aristotelian assumptions (as, for instance, his misconception, corrected by Copernicus and Galileo, that the earth is the center of the universe) which had become gospel among medieval scholars.

Bacon, Descartes, and Locke were effective propagandists for a new faith in knowledge based on sense perception and logical reasoning. Scientific theories changed rapidly with the development of inventions such as the microscope ($c.$ 1590), the thermometer ($c.$ 1593), the telescope (1608), and the barometer (1643), and with the subsequent flow of unexpected discoveries. Every field of knowledge flourished. During the seventeenth century, Harvey, Hooke, Leeuwenhoek, and Redi revolutionized biology. Boyle, Stahl, and Boerhaave disproved the theory of the four elements (which had been espoused in ancient times by Empedocles) and thus made possible the eventual development of organic chemistry. During the eighteenth century Lavoisier founded modern quantitative chemistry; Hutton established the scientific approach as the basis of modern geology; continuing the work begun by Galileo and Kepler in the seventeenth century, Newton, Bradley, Laplace, and Herschel transformed the concepts of astronomy; and Lamarck announced the principle of organic evolution which Darwin was shortly to modify and explain by means of ample evidence. New discoveries and hypotheses multiplied. Extraordinary novel approaches were developed in the twentieth century, such as the quantum and relativity theories which ushered in our Atomic and Space Age. Only the scientific methods of analysis and prediction of events have remained constant, requiring unbiased observation and experimentation, logical reasoning (inductions, hypotheses, comparisons, deductions), measurement, and classification of experience.

History of Educational Psychology

During the nineteenth century, educational psychology remained a theoretical discipline dominated by Cartesian dualism (which divided the universe into matter and mind), Locke's principles of learning through sense perception and association of ideas, and the faculty theory of human intellect. The faculty theory, which had been espoused in a simple form by Saint Augustine, divided the mind into distinct powers or faculties, each of which could, it was assumed, be developed independently through exercise and discipline. Educational practice emphasized memorization, compulsion of body and mind (including physical control and corporal punishment), and the formalized manipulation of concepts to prepare children for the anticipated duties of adulthood. However, social changes, reflected in the revolutionary, negative, naturalistic ideas of Rousseau (1712–1778), who advocated individual freedom, self-expression, and learning through experience, paved the way for more positive and constructive reformers such as Johann Heinrich Pestalozzi (1746–1827), Johann Friedrich Herbart (1776–1841), and Friedrich Froebel (1782–1852). Pestalozzi advocated education through sense perception, reasoning, and the use of real objects. Herbart contributed five formal steps of learning: (1) preparation, (2) presentation, (3) comparison or association of new with old ideas, (4) organization or generalization, and (5) application. The first and fourth steps, though more artificial, resemble contemporary concepts of readiness (or experiential background) and generalization. Froebel demanded that education be adapted to the psychophysical needs and social nature of the child. The followers of Herbart became most influential, winning popular acceptance of two main principles: intellectual development through combinations of ideas, and character development through acquisition of ethical ideals. Herbartianism introduced a new formalism but, in so doing, stimulated objective investigation of mental functions. In England, James Mill (1773–1836) interpreted mental behavior as the chemistry of ideas, an associationist doctrine which his son, John Stuart Mill (1806–1873), and other English philosophers ably defended.

Simultaneously with the work of these philosophers, numerous biologists, physiologists, and physicists initiated the modern science of psychology. In 1826 Johannes Müller (1801–1858) expounded his Doctrine of Specific Nerve Energies, which stated that a variety of stimuli may cause the same nerve response. In 1834 Ernst H. Weber (1795–1878) investigated the relationships between stimuli and receptors, especially the increased energy required for an individual to judge the difference between two stimuli. Hermann von Helmholtz (1821–1894) measured the rate of nerve action and analyzed vision and hearing experimentally, with astonishingly accurate conclusions on these sensory processes. Gustav T. Fechner (1801–1887) discovered new techniques for measuring sensations, deducing from Weber's law a new principle that the intensity of a sensation varies with the logarithm of the stimulus. Edouard Seguin (1812–1880) devised methods of diagnosis and instruction of mentally retarded children.

Shortly after the mid-point of the nineteenth century came the revolutionary influence of Darwin, who, in 1859, supported the doctrine of evolution by means of abundant evidence, leading to significant researches in animal psychology and human heredity. In 1869 Francis Galton (1822–1911) set forth his famous studies on the inheritance of genius. He completed numerous investigations of mental imagery and individual differences. There followed the experiments of Wilhelm Wundt (1832–1920), who contributed many psychological findings applicable to education. Wundt's laboratory of experimental psychology (established in 1879 in Leipzig) inspired a long list of pioneering students, including G. Stanley Hall (1844–1924), who arrived at useful principles governing the stages of human growth and thus gave impetus to the child study movement. Hall also devised a questionnaire method of investigation. Testifying to the new faith in science, Herbert Spencer (1820–1903), Thomas H. Huxley (1825–1895), and Charles W. Eliot (1834–1926) became foremost exponents of science studies in the field of formal education.

The American physicist-philosopher Charles Sanders Peirce (1839–1914) founded pragmatic philosophy based on the premise that if an idea or theory works in practice, it must be accepted as true. Conversely, as William Ernest Hocking (1873–1966) pointed out, the pragmatic view is that if an idea or theory does not work in practice, it cannot be true. (Teachers have accepted many of the tenets of the pragmatists, although with some qualifications, realizing that an apparently successful idea or theory may work well for a time, only to be proved to have a merely temporary value.) Peirce's followers William James (1842–1910) and John Dewey (1859–1952) demanded strictly practical, instrumental, and scientific analyses in psychology. James adapted experimental methods to the problems of emotional, intellectual, and moral development. He completed significant studies on memory, the transfer of training, and emotional reactions, and he attributed emotions to the awareness of bodily changes. Dewey synthesized many of the ideas of Rousseau, Pestalozzi, Herbart, and Froebel, advocating particularly the project and problem methods of learning through individual and group activities. His views also stimulated hundreds of experimental researches on methods of thinking and problem solving. James, Dewey, and James R. Angell (1869–1949) advocated functionalism (study of the organism as an active, purposive whole) as contrasted with the structuralism (analysis of consciousness through introspection) represented by another of Wundt's students, Edward B. Titchener (1867–1927). Angell made special contributions to the study of auditory localization and reaction times.

Toward the end of the nineteenth century, the work of James McKeen Cattell (1860–1944) and Livingston Farrand (1867–1939) at Columbia College speeded the tests and measurements movement. These psychologists used objective tests to measure individual differences among students. Hermann Ebbinghaus (1850–1909) used a similar approach in studying memory and devised the first completion test. Ernst Meumann (1862–1915) applied Wundt's experimental techniques and the new testing procedures to the study of learning and teaching methods. (The eminent teacher of experimental education, Paul R. Radosavljevich, who later added new experimental findings to Ebbinghaus's data, was Meumann's research associate.) In 1905 Alfred Binet and Theodore Simon constructed a test in point-scale form to measure individual intelligence. Their test was intended for subnormal children but was found useful for measuring intelligence of normal children as well. Widespread interest in mental retardation was reflected in the work of Emil Kraepelin (1856–1926) who pioneered in the study of mental illness, fatigue, and the psychological influence of drugs—dominant topics of investigation today; and in the researches of Pierre Janet (1859–1947) on the diagnosis and treatment of psychoneuroses. Karl Pearson (1857–1936) developed correlation techniques for use in the study of individual and group differences. In 1909 Edward L. Thorndike (1874–1949) devised a handwriting scale. The field of testing grew rapidly; standardized tests of intelligence, aptitudes, and achievement became popular tools in education.

Thorndike, who did not adhere to any one school of psychology, studied animal behavior and human learning. As early as the 1890's he completed some of the first experiments (using cats that learned to open the bolted doors of boxes) to investigate the learning process in animals. He formulated suggestive laws of learning: the laws of readiness, exercise, and effect and, later, a theory of "belongingness" which was reminiscent of associationist psychology.

The main trends in educational psychology during the first half of the twentieth century may be indicated by reference to a few representative investigators and theorists. W. B. Cannon (1871–1945) studied emotional behavior, especially the relation between emotions and the adrenal glands. John B. Watson (1878–1958) investigated animal psychology, particularly maze learning, described the emotional reactions of infants, and was a leader in the behavioristic school of psychology. He was influenced by the researches of Ivan P. Pavlov (1849–1936) on the conditioned responses of dogs and the use of conditioning to induce frustration and neuroses in animals. Max Wertheimer (1880–1943) experimented on the integrated perception of movement and in 1912 led in the formation of the Gestalt school. Kurt Koffka (1886–1941), Wolfgang Köhler (1887–1967), and Kurt Lewin (1890–1947) developed Gestalt theories in considerable detail. Koffka and Köhler analyzed visual perception and the intelligence of apes. Lewin studied child personality as a whole and the development of inner conflicts and frustration. Alfred Adler (1870–1937) postulated a will-to-power as the driving force of human behavior, assuming that frustration of this force causes an inferiority complex. Carl Gustav Jung (1875–1961) set forth a similar principle, the will-to-live. He advocated the treatment of neuroses by analysis of the individual's immediate environment and needed adjustments to that environment. For this purpose he devised a free association test. Sigmund Freud (1856–1939), on the other hand, who founded psychoanalysis, stressed sexual desire, repression of such desire, and repressed past experiences as the factors responsible for abnormal behavior. According to Freud, the individual's motives must be redirected and free self-expression encouraged. William McDougall (1871–1938) founded the hormic school, based on the purposive character of organic behavior. His studies of group life stimulated development of the field of social psychology.

Other significant contributions to psychology and education include the studies of Charles S. Sherrington (1861–1952) on the functions of the neuron; Edwin G. Boring (1886–   ) on sensations and space perception; Leonard T. Troland (1889–1932) on the psychology of vision; Karl S. Lashley (1890–1958) on the motor areas and integrated functions of the brain as a whole; Charles H. Judd (1873–1946) on the transfer of training; John A. McGeoch, Willard L. Valentine, Leonard Carmichael, and B. F. Skinner on animal behavior and motivation; Herbert H. Woodrow on rhythm, retention, and transfer of training; W. S. Hunter, J. P. Guilford, E. R. Guthrie, and B. F. Skinner on learning and conditioning; N. R. F. Maier on problem solving by animals and man; Floyd H. Allport, Gordon W. Allport, Robert G. Bernreuter, L. E. Cole, Arthur I. Gates, Frederick Kuhlmann, Carl Seashore, Rudolf Pintner, Charles Spearman, William Stern, Lewis Terman, L. L. Thurstone, and Robert M. Yerkes in the field of tests and measurements; and Adelbert Ames, Jr. on apperceptive background as a determiner of perception.

Ames's experiments on the relativity of perception demonstrated that the forms of objects depend to a large extent on preconceived assumptions which the individual percipient has developed through previous experience. Thus, an observer who examines a distorted room with slanted floors judges two identical objects to be vastly different in size. This is because he interprets the objects in terms of his familiar experiences with rectangular rooms. Ames's experiments provided laboratory evidence for the naturalistic, pragmatic views of John Dewey and other adherents of the emphasis upon the role of experience in education. They also pointed the way to a new field of investigation into the backgrounds of perception and reasoning. In recent years researches have been in progress which employ drugs to explore the intellectual reactions of individuals to their environment.

The child study movement engaged a host of scientific investigators, such as Arnold Gesell who constructed tests to measure the intelligence of infants, charting the physical and mental growth of children from the fetal stage to adolescence. Experiments in the use of projects and purposeful activities in elementary schools were encouraged by the Progressive Education Movement and left their mark on teaching methods. Hundreds of monographs and books on child development contributed greatly to the rapidly expanding scientific and popular literature of educational psychology.

Worthy of special attention is the recent attempt by means of programed textbooks and teaching machines to divide learning problems or tasks into a step-by-step sequence of very small units or facts which the learner can easily master as he proceeds from one point to the next in a subject field. Pioneers in this field have been S. L. Pressey and B. F. Skinner, and research has borne out their claims that programing aids motivation because of the large measure of success achieved by the learner. On the other hand, since much of the material subdivided minutely is already known to the learner, programed textbooks seem to offer him less challenge and to discourage interest. A more promising current emphasis in teaching is that upon the whole view of a large topic, upon critical judgment by the learner, and upon the allocation of learning assignments and time in accordance with his actual need.

Scope and Methods of Educational Psychology

Educational psychology is one of the many branches of the science of psychology. Psychologists discover, organize, and interpret facts about the mental and emotional behavior of organisms in their various aspects. Psychology may therefore be defined as a body of data and verifiable laws regarding the mental and emotional phases of organic life.

As distinguished from psychology proper, educational psychology concentrates attention on the processes of emotional, intellectual, and moral development. Educational psychologists do not merely use the discoveries of individual and social psychology to solve problems of education; they apply their own special experiments, research techniques, and hypotheses to learning and growth—the specific field of educational psychology. Within this field the main topics covered (but only so far as they relate to education) are: heredity and environment; physical structure; growth; behavior processes, including many perceptual and motor adjustments to the environment; learning; aptitude, intelligence, and achievement; character development; mental hygiene; and acquisition of knowledge.

Note that there is much overlapping among the special field of educational psychology and various other branches of psychology. Thus, social psychology studies the behavior of groups and of individuals in their relationships to groups. Obviously, the data of social psychology are pertinent to many problems of teaching and learning. Child psychology is another broad field of psychology which inquires into the behavior of children from birth to maturity, and its researches have contributed significantly to educational psychology and practice. The findings of abnormal psychology, the study of mental and emotional maladjustments, have enabled many school systems to employ specialists, such as clinical psychologists and psychiatrists, who can diagnose and treat children in need of their assistance. There is a reciprocal relationship—a sharing of information—among all these branches of psychology, each of which concentrates its attention upon its own class of problems.

Methods of Research in Educational Psychology. Educational psychology has developed useful methods and instruments of research, ranging from the early introspective techniques of the structural school of psychology to the recent emphasis on statistical evaluation, testing, and guidance.

Introspection is a method of attending to and recalling one's "mental" experiences. This method cannot accurately duplicate prior experiences: it may fail to disclose significant factors; it depends on the individual's capacity for self-investigation; and it tends to overemphasize unusual experiences which attain prominence because of personal bias. Introspection is of value, however, for exposing the intimate poignancy and intensity of certain experiences which cannot as yet be measured or evaluated thoroughly in any other way. It has the further merit of raising questions about intricate or obscure "mental" activities. What children say or write about their inner experiences—thoughts, doubts, emotions—reveals much about their educational progress and needs.

Experimentation is the most dependable method of research but is not always possible in practical classroom situations. It emphasizes accurate observation, the collection and organization of pertinent data, the formulation of careful hypotheses, the development of tentative explanatory theories, and the testing of theories by trial under controlled conditions and by practical applications to life situations. Experiments may be conducted in a laboratory, in a classroom, or elsewhere in the community. They usually involve comparisons between the behavior of a control group and that of an experimental group. The experimenter tries to isolate or pinpoint the factor or factors responsible for differential behavior in the two types of groups. To the greatest possible extent he must eliminate preconceptions and personal bias concerning the problem under investigation. All factors and conditions in the observation and measurement of behavior must be so far as possible controlled by the experimenter in order to insure validity (the fact that the findings actually reflect the behavior being investigated) and reliability (the chances that the conclusions will be found accurate in subsequent experiments and in practice).

Experiments ordinarily involve an independent variable (a factor modifiable by action of the investigator) and a dependent variable (the factor to be observed and measured in order to analyze the changes produced by the independent variable). All other variable factors, such as the characteristics of the persons in the experimental and control groups and the conditions of the experiment, are kept constant. Furthermore, due account is taken of any effects of the experiment itself upon the behavior of the participants. The results can often be interpreted mathematically by ascertaining the correlation (mathematical relationship) between the observed behavior patterns before, during, and after the experiment. The figures for a positive correlation will fall at some point between zero and 1; for negative correlation, at some point between zero and -1. (See Chapter 11 for explanation of the statistical procedures required.) The experimenter's conclusions will be subjected to the test of additional experiments. Mathematical analysis will indicate the statistical significance of the findings, that is, the degree of probability that the results in any experiment could occur by pure chance.

Observation is a visual and aural method of examining, describing, and interpreting the reactions of individuals and groups in laboratory, classroom, or out-of-school situations. The method requires trained observers who carefully delimit each investigation, make objective reports, eliminate extraneous or disturbing influences so far as possible, and check their conclusions against repeated observations. In analyzing and interpreting observed data, the observer should bear in mind the child's background of experience and the family relationships or other human relationships which might help to explain or clarify the reactions being observed.

Case studies comprise many-sided inquiries into diverse factors of a situation, often including analysis of an individual's life history, health record, home environment, school progress, social relations, and psychological equipment for educational tasks. *Anecdotal records* of specific events or episodes may be part of the basic data in a case study of a child's development. Great care must be taken in arriving at conclusions about the motives and adjustment needs of the child, and such conclusions must be regarded as merely tentative hypotheses, pending further repeated studies of his behavior.

Questionnaires and *interviews* make use of questions and answers, or of discussion, to ascertain an individual's opinions, problems, and recalled experiences.

Two closely related instruments of research are *statistics* and *tests*. Statistics involves the enumeration, classification, correlation, and interpretation of data. Tests are used for the measurement of physical and psychological traits, capacities, accomplishments, and needs. During the past ninety years, progress in statistical methods and the development of standardized tests have helped to build a scientific foundation for educational psychology.

Principles of Research in Educational Psychology. The following principles utilized in all scientific work are of special interest in educational psychology: strict application of the *scientific method* (elimination of bias and preconceptions); the *principle of universality* or the *uniformity of nature,* the theory that similar effects result from similar antecedent conditions and that the laws of nature are valid under all circumstances; the *law of parsimony* (applied to psychology as Lloyd Morgan's Canon in 1899), which permits the scientist to select from several theories the one that explains most and is the least complicated; the *principle of probability,* the thesis that various explanations may be arranged in the order of their probability prior to further investigation, and that a high correlation among data increases the probability of a conclusion and justifies tentative reliance on its validity; the *principle of piecemeal research,* the contention that efficiency requires limitations on the extent of subject matter to be investigated—for example, the philosopher generalizes about the entire universe, but the scientist tends to restrict his experiments to specific problems.

These principles of research are applicable to everyday classroom situations. For example, the teacher may have formed a general impression about the work of his class. *Scientific method* subjects such an impression to objective investigation, including careful observation of the learning activities of the group and factual analysis of what has been achieved. The administration of achievement tests may help to correct or to verify the teacher's impression and indicate a need for changes in the program of the class. Instead of depending upon complex explanations or broad generalizations, he deals with specific problems of the class, for which he seeks concrete solutions, and thus he applies the principle of piecemeal research.

Problems of Concern to Educational Psychologists. The problems with which educational psychologists are concerned may be classified as follows: *problems of behavior,* including consideration of human equipment, reflexes, temperament, motives, behavior controls, affections, psychophysical structure, and dispositions; *problems* of learning, including consideration of responses to learning situations, practice and drill, motivation, methods of learning, ability to learn, transfer of training, psychology of school subjects, intellectual understanding, and growth; and *problems of individual differences,* including consideration of the rate, stages, and types of growth among individuals, the distribution of characteristics among individuals and groups, and the analysis of differential needs.

Approaches to Educational Psychology

During the past half-century, there have been six distinct approaches to the science of educational psychology, each of which attracted substantial interest and support of teachers. In addition to the following six points of view, many psychologists and educators adhere to no one school of thought but draw upon the concepts and findings of all of them, and therefore comprise the eclectic group. The emphasis is placed currently upon whatever theories and findings contribute to the economy and efficiency of learning (the functional approach).

The introspectionists (structuralists) (Titchener *et al.*) stress self-analysis and the careful scrutiny of details in psychological experience. Their attention is concentrated on psychological states or evidence of psychological conditions rather than on overt behavior.

The behaviorists (J. B. Watson *et al.*) represent a somewhat mechanistic view of human behavior. Man is regarded as a machine-like organism reacting to specific stimuli, an organism whose emotions, thoughts, and actions can be explained entirely by reference to his overt behavior. In recent years the behaviorists have concentrated upon the study of perception, thinking, and problem solving.

The functionalists (Angell, Dewey, *et al.*) seek to establish principles of psychological behavior in terms of functions instead of the structure of consciousness as such. For them, the main problem is not to discover the structures determining conscious behavior, but to investigate how and why human beings perceive, think, and act as they do.

The Gestalt psychologists (Wertheimer, Koffka, *et al.*) regard man as a unitary whole and maintain that the investigation of behavior can be successful only to the extent that it emphasizes the entire reacting organism (in its entire environment) and not merely its parts or isolated responses. This approach emphasizes the whole view of the learner and learning task and thus stands in opposition to the minute dissection of subject matter as set out by programed textbooks and teaching machines.

The hormic psychologists (William McDougall *et al.*) regard man not only as a unitary whole but also as a purposive, striving organism, and are strongly opposed to the mechanistic or behavioristic point of view.

The psychoanalysts (Freud, Jung, Adler, *et al.*) assume that human desires and primitive impulses are the central factors in behavior. Thus, inner conflicts of the individual are attributed to his repression of desires which then remain submerged in his subconscious.

Contributions of Educational Psychology

The discoveries and ideas contributed by educational psychologists have proved helpful to the teacher, learner, and community. They have helped the teacher to gain understanding of the child's motives and to provide for the child's needs. Data about the principles and proper conditions of learning have made it possible for teachers to adjust school activities to the requirements of the individual and to the community. Researches of educational psychologists have shed light on effective methods of study and learning. Studies of child development have done much to improve school programs, and in this way to enrich and deepen the pupil's learning experience, stimulate his interest, and facilitate his physical, intellectual, social, and moral growth. Children today are doing more of what they can do best, and in a better psychological environment, thanks to the increasing adaptation of education to those individual differences and needs disclosed by numerous experiments and research investigations. Furthermore, educational psychologists have helped to clarify human motives and thus to achieve better understanding among individuals and groups. Their scientific data have been useful instruments in such fields as juvenile delinquency and intercultural and interracial relations, contributing to improved programs for the disadvantaged groups of the community and to the special problems of mental retardation and of physical or social maladjustment.

The classroom teacher's lesson plans cannot ordinarily be subjected to the test of experimentation. Daily plans must be made in the light of the best available theory and past experience. Nevertheless, the scientific attitude and many of the techniques of the experimenter can be utilized by the teacher as bases for important decisions. Certainly the teacher has the obligation to obtain, organize, and interpret facts about pupils' needs; to apply the most promising principles and theories as indicated by available evidence, past and present; to measure and carefully evaluate progress in learning; and to modify teaching practices in accordance with new conditions and situations in order to facilitate and deepen the pupils' educational experience.

PART ONE

Human Equipment and Behavior
by Rudolf Pintner

Chapter 1
Heredity and Environment

The interaction between man's inherited equipment and his environment determines the nature of human nature. Heredity can be a potent factor in and of itself. Nevertheless, modern research indicates that the environment is the decisive factor in shaping many of the physical, mental, emotional, and moral characteristics of the individual. Every effort should therefore be made to provide for all children the most desirable conditions of learning. On the other hand, due account must also be taken of inherited advantages and disadvantages.

The Mechanism of Heredity

The inheritance of physical and anatomical characteristics has been well established. Like begets like.

Germ Cells. The process of perpetuating the species takes place through the transmission of characteristics from one generation to the next by means of the germ cells of the two parents. In the genetic mechanism, one sperm cell is drawn into the protoplasm of the ovum. Fertilization of the ovum initiates cell division which continues and thus forms the various masses and layers of cells from which the organs of the embryo develop.

The animal cell is made up of protoplasm and other substances within a thin sheet of tissue or membrane and ranges in size from .002 millimeter to 2 inches or more (egg yolk of ostrich). In the nucleus of the cell are a membrane, small particles of chromatin, filaments, and nucleoli or spherical bodies. The human body cell has 46 chromosomes (arranged as 23 pairs in long strings) which are regarded as the material basis of heredity, for they contain the genes or hereditary units. Many such genes are necessary to produce even the simplest physical characteristics of the animal. Unit characters are produced by various combinations of the genes. It is estimated that on the average a human body cell contains about 40,000 genes, innumerable combinations of which are responsible for specific traits. Consequently, inherited characteristics are almost infinite in number; they range from such familiar qualities as the individual's eye color to such extraordinary factors as those producing an excess of certain body enzymes that may concentrate acids in the blood, damage the nervous system, and thus cause mental retardation. Any attempt to modify the genes will involve their complex relationships to amino acids and cellular enzymes.

Mendel's Experiments. By propagating plants or by breeding animals it is possible to track down the inheritance of traits in succeeding generations. For example, animals which possess a specific characteristic are bred with others which do not possess that characteristic. This method of experimental study of heredity is called the *monohybrid cross*. In 1866 Gregor Mendel published the results of his experiments of this kind in the hybridization of peas. He showed the difference between dominant and recessive traits. He had discovered that terminal-flowered plants provided pollen which, when placed on the pistil in axial-flowered plants, formed seeds that developed into axial-flowered plants in all cases, but that the seeds from self-pollination of the new plants grew into plants with a ratio of three axial-flowered to one terminal-flowered types. He noted that the dominant characteristic, when present in the seeds, always reappears. The recessive characteristic can appear only when the dominant one is not present. The Mendelian Ratio (3 to 1) indicates the expectation of the appearance of the dominant and recessive characteristics in the offspring of the second generation of two pure types. The ratio means that among large numbers of offspring the chances will be about three to one that any one individual will possess the dominant characteristic.

The Inheritance of Physical and Psychological Traits

Only characteristics inherited by the parents are passed on to their offspring. Characteristics acquired by the parents are not inherited by their children. This point has been for a long time and still is much debated, but the evidence at present is against the possibility of the inheritance of acquired characteristics. (Rare exceptions may occur, as in the case of drastic environmental forces, such as radiation, which can affect the genes of the parents.) Many of the physical characteristics of man are found to be inherited in the Mendelian fashion.

On the other hand, any inherited physical equipment may require a favorable environment for its full development. Furthermore, a changed environment may alter the normal development of inherited characteristics by affecting the metabolic and growth rates of the organism.[1]

Anastasi has pointed out that heredity may affect child growth profoundly in several ways: (1) a metabolic or other physical defect may impede or prevent normal growth; (2) an inherited defect may make subsequent adjustment to people difficult and therefore require special retraining; (3) inherited illnesses or susceptibilities may retard educational or social progress in later years; (4) some inherited physical features (such as skin color or physical build) may handicap the child or require special compensatory measures.[2]

It is apparent that hereditary and environmental influences are closely intertwined. Teachers should note that something helpful can be done about many individual cases of inherited deficiencies and that much may also need to be done for children endowed with excellent exceptional hereditary equipment. Further, depth psychology, as shown in the scientific work of Sigmund Freud and others, indicates that human relationships during the earliest experiences of children may turn out to be

---

[1] See D. H. Eichorn, "Biological Correlates of Behavior," in Part I, *Sixty-Second Yearbook of the National Society for the Study of Education*, Chicago, 1963.
[2] See Chapter 7 in *Individual Differences* by Anne Anastasi (New York: John Wiley & Sons, 1965).

controlling influences upon their later personality growth and adult behavior.

Francis Galton. Interest in the inheritance of psychological traits was first stimulated by Francis Galton. His epochal work *Hereditary Genius* (1869) begins as follows: "I propose to show in this book that a man's natural abilities are derived by inheritance, under exactly the same limitations as are the form and physical features of the whole organic world." He studied the family histories of many eminent men and finding that a certain trait or ability appeared frequently in a family, he concluded that this trait was inherited. In this way, therefore, he began the family history method for the study of inheritance. He was one of the first to recognize the significance of the study of twins. He gathered data by means of a questionnaire. By showing the greater similarity of more closely related individuals and by studying large numbers of people, Galton may also be said to have started the correlational method for the study of inheritance. We shall now briefly describe these two methods and review the chief results found by each method.

The Family History Method. The pioneering work is Galton's family histories of eminent British men. Notable also is his study of the Wedgwood-Darwin-Galton family, which abounds with eminent scientists and scientifically inclined individuals. Karl Pearson later extended this family tree, tracing it back many hundreds of years, and finding individuals of outstanding ability all along the line. The pioneer work in the study of the inheritance of inferior mentality was completed by Dugdale (1877), whose Jukes family has become famous. In this family we find numbers of prostitutes, criminals, and paupers. The author intimates that prostitution, criminality, and pauperism are inherited traits. That view is now mainly of historical interest, for today we should not consider such complex traits inherited. We should be inclined to say that this family inherited certain physical equipment which could readily lead to anti-social behavior in the poor environment in which the Jukes lived.

Among numerous family history studies stimulated by the early work of Galton and Dugdale, Goddard's history of the Kallikak family is one of the best known, although much doubt has developed concerning the validity of his conclusions on the inheritance of mental traits. Here we have two collateral lines, one highly intelligent, the other retarded, both going back to the same progenitor at the time of the American Revolution. This man contracted two unions, one with a mentally retarded woman, from which the inferior line descended, and the other with an intelligent woman, from which the superior individuals descended. Goddard also studied the family histories of 327 retarded individuals. He concluded that mental retardation is inherited in about 54 per cent of these families. Today, however, it is agreed that environmental conditions are of pre-eminent importance and that even mentally retarded children can learn and make considerable progress in self-direction if they are properly encouraged and assisted. Teachers can accomplish much in behalf of the very slow learners who are in need of special attention if they are to become efficient human beings and good citizens.

The Correlational Method. By means of correlations between the measurements of physical or personality traits of individuals, we can compare the degree of similarity among individuals of different degrees of blood relationship. Among chance pairs of unrelated individuals we find no or insignificant correlations, but among related individuals we find positive correlations increasing in size with an increase in the degree of relationship between the paired individuals. Galton maintained that personality traits are inherited in the same manner and degree as physical traits. Pearson found a correlation of about .5 between siblings for such physical traits as height, cephalic index, color of eyes and hair; and he also found a correlation of about .5 for such personality traits as vivacity, self-assertiveness, temper, ability, and the like. Environment has no influence on the color of the eyes of siblings, and hence the degree of such resemblance is attributed to heredity. We find the same degree of resemblance in regard to personality traits, but in these instances, related individuals may also share similar educational opportunities so that the contribution of heredity to the end results cannot be precisely determined. The early studies gave reason to believe that heredity is important both for physical and for mental development. More recent correlational studies can be grouped under (1) twins and (2) siblings.

Twins. Twins are of two kinds: identical and fraternal. Identical twins are the result of the germination of one ovum. Fraternal twins arise from the germination of two separate ova. The study of twins, especially identical twins, is, therefore, of great interest for heredity. Here we have the closest possible relationship between two individuals. Many studies of twins have been made to discern their *concordance,* that is, the percentage of their similarity, notably by Thorndike, Merriman, Wingfield, Holzinger, Gesell, and F. N. Freeman. The correlations between pairs for intelligence range from .62 to .92. The correlations for identical twins cluster around .90; those for fraternal twins cluster around .75.

Winchester (1962) reported a study of twins one of whom in each pair had committed major crimes. Among identical twins, 68 per cent of the brothers and sisters of the criminals also had a criminal record; among fraternal twins of the same sex, only 28 per cent of the brothers and sisters had a criminal record. Environmental influences may have affected both types of twins, but with a much stronger impact upon the identical twins, drawing 68 per cent of their brothers and sisters in the wrong direction.

What happens to identical twins if they are separated at an early age and reared apart from each other for most of their lives? Newman and Müller investigated numerous such cases, on ten of which they reported in detail. Schwesinger summed up the results. Let us subtract the I.Q. of one twin from the I.Q. of the other and compare the average intra-pair differences with similar I.Q. differences found for other groups:

	Average I.Q. Difference
Identical twins reared together	5.3
Identical twins reared apart	7.7
Fraternal twins reared together	9.9
Re-tests of same individuals	6.8

Identical twins reared apart since infancy differ somewhat more than do identical twins reared together, but they still remain more alike than fraternal twins reared together and they differ from each other on intelligence tests only a little more than the same individual differs from himself when re-tested on intelligence tests. Nevertheless, the precise influence of heredity upon individual intelligence is unknown, since environmental factors also play a major role in each stage of the child's development; it is believed that even in physical structure, boys and girls seem to have grown taller and healthier than children of past generations because of superior diets and greater participation in sports activities.

Siblings. The relationship between siblings (brothers and sisters) is not so close as that between twins. Many correlations between the I.Q.'s of sibling pairs have been reported. They range from .27 to .68 and cluster around .50. Hartshorne and May found a similar correlation between siblings in tests of honesty. We may note that this correlation of .50 is about the same as that found between siblings for physical characteristics. The fact that superior intelligence often accompanies superior physical qualities does not prove that both types of superiority are hereditary. The environment may contribute decisively to both aspects of growth. However, there must be an inherited basis upon which environmental influences can build.

Other Relationships. A number of studies have disclosed correlations between parents and children and between cousins. The correlation between the child and one parent (either father or mother) is always smaller than that between the child and the mid-parent (the average of the father and mother). In general, the correlation between a parent and child seems to be about .45, between a child and the mid-parent about .60. We have only a few correlations for cousins, about .25.

Summary of Correlational Results. If we set down these general findings, we will have a series of correlations:

Identical twins	.90
Fraternal twins	.75
Mid-parent and child	.60
Siblings	.50
Single parent and child	.45
Cousins	.25
Unrelated children	.00

The exact values in these correlations are not important. It is the order of the correlations which is important. The correlations decrease in the same order as the closeness of the relationship between the individuals decreases. People are more alike in general verbal intelligence the more closely they, are related. Perhaps they benefit from a superior identical environment (or are handicapped by an inferior shared environment) if they are closely related; or there may be something in the inherited physical constitution upon which the fullest development of general verbal intelligence depends. Whether these considerations apply to other traits, we do not yet know.

Other Evidence for Inheritance of General Intelligence. If we study the intelligence of children according to the social status of their families or according to the occupations of their fathers, we generally find a ranking of I.Q.'s from high to low which corresponds to the social status or occupational rating of the family. We find the highest average I.Q. among children in professional families; then follow business or clerical, skilled workers, semi-skilled, and unskilled. This hierarchy is found among pre-school children, as well as among elementary school, high school, and college groups. The actual values of the I.Q.'s vary, of course, among the different groups of children, but the general hierarchy of occupations remains the same. Such results have been reported frequently in the United States and in Great Britain, and also in Germany. The results for the pre-school groups show that all these differences cannot be due to the superior education of those in the upper social classes. Such results as these do not, however, prove that intelligence is inherited; they merely fit into such a theory. In general, we find more intelligent individuals in the higher occupations because such occupations demand higher intelligence. The children of these individuals are found to have higher intelligence, and this is true at all educational levels and also before schooling has begun; hence it is reasonable to suppose that something basic has been inherited which develops in response to a favorable early environment and upon which their general verbal intelligence partly depends.

Environmental Influences on the I.Q.

No one believes that the actual score or I.Q. obtained by a child on any intelligence test is due wholly to heredity in the sense that it could not be changed by environmental forces working upon the child. The score or I.Q. is an index of the child's present ability to respond to certain situations; in a sense it is a measure of what he has learned in a given environment. We deduce his native ability from his present performance by comparing his score with the scores of other children who have a common background. We can change any child's score on any intelligence test by repeated practice on the test material or by teaching him similar material. In this way we can easily increase his presumed mental age by a year or two, or his assumed I.Q. by 10 or 20 points, but we do not thereby change his general intelligence. We only make it impossible for us to assess his intelligence in terms of the standard norms; we cannot compare him with other similar children if we coach him, for we have thus removed the common basis for comparison. Finally, the specific background of experience and education in the home and community may profoundly affect performance on any kind of intelligence test from time to time; and some recent studies suggest the probability of wide changes in the individual's I.Q. as a consequence of drastic changes in his environment. The researches of Terman and Merrill (1960), for example, indicated the occurrence of large changes in the I.Q. over extended intervals of time.

The most important studies attempting to measure the influence of general home background on the Binet mental rating have been those of Freeman *et al.* and Burks. These workers agree that young children removed from a poor environment and placed in a good environment show an increase in Binet mental rating. They disagree as to how great a change in I.Q. can be effected. Their studies indicate that the shift in environment must be a large one (from very poor to very good), and that such a shift must be made at a very early age (pre-school age) if there is to be appreciable change in the I.Q. on the Binet. Gesell has reported studies indicating that serious retardation may result from a poor environment, as in cases of long-term hospitalization and impoverishing institutionalization. He has cited instances where removal of a child from an institution to a family home environment stimulated growth so that symptoms of mental retardation disappeared.

Conclusion

Most psychologists are inclined to believe that the individual inherits something basic in his nervous system upon which the future development of his intelligence depends. How much this development can be influenced by environment is still controversial. Some believe that environment can do a great deal; others that it is very limited in its effects. Heredity determines the limits between which the I.Q. will vary. Environment determines the specific I.Q., within these limits, which a child will receive on a given test. If the environment is the same for all children, heredity will be the factor determining the differences in their I.Q.'s. If the environment differs greatly, then it may be the determining factor in the I.Q. differences. Except within rather narrow limits, we do not know how to alter the I.Q. by manipulating the environment. Despite recent studies which indicate that wide changes in the I.Q. do occur in response to drastic changes in the environment, it is still remarkably difficult to achieve any permanent large change in the I.Q. of a child, even on the Binet scale or on the usual verbal group intelligence test—tests which seemingly contain many items of a scholastic type. Perhaps further research with non-verbal and non-language intelligence tests will show still less modifiability of the I.Q. by environmental influences, because these tests may contain fewer items of a scholastic type likely to be specifically learned in school or at home.

Lastly, we must remember that almost all·of our evidence for the inheritance of psychological traits has been limited to intelligence testing. This instrument of measurement, despite its imperfections, is considered much more reliable than subjective opinions about the individual's mental ability. Psychologists have begun to construct similar instruments for measurement of personality and temperament.

Differences in attitudes, interests, and the like seem to be greatly determined by environmental factors. Differences in temperament or disposition may be more dependent upon hereditary than upon environmental factors, but the solution of the problem of exact hereditary influence remains for the future.

Chapter 2
Physical Structure

In this age of atomic power, space travel, automation, and the computer, we may be prone to underestimate the facts that individuals remain the backbone of human progress and that the achievements of individuals depend on their physical structure as well as their psychological equipment and educational experience. Physical and psychological factors are so closely intertwined that it is difficult to draw a line between them. Experiments with the use of drugs (such as LSD) have shown, for example, the profound effects of physical and chemical factors on human perception, thinking, and emotions.

The physical structure of man is particularly significant for psychologists because it determines what aspects of the environment will affect him and also what kinds of reactions he will be able to make. We inherit a certain type of body, a definite type of nervous, muscular, and glandular organization, which conditions all our behavior. Not all the stimuli in our environment can affect us. We are deaf to many tones and blind to many light vibrations because our sense organs are constructed in a certain definite way. And there are numerous things we cannot do (fly like a bird, for instance) because we have inherited a given muscular system. In his work, the teacher must always bear in mind the child's physical equipment, capacities, and limitations. Thus, a child's faulty eye movements and visual defects may require altered instruction or referral to specialists for therapy. It is highly desirable, therefore, for the teacher to have an elementary knowledge of man's physical structure. The areas of the physical structure most directly involved in psychological processes are: (1) the receptors or sense organs; (2) the connectors or nervous system; (3) the effectors or reacting mechanisms, principally the muscles and glands.

Receptors

We possess a great number of sense organs for the reception of stimuli from the outside world. People still speak of the five senses—sight, hearing, smell, taste, and touch—but the psychologist recognizes many more. The first four are very distinct, having specific sense organs which are prominent characteristics of the human head. The last sense—touch—is too vague for the psychologist because the sensations arising from the skin come from different sense organs and give rise to very different sensations.

So the psychologist differentiates temperature, pain, and touch. In addition, he distinguishes kinaesthesis (sense of movement), equilibration (sense of balance), and visceral sensitivity. All of these senses are necessary for the proper functioning of the body. However, students of education do not need detailed knowledge of all of them. For these students the most significant are the two so-called "higher" senses of vision and audition. These two play the most influential role in the education of the individual, granted an adequate functioning of the other senses.

Vision. The main structures for human vision consist of the eyeball, the accessory structures (eyebrows, eyelids, conjunctiva, lacrimal apparatus, and ocular muscles), and the orbits which contain the eyes and certain bones, blood vessels, fascia, and nerves. The eyeball consists of three coats: (1) the outer, fibrous sclera, the front part of which constitutes the transparent cornea; (2) the middle coat, which includes the choroid membrane, the ciliary body, and the iris; and (3) the inner coat, the retina. The lens of the eye is enclosed within an elastic capsule connected to the ciliary body. There are two chambers of the eye: (1) a posterior, smaller chamber between the lens and the iris, filled with an alkaline watery fluid (the aqueous humor); and (2) an anterior, larger chamber between the lens and the retina, filled with a jelly-like substance (the vitreous humor).

Evolution of the Eye. A diagram of the human eye shows that it is a highly complicated structure. In the evolutionary series we find the earliest beginnings in the pigmented spots on the surface of the body of certain lower animals. These spots are more sensitive to light than the unpigmented parts of the body. And so we can trace the eye up through stages, where only gross differences of light and darkness are differentiated, to the human eye with its sensitivity to color as well as brightness, and with its marvelous focusing ability.

Focusing. Light enters the eye through the aperture called the pupil. The iris surrounding the pupil controls the size of the aperture and in this way regulates the amount of light allowed to pass to the lens. The muscles of the iris contract or relax in accordance with the degree of illumination. In relative darkness the muscles of the iris relax so that the pupils of our eyes are large and we need all the illumination we can get in order to see. In bright light the muscles of the iris contract so that the pupils become small and we do not need so much illumination in order to see distinctly. The light penetrates the lens, which is just behind the pupil. The lens is a focusing instrument; by means of the ciliary muscles it is made thicker or thinner, depending upon whether the object looked at is near or far away. Then the light rays penetrate the vitreous humor which fills the eyeball and strike the sensitive retina at the back. The retina (the innermost coat of the eyeball) is a nerve membrane made up of three sets of neurons whose cell bodies and processes are arranged in layers; of these, one layer contains the specialized nerve endings, the rods and cones, which function as the receptors of light rays reaching them through the outer layers. Rods seem to be insensitive to color and to function best under weak illumination (twilight vision), while cones are sensitive to both light and color.

Adjustments. In addition to the focusing quality (accommodation) of the lens, we have the adjustment of the whole eyeball by means of the muscles of the eye. These control the movements of the eyes. The two eyes are turned slightly toward each other (convergence) when looking at a near object. We can see with one eye (monocular vision), but two eyes (binocular vision) are much superior. Each eye receives a slightly different retinal image. The right eye sees more of the right side of an object, the left eye more of the left side, and thus from the two images we get many of our perceptions of mass, relief, and distance.

Visual Sensations and Interpretations. The stimuli we receive from the eye are of two kinds—colors and grays. All kinds of combinations of these make up our visual world. A study by Riesen (1960) indicated that normal development of the retina in the child depends upon previous use of the eyes. Another study by von Senden (1960) showed that efficient visual discrimination of objects depends upon repeated experiences with visual patterns over a long period of time.

A very simple experiment by the present editor shows that the brain is often compelled to interpret sensations in a specific manner even when the individual knows his interpretation to be incorrect. If we close one eye and with the other eye look through a pinhole (in a card held close to a light) while holding a pin upright and passing the head of the pin very slowly up and down and from side to side between our eye and the pinhole, we will see a reversed, inverted image of the pin, just as if it were in the pinhole itself. When passing through the pinhole, the rays of light strike the lens of the eye at such angles that the image of the pin is not reversed and inverted by the lens but remains upright and normal. Ordinarily the images of objects become reversed and inverted after striking the lens of the eye, and the brain again reverses and inverts them so that we see the objects correctly in their upright position. When an object close to our eye is viewed in front of a pinhole, however, the image seen in the pinhole is not inverted but remains normal; the brain then still reverses the image so that we see the object as if it were upside down and reversed. Evidently the action of the brain in manipulating and interpreting sensory impulses of this kind has become rigid and inescapable.

Eye Movements. If we photograph the eye while it is looking at something, we note that it jumps from one spot to another. It fixates one spot and then jumps on to another. It is during these fixation periods that the eye sees. During the rapid jump from one point to another, nothing is seen. We do not read by sweeping our eyes along the printed page, but by jumping from one spot to a different one until we come to the end of the line, and then we jump back to the beginning of the next line. The efficient reader takes in a wide span, a great many words, at each fixation period, and he also jumps back unerringly to the beginning of the next line. The poor reader makes a great many jumps along each line, sees relatively few words at each fixation period, sometimes has to go back along the line to make sure of what he has seen, and may also miss the right line when he jumps back from one line to the next.

Eye Dominance. The two eyes work together in binocular vision, but in almost all people one eye is dominant. One eye is used for "sighting." Some people are right-eyed and others are left-eyed, just as everyone is more or less right-handed or left-handed. Right-eye dominance is much more frequent than left-eye dominance. The great majority of right-handed people are also right-eyed. Left-handed people are about evenly divided between right-eye dominance and left-eye dominance.

Color Blindness. Some eyes cannot differentiate colors as well as the normal eye. There seem to be all degrees of this inability. If this inability is slight, we speak of "color weakness"; when it becomes rather marked, we designate it as "color blindness." The most common type of this defect is red-green color blindness. The red or the green or both are not sharply differentiated from the adjacent colors of the spectrum. There are a few cases of blue-yellow blindness and a very few where all perception of color has been lost. Color blindness is of great interest to the student of heredity because it seems to be a good example of the sex-linked type of hereditary trait. It rarely appears in females (less than 1 per cent), but it can be transmitted by them (through variant genes on their X-chromosomes) to their male descendants. From 3 to 8 per cent of males are thought to be color blind.

Visual Defects. Few eyes are perfect; most have slight defects. Happily, many of the slight defects can be corrected by means of eyeglasses. Myopia (nearsightedness) is one of the most common of such slight defects. In myopia the distance from the lens to the retina is too long and the light rays focus in front of the retina, a condition often correctible by use of concave lenses that disperse the rays before they reach the lens. In hyperopia (farsightedness) the rays focus behind the retina; convex eyeglasses can often correct this condition by making the rays converge on the retina. Other common defects include "cross-eye," an excessive convergence of the two eyes caused by muscular weakness or by differences in the curvatures of the two lenses; "walleye," an excessive divergence; and astigmatism, an irregular curvature of cornea or lens causing indistinct vision requiring cylindrical lenses for correction.

Because we use our eyes so much for reading, even the slightest defect should be discovered and remedied as soon as possible. All school children should have their eyes examined periodically. Reading difficulties may be caused by visual defects. Among 148 poor readers examined for visual defects, Gates found indistinct vision of a mild nature present in 12 per cent, and indistinct vision of a serious type present in 2 per cent. Lack of interest in reading may start because the use of the eyes for printed material causes discomfort. Visual defects are very numerous among school children. Reports from surveys in several cities run from about 10 per cent to as high as 40 per cent. Such large differences are due to different standards set by different examiners. Perhaps 25 to 30 per cent of children in our schools have defects that need attention.

Partial Vision. The vision of some children is so poor that, even after they have been fitted with the best glasses, they cannot properly see the printed page. These "partially seeing" children need special methods of education and are taught in "sight-saving" classes. They use books with very large print and their work must be carefully supervised to prevent injury to their eyes. It is estimated that there are about 75,000 such children in our schools today.

The Blind. When vision becomes so poor that the individual must depend on other senses entirely for orientation, he is called blind. Blindness does not bring with it, as a compensation, increased acuity of hearing or touch or a special sense of location, which could prevent the blind man from running into things. The blind learn to substitute hearing and touch for vision, and hence they pay attention to sensations which the seeing individual habitually disregards, because he does not need them. The education of the blind requires special equipment and special teachers.

Audition. All three divisions of the ear (external, middle, and inner) contain structures which are necessary for normal hearing. Disorders of hearing or deafness may be either congenital or acquired; such defects may greatly handicap the child's education and require special attention from the teacher.

Structure. The ear is a complicated organ. Sound waves enter the external ear canal and strike the tympanic membrane (eardrum) causing the latter to vibrate. Attached to the tympanum are three bones (ossicles)—the hammer (*malleus*), the anvil (*incus*), and the stirrup (*stapes*), each of them connected to the others by joints—and these conduct the vibrations across the middle ear to the inner ear, magnifying the vibrations in the process. The Eustachian tube leads from the pharynx to the middle ear to allow for the admission of air and thus keep the pressure on both sides of the eardrum equal. In rapid ascents or descents (as on mountains or in airplanes) the change in air pressure causes unpleasant sensations because of pressure on the tympanum. When the vibrations are transmitted by the three bones, they stimulate a fluid in the cochlea of the inner ear, and these fluid vibrations act upon the hair cells in the cochlea. The hairs bend against the tectorial membrane and thus send the wave impulses along the cochlear nerve (the auditory branch of the eighth cranial nerve) to the brain. The brain interprets the wave impulses as sound sensations. (Note that connected with the cochlea and also filled with fluid are three small loops, the semicircular canals, but these have nothing to do with hearing; they contain the receptors for our sense of equilibrium or balance.)

Sound Sensations. Sound sensations have pitch, quality, and intensity. Pitch is caused by the number of vibrations per second. The normal ear is sensitive to a wide range of vibrations, from about 12 per second to about 25,000 to 30,000 per second, but people vary greatly in this respect. The vibrations from about 30 to 4,000 per second are used in music. Ability to distinguish differences in pitch is one of the factors necessary in musical performance. People vary tremendously in this ability, and only those who excel in it should attempt to become professional musicians. There are standard tests (the Seashore Measures of Musical Talent were among the earliest) to measure this ability as well as other capacities necessary for the musician. Quality or timbre depends upon the number of overtones that go along with the fundamental tone; and thus we get the different qualities of tones on different instruments or with different voices. Intensity refers to the loudness or softness of sound sensations.

Localization. The fact that we have two ears helps in the localization of sounds. A sound coming from one side affects one ear differently than the other. The farther away the sound, the more difficult it is to locate accurately. We move our heads from side to side to help us. When we think we have located the source of sound by vision, the sound truly seems to come from that location, but we all know what ridiculous mistakes we can make.

Auditory Defects. Auditory defects may result from disease or injury affecting the structures or pathways of the hearing apparatus. Deafness can be congenital, and the recessive genes causing the condition can be transmitted by parents with perfectly normal hearing. There are many different kinds of auditory defects, but for educational purposes two groups of individuals need special consideration here, namely, the hard of hearing (the hypacousic) and the deaf. The hard of hearing are those who have established speech and ability to understand speech, and have later developed some impairment of hearing. The deaf are those who because of hearing deficiency have not been able to establish speech in the ordinary manner. There is, of course, no sharp dividing line between the two groups. The educational problems of the two groups are, however, quite different. Teachers should be alert to evidence of hearing impairment, including temporary difficulties of the child due to infections of the middle ear or to excessive wax secretions, and refer the problem to parents or to professional personnel (nurses, psychologists, or physicians) connected with the school.

The Hard of Hearing. The hard of hearing range from those with very slight deficiency to those who can just hear conversation if given sufficient assistance, either by means of a favorable location with respect to the speaker or by means of mechanical aids. (Sound vibrations passing through certain bones in the skull to the cochlear fluids of the inner ear can be heard with the help of sensitive instruments utilizing the alternative route of bone conduction.) Accurate instruments (audiometers) for the measurement of hearing acuity have been devised. It is estimated that there may be three million hard of hearing children in the United States. Many of these children are considered dull or disinterested because they cannot understand all that is going on around them. The educational problem with such children is to help them utilize, in the most efficient way, all the hearing that they have, and to supplement their loss by means of lip-reading. The plan usually recommended is to form special classes for these children, where they will spend part of their time. They should not be entirely segregated, for they must learn to adjust to a normal speaking environment.

The Deaf. The deaf need special education so different from the hearing that special schools or classes are necessary. There are many thousands of such children in the United States. They must be taught language from the very rudiments, because practically none of it has come to them naturally as it comes to a child who hears. To them our conventional language is stranger and harder to learn than is a second (foreign) language to a normal hearing child. If left to themselves they communicate by means of signs. Most deaf children are taught to speak and to read the lips. These two arts are extremely difficult, and some deaf children can make little headway. Finger spelling by means of the manual alphabet, and sign language or conventional signs to represent words or phrases are additional means of communication, and the deaf make use of these very largely among themselves.

The deaf are unable to speak simply because they do not hear. Because we can hear, we are able to speak, and because we can speak and hear we learn language easily and rapidly. Upon our knowledge of language much of our thinking depends, especially our abstract thinking. Some psychologists believe that most thinking depends upon speech (sub-vocal speech), and since the acquisition of speech depends upon hearing, it can be realized how greatly handicapped the deaf are and how very important is our sense of hearing.

Connectors

Stimuli affect our end organs (receptors), and the nerves attached to these end organs transmit impulses to different parts of the body. There is an intricate system of connectors, and we shall outline it only briefly. We should distinguish between the nerve fibers (the groups of fibers which conduct the nerve impulses) and the nervous system. The nerves that bring nerve impulses into the central nervous system are called afferent nerves, and the nerves that conduct impulses to the reacting mechanism (muscles, glands) are called efferent nerves.

Nerves. Each nerve consists of a more or less independent bundle of fibers and their coverings. The nerve tissues which serve as the pathways for nerve impulses consist of neurons and their supporting cells. The neuron is the essential element of the entire nervous system and is composed of a nerve cell with axons and dendrites. The axons and dendrites are the means of communication from one neuron to another. The place where the axon of one neuron comes into relationship with the dendrites of another neuron is called the synapse. The nerve impulse passes across the synapse and in so doing it is supposed to lower the resistance at the synapse, so that a second nerve impulse may pass across more easily. The greater the number of impulses, the lower the resistance becomes. In this way a preferred path or pattern is formed. This process is the physiological basis for habit formation and learning.

The Nervous System. When we speak of the nervous system, we generally refer to the central nervous system made up of the spinal cord and brain. There are, however, three systems: the central, the peripheral, and the autonomic. (The autonomic system is actually a functional system which utilizes mainly portions of the peripheral nervous system and is therefore often referred to as a subdivision of the latter.) As the central is by far the most important for the psychologist, we may merely say, in passing, that the peripheral system comprises various nervous structures outside the brain and spinal cord, while the autonomic system (i.e., the autonomic division of the peripheral system) extends parallel to the spinal column from neck to pelvis and to some extent controls heart action, respiration, the activities of many glands, and nearly all the smooth muscles.

The central nervous system consists of the brain and the spinal cord. Sensory and motor nerves in great number enter and leave the spinal cord, coming from and going to all parts of the body. Nerve fibres in great number run up and down the cord to the brain. The brain is made up of the cerebrum, cerebellum, pons, and medulla oblongata. The brain contains countless neurons, and we may think of it as an organ whereby nerve impulses from any part of the body may be switched over to any other part of the body; or again, as an integrating mechanism, where the countless afferent and efferent impulses are regulated and controlled. The analogy to a central telephone exchange may be useful but it is obviously much too simple a comparison to explain the complicated interlocking and interdependence of the neurons in the central nervous system.

Connection Levels. Some psychologists differentiate three levels in the organization of connections between stimulus and response. At the first or simplest level we have a stimulus activating a neuron or group of neurons which connect in the spinal cord with another neuron or group leading to a group of muscles. This is called a reflex arc, and it functions automatically and quickly. Simple reflex acts, such as the knee jerk, the eye wink, and the like, follow this pattern. The second level of organization consists of connections that involve the mid-brain and cerebellum. Several stimuli are concerned and the response is more complex. Such complicated habitual reactions as walking, sitting, or standing erect, turning the head to a sound, and the like, are dependent upon the mid-brain and cerebellum. The third level connections depend upon the cerebrum and include all higher responses. Thinking depends upon the cerebrum.

Localization. The cortex or covering of the cerebrum has been divided into so-called "cortical areas." These are the places in the cortex to which the main nerve tracts come from certain sense organs, and from which the main motor nerves start out to certain groups of muscles. This is called the localization of areas of the cerebrum. Three kinds of areas are distinguished: (1) motor, (2) sensory, and (3) associational. The associational areas are made up of neurons connecting different parts of the cerebrum. From these anatomical facts and from numerous experiments in stimulating specific points of the cortex, it was concluded that the functions of the cerebrum are also specifically localized, and hence in our textbooks of psychology we find many diagrams showing the location on the cortex of speech, vision, movement of the arm, even writing and the like. However, recent experimental work has cast grave doubt upon such specific localization. Destruction of any part of the cortex seems to impair the whole behavior of the animal. Destruction of a specific part may for a time interfere with certain types of reactions, but they can be re-learned. Evidently another part of the cortex can take over such functions. This is called vicarious functioning, and the cortex seems to have great possibilities in this respect. Specific localization seems to be only partially true. The cerebrum as a whole seems to be more or less concerned in almost all reactions, certainly in most connections beyond the first level.

Effectors

Muscles and glands constitute the principal reacting mechanism of the body. Muscles consist of specialized body tissues which produce movements of the body or its parts by means of contraction and relaxation. Glands are aggregations of cells which produce substances that are either absorbed by body tissues or discharged from the body. The muscles and glands are the main effectors, the structures which react to stimuli.

Muscles. The muscles may be divided into three types: cardiac, striped or skeletal, and unstriped or smooth. Cardiac muscles comprise the wall of the heart. The striped muscles are closely connected with the skeleton; the motor nerves coming from the brain or spinal cord cause them to contract and relax, releasing mechanical energy so that some kind of movement takes place. The obvious contractions of the skeletal muscles produce the overt physical behavior of the organism, including locomotion, manipulation, vocalization, swallowing, eye movements, respiration, and some of the activities of the abdominal organs. Along with the contractions, there is a sort of tension or muscle tonus (partial contraction) dependent upon the action of the cerebellum of the central nervous system as well as upon impulses coming from the autonomic nervous system. The unstriped or smooth muscles are found in the visceral organs. They control the alimentary tract, the blood vessels, the pupils of the eyes, the trachea and bronchi, the gall bladder, and the urinary and genital organs. They are characterized by relatively slow contractions and by a tendency to maintain muscular tone. They are stimulated in many cases by the hormones (secretions) of the ductless glands as well as being subject to control by the nervous system.

Glands. The glands are masses of cells which transform the materials they obtain from blood or lymph fluids either for absorption by or for discharge from the body. The two kinds of glands are the duct (or exocrine) and the ductless (or endocrine) glands. The duct glands, such as the salivary and sweat glands, pour their secretions down ducts into body cavities or onto the body surface. The ductless or endocrine glands have no outlet, and their secretions are absorbed by the blood or lymph; examples are the thyroid, adrenal, pituitary, duodenal, and sex glands, and possibly the thymus gland. (Certain glands, such as the pancreas and the liver, combine duct and ductless modes of discharging their secretions. Thus the pancreas pours its digestive juice through the pancreatic duct into the duodenum, but its ductle secretion is insulin, which is absorbed directly by the blood

Our knowledge of the psychological accompaniments o secretions (hormones) of the glands is very recent and ru tary, but endocrine secretions seem to be correlated clo different emotional states. Adrenalin (the hormone epi secreted by the adrenal glands (located above and the kidneys), affects visceral movements. Increa secretion accompanies states of fear and rage. D turbed if we eat during or immediately following outbursts of anger or in a state of fear. But increased adrenalin secretion also stimulates the muscles and thus increases our strength; we achieve feats in fear and anger which are ordinarily beyond us. The thyroid gland is situated in the neck, just above the trachea. If the secretion of this gland is defective, we have all sorts of bodily symptoms. Defective thyroid functioning from birth causes cretinism, usually accompanied by mental retardation. If the condition starts in adult life, it may cause bodily changes accompanied by general lethargy and mental inertia. Hyperfunctioning of the thyroid leads to general restlessness and the individual becomes exceedingly nervous.

Chapter 3
Human Growth and Development

As we have seen in the preceding chapter, the individual inherits a specific bodily mechanism capable of reacting in various ways. At birth it is immature, but there follows a long period during which it grows or matures. During this period of maturation, what happens to it depends upon the intrinsic factors of growth and the extrinsic influences of the environment. The environment determines the kinds of learnings or modifications that will take place, while maturation determines the amount of such modification for each individual. Growth and environment can never be separated. They are closely interwoven at all stages of the organism's life.

Steen and Montagu divide the life span of the individual into the following periods: (1) Neonatal (the period of the newborn), from birth to the end of the first month; feeding reflexes develop rapidly although many reactions are of a generalized character, with several body parts participating therein together. (2) Infancy, from the second month to the beginning of the second year. (3) Childhood, including early childhood, ages one to six years; middle childhood, ages six to ten years; and late childhood (prepubertal period), ages ten to thirteen or fourteen years. (4) Puberty, beginning at about fourteen years with females and at about fifteen with males; the period is extremely variable. (5) Adolescence, from puberty to about twenty-one years in females, twenty-four in males. (6) Maturity, including early maturity to thirty-five years; later maturity to fifty-five or sixty years. (7) Terminal age, following later maturity.

Piaget has suggested a different classification of the stages of human growth: (1) birth to two years of age, a period during which the child learns reflex actions and responses to single objects rather than to groups or classes of objects, and with a minimum of generalization or abstraction. (2) Early and late childhood (pre-adolescence), a stage of learning to classify objects and to apply logical reasoning. (3) A stage of emphasis on theory, generalization, and abstraction based on comparison, contrast, and deduction from recalled facts.

We shall here discuss briefly the growth factors of special interest to teachers as applied to infancy and early childhood, childhood, adolescence, and maturity.

Infancy and Early Childhood

We may assume that infancy refers technically to the first year of life, a period of tremendous importance to the progress of the individual. (Early childhood will then begin after age one and continue through age six.) Physically and mentally the infant is growing rapidly. Recent investigations have given us much information about the first three or four years of life. Of course, even before birth, during the prenatal stage, a great amount of growth has taken place. The embryonic period (lasting about fifty days, to the end of the second month), in which the bones, nerves, muscles, and sense organs develop, is followed by the fetal period (about seven months) in which the sense organs are well formed. The fetus weighs about seven pounds at full term (the tenth lunar month). At birth the brain is almost one-fourth of its final weight of two pounds and twelve ounces, while most of the other organs are relatively much less developed. The brain continues its rapid growth during the first few years of life and at the age of five or six has attained about 90 per cent of its ultimate weight.

Research Studies. Careful studies, such as the studies by Gesell and McGraw, reveal the rapid maturation of these early years. Gesell differentiated four types of behavior—motor, language, adaptive, and personal-social. He showed how the normal child develops in a normal environment in these four respects from month to month. Thus in motor development, at one month he lifts his head from time to time; at two months he holds his head erect for a short time; at five months he sits if propped up; at eight months he sits without support and stands with some help; at twelve months he is walking with help; at eighteen months he is climbing stairs; at twenty-four months he is running. We are all familiar with this rapid motor development of the child. Gesell provided the details for each month during the first year of life and for longer intervals thereafter. Weight increases 200 per cent during infancy. Physical maturation follows a cephalocaudal direction: the rate of growth is faster at the head in initial stages until this area has been well developed; growth then becomes more rapid toward the lower parts of the body. In language development the early life of the child is no less, and perhaps even more, remarkable. For a few months he makes no vocal response of a language type; at six months he has well-defined vocal expressions; at twelve months he can use one or two real words; at two years he is prattling gaily, and from then on his vocabulary increases by leaps and bounds.

M. E. Smith as long ago as the 1920's studied the size of vocabulary for children from eight months to six years. Below are the results by years.

Age	8 mos.	1 yr.	2 yrs.	3 yrs.	4 yrs.	5 yrs.	6 yrs.
Number of words	0	3	272	896	1540	2072	2562

And this goes on increasing to a vocabulary of fifteen or sixteen thousand words at the high-school level and to higher figures for educated adults. The interesting point here that we wish to emphasize is the rapid development during the first few years of life. As with motor and language development, so it is with all other types of behavior.

Foundations of Growth. Some psychologists believe that characteristics of fundamental importance to the child's later personality development may be formed in the pre-school period. Freudian psychology emphasizes the significance of early childhood, asserting that submerged experiences of the very young persist throughout their lifetime. Behaviorism stresses the importance of early conditioning for later development. Certainly the child living in a one-sided or meager or repressive environment (and this may be true of rich as well as of poor children) needs the special attention of skilled teachers (as in nursery schools) to counteract such deprivation and help him to build the foundations of his future growth.

Childhood

Childhood is the period from infancy to adolescence. It is preeminently the period of elementary schooling. In all civilized countries childhood is devoted to learning and the child goes to school for a certain number of hours a day for formal schooling, preparing to become an adult.

During this period growth is still proceeding vigorously. Perhaps it is not so rapid as during the first four or five years of life, but certainly it is rapid enough so that there are obvious differences mentally and physically between the seven-year-old, the nine-year-old, and the twelve-year-old. For example, the seven-year-old can repeat ten-word sentences and numbers through five digits; describe similarities in objects; relate events in his experience; and use about three thousand words orally. The nine-year-old can read and report on simple paragraphs; explain why events in his experience happened, and use about four thousand words orally.

Curves of Growth. The physical growth curves for weight and height show a steady increase during childhood. The average weight and height among thousands of children have been calculated by many investigators. The height of boys, according to Baldwin, begins at birth at 52 centimeters, increasing to 106 centimeters at age five, to 131 at age nine, to 151 at age thirteen, and so on. The rate is rapid at first and then slows down between ages eight and eleven, increasing again slightly during adolescence. In all periods of growth except about three years during middle and late childhood, girls are shorter than boys, on the average, but the curve for them has much the same characteristics as for boys. These are the general curves, but there are tremendous individual variations. Some children are short and some are tall. Repeated measurements of different children during the whole period of childhood show that the boy who is short in early life tends to remain short at adolescence, and the tall boy at age six or seven is the tall boy at fifteen or sixteen.

Other Aspects of Physical Growth. The curves for other aspects of physical growth are by no means all of the same type. Different features grow at different rates and reach their maximum growth at different times. The weight of the brain increases most rapidly in early childhood. Many head dimensions increase rapidly during the first six years of childhood, then more slowly for two or three years, and comparatively little thereafter. Up to about twelve years of age, the lymphatic organs grow rapidly, then cease abruptly in growth; and sex characteristics and sex organs develop at a rapid rate from the twelfth or thirteenth year onward through adolescence.

Adolescence

This is the period which begins with puberty and ends with the general cessation of physical growth. It emerges from childhood and merges into adulthood. It covers about seven or eight years, from age twelve to twenty for the average individual, with large variations in many cases. During this period bodily growth in general is slowing down, but at the same time the maturation of the sex function is taking place. It used to be thought that adolescence was marked by a sudden spurt of growth, that a "new birth" took place, that new traits and powers suddenly appeared. But recent study of the growth of all sorts of characteristics and functions lends no support to this view. Adolescence is simply the period during which the individual prepares himself for adulthood. This does not mean that the period is not different from childhood on the one hand or adulthood on the other. It is very different. It presents certain problems which arise from four basic needs, according to Hollingworth. These are: (1) need for freedom from dependence upon family; (2) need for association with the opposite sex; (3) need for self-support; (4) need for a theory of life.

Need for Freedom from Dependence. We may briefly describe these needs as Hollingworth presents them. The first she calls "psychological weaning." The adolescent must learn to stand on his own feet, to accept responsibility. The family or the parents in particular must learn to treat the adolescent as a separate, responsible individual and not as a dependent child. Friction arises when the adolescent wants to proceed too fast, and the parents lag behind. If the adolescent wins out, he may achieve independence before he is able to use it wisely. On the other hand, if the parents dominate, the individual may grow into maturity still dependent upon his parents. Whatever interferes with a normal "growing up" will handicap the individual in later life.

Need for Association with Opposite Sex. The need for association with the opposite sex arises because of the maturation of the sex function during the period of adolescence. The peak for frequency of love affairs occurs during this period. The attraction of one sex toward the other leads to an emphasis upon physical appearance. Clothing becomes very important during this period. Deprivation of association with the opposite sex may lead to various personality maladjustments. In extreme cases homosexuality (association with the same sex) is eventually established, instead of the normal heterosexuality (opposite sex).

Need for Self-Support. The need for self-support indicates the desire on the part of the adolescent to find his place in the world. He begins to think seriously of what he would like to be or to do. The childhood ideals of fireman and cowboy begin to change to those of doctor, lawyer, and the like. The function of the school here is to endeavor to find the vocational outlet suited to the adolescent's intelligence and interests. The professions require high intelligence, and adolescents of average or below average intelligence will meet difficulties and frustration if they are persuaded by family considerations to undertake the required preparation. Educational and vocational guidance is important during the high school period.

Need for a Theory of Life. The need for a theory of life does not imply always a consciously thought-out philosophy. It implies merely a certain integration or balance between the conflicting desires, impulses, and ambitions that beset the individual. It implies a certain point of view or attitude toward the self, others, the world, and so forth. During adolescence the problems of origin, destiny, conduct, God, begin to engage the adolescent, and so religion becomes a problem. The individual either grows into the religious atmosphere of the family group or else revolts against it. He may emancipate himself successfully or else he may carry the scars of an emotional conflict for the rest of his life. Problems of moral conduct loom large in adolescence. Ideals are potent forces of behavior. The adolescent selects individuals to imitate, shifting from the parent to the teacher or to some other living or historical personage. All of these questionings in the normal individual lead eventually to a more or less well-integrated mature individual. Failure to do so may result in delinquency, insanity, or suicide.

Maturity

Adolescence gradually merges into maturity. At no specific chronological age can maturity be said to begin. It is the period when growth has reached its highest point. But, as we have seen, the growth of various parts of the body, of various psychological functions, ceases at different times, so that maturity does not begin at a definite age. The end of the teens, the beginning of the twenties, is in general the period when most individuals have grown up and begin to accept the responsibilities of adults. They are able to make their own way in the world and behave like men and women. But, of course, many people never completely reach this stage. They remain psychologically immature all their lives, more or less dependent upon others, and their behavior shows traces of infantilism.

The Growth of Intelligence and Learning Ability

For psychologists the ability to learn and general intelligence are very important. Studies of these two functions (or two aspects of the same function) have been made from birth to senescence.

Studies by Thorndike.[1] Thorndike gave many individuals of various ages different sorts of things to learn. From the results of these experiments, the ability to learn is shown to increase greatly from early childhood to the early twenties, after that it declines very slowly (about one-half of one per cent a year) to about forty-five, and then somewhere about age fifty-five the steeper decline of senescence begins. Individuals of superior and inferior intellect show the same type of curve. Superior intellects reach their highest point at about the same age as (or at most one or two years later than) inferior intellects, and similarly with the age of decline. Learning a foreign language is not easiest in childhood. Given equal interest and incentive, adults between the ages of twenty and forty can learn it more rapidly than children between the ages of eight and twelve. Ages from twenty-five to forty-five are superior to childhood and quite equal to adolescence in general ability to learn. Nobody, said Thorndike, who is under forty-five should draw back from learning anything he wishes to learn because of a fear that he is too old to learn it. From such facts as these the great possibilities in the way of adult education become obvious. We can teach adults those things within their intellectual scope just as well as we can teach children.

Other Studies. The growth and decline of intelligence with age have been studied by many workers. The two most comprehensive reports are by Miles and Miles, and by Jones and Conrad. Both reports show a rapid increase in intelligence from early childhood to adolescence. The Miles report shows the peak of intelligence reached at about seventeen to eighteen, remaining at this level in the twenties. The Jones and Conrad report shows the peak reached a little later, between eighteen and twenty-one. During the twenties there is no decrease in intelligence. During the thirties and forties there is a steady slight decline. This decline is not great, for even in the fifties the intelligence is still equal to the teens. After this period the curve for intelligence begins to show a definite decline. Both reports emphasize the

---

[1] See E. L. Thorndike *et al.*, *Adult Learning* (New York: The Macmillan Co., 1928).

enormous individual differences in intelligence at all ages. Miles estimates that the average individual at age seventy-five falls to the 6th percentile in intelligence, whereas the very intelligent individual, in the upper ten per cent, is, when he reaches seventy-five, still as intelligent as the average individual ever was. In 1955 Thurstone reported on studies of adult learning which showed that adults continue to progress in such areas as vocabulary even though their abilities in other areas may decline somewhat with old age.[2]

A recent study by the National Institute of Mental Health compared healthy men aged sixty-five to ninety-two years with a group of young men averaging twenty-one years of age. The Institute reported that the older group were superior in verbal intelligence and just as mentally "vigorous, interesting, and deeply involved in everyday living." Physical aging is often accompanied by mental and spiritual growth.

These studies on the growth of intelligence and the growth of learning ability all show that childhood is eminently the period of rapid growth, adolescence the period when growth begins to slow down, early manhood the period of full mental power. This full mental power maintains itself with only slight diminution into the forties or fifties, but from then on decline sets in definitely. But the drop in old age is not nearly so steep as the rise in childhood.

Training and Growth

Recent studies have indicated that some animals must receive prompt training in certain necessary skills and that failure to provide such training at the most appropriate or opportune time may make subsequent learning efforts more difficult or even useless. Of course, if there is a best time for learning certain tasks, there is also need for the best methods and effective motivation to be used; otherwise, the advantage of proper timing will not be realized.

---

[2] See L. L. Thurstone, *The Differential Growth of Mental Abilities* (Chapel Hill: University of North Carolina, 1955).

Of great importance to the educator is the question whether the training or education of the child can speed up the process of growth or maturation. If we take great pains to train a child to walk or to talk, as early as possible, will he profit by it later on, in the sense that he will ever after be more capable in these functions than he would have been if left to develop these functions by the customary incidental learning of the normal environment? Is it the business of education to train as many functions as early as possible? Or is this procedure more or less futile, because these functions will develop normally as the child matures and ultimately reach their full efficiency? Will the untrained child catch up to the trained child owing to the ordinary processes of maturation and growth? Two methods have been used to help in answering these questions: the method of co-twin control and the method of comparing trained and untrained equated groups.

Gesell. The method of co-twin control was used effectively by Gesell. It depends upon the similarities of identical twins. One of the pair is trained in certain functions and the other is used as an untrained control. In this way training in climbing stairs, manipulating cubes or blocks, and language have been studied in young children. The trained twin always forges ahead as a result of the special practice. At the end of such practice the trained twin is much superior to the control. As time goes on, however, this difference is gradually wiped out and the two children become more or less alike. Over a period of several months, such as these experiments usually cover, the advantages of early training are not permanent. Maturation is of greater influence.

Jersild. The other method is to employ equated groups of children instead of a pair of twins. Several such experiments have been carried out. Extensive results have been reported by Jersild. His children ranged in age from two to eleven. He trained them in different mental, motor, and musical performances, such as tapping, vital capacity, strength of back, free association, color naming, strength of grip, the singing of tones and intervals. In all cases the practiced children forged ahead of the unpracticed because of the special training, as we should expect. When training stopped they were, more or less, superior to the unpracticed. Three months later there was no difference between the practiced and unpracticed, except in strength of grip and singing. After seven and a half months the differences in strength of grip disappeared. With reference to singing, reliable differences in favor of the practiced group remained after four months. How long this group would have remained superior or whether it would remain superior in vocal ability permanently, we do not know. The experimenter is inclined to think that the latter result is possible in the sense that they may have been started "on the way toward making full use of their vocal powers." And he adds, "without training a child might readily become fixed in the habit of using only a limited portion of his vocal range."

Effects of Early Training. In general we may say that in most mental and motor capacities that have been investigated, we find that early training seems to lead to mere temporary improvement. Maturation is the determining factor. But there is the suggestion that early training may lead to an extension of knowledge or skill, which otherwise may not be obtained, and thus result in a permanent advantage for the rest of one's life. This last suggestion is at present purely hypothetical.

Growth in General

Growth in general, both mental and physical, so far as it has been studied, is found to be continuous and not saltatory. It proceeds at an even pace and not by leaps and bounds. There are great individual differences in rate of growth, and various traits within the individual grow at different rates. In general the development proceeds at the rate at which it starts. The tall child becomes the tall man; the dull child becomes the dull man. But Terman and Merrill reported (1960) that intelligence test scores in early childhood do not indicate precisely what the intelligence test scores of the same children will be in later years. The tests may be imperfect or they may measure different factors at the different age levels. Further, according to F. Riessman (1962), the cultural opportunities and wealth of the community affect the intelligence test scores of children.[3]

---

[3] See F. Riessman, *The Culturally Deprived Child* (New York: Harper and Brothers, 1962).

Physical growth slows down and practically ceases before or in the early twenties; some aspects of intelligence and ability to learn remain on a high level and do not markedly begin to decline until the late forties or fifties. Maturation is a highly significant factor in the development of our capacities. Training does not seem to affect permanently the stages or patterns of growth in fundamental motor and mental abilities.

Unconventional behavior of children may annoy the teacher but may reflect highly creative tendencies in some instances. Investigations by J. P. Guilford, J. W. Getzels, and P. W. Jackson reported in the 1960's on the differences between originality, high intelligence, and creativity (e.g., musical, artistic, or mechanical capacities), indicating that the most creative pupils often tend to place little value on the standards or conventions most prized by adults. The teacher must, nevertheless, recognize and encourage the fullest development of creative abilities.

Retardation in any aspect of growth, resulting in such things as an exceptionally small stature for a boy or a very tall stature for a girl, may cause social and psychological maladjustments of the individual. The teacher must take handicaps of this kind into account in helping the child to cope with these disadvantages. Among American children, boys tend to develop a larger build and greater strength than girls in all stages except a brief period during middle or late childhood (about eight to eleven years of age) when girls spurt ahead temporarily in physiological development. These growth differences may affect individual boys or girls in regard to their self-respect, ability to master assigned tasks or skills, and relationships in school, home, and community.

Chapter 4
Behavior Processes

Teachers are interested mainly in the kinds of behavior that can be changed or learned. Nevertheless, learning takes place within limits set by the child's physical endowment and inherited equipment. Psychologists have therefore made intensive studies of the behavior patterns of infants and of other children during the pre-school period. They have investigated the entire range of the child's earliest reactions and have attempted to describe the neural basis for the modification of behavior. Such modification can be achieved by means of environmental influences, i.e., by eliciting repeated responses to stimuli. Examples are the use of rewards for approved reactions and the providing of desirable social experiences. Although some behavior patterns may be difficult to modify, a great many desirable responses can be reinforced so that they become habitual, while certain less desirable ones can often be counteracted or eliminated. Some contemporary psychologists believe that any task of learning can be broken down into small units or steps, each requiring specific reactions, and that the child can thus master skills and knowledge perfectly in an orderly progression. The recent development of programed instruction is based upon this belief in the ready modifiability of the learner's reaction patterns.

Early Behavior Patterns

The newborn infant's earliest tendencies seem to depend upon inherited connections in the nervous system, perhaps upon the growth of synaptic connections in the central nervous system, establishing neural pathways which lead to more or less specific responses to stimuli. Some reactions are highly specific, while others are relatively indefinite. The most specific reactions are the reflexes. Warren listed about 70 reflexes and grouped them into categories according to the possibility of modification. As least modifiable he listed such reflexes as the pupillary reflex, hand withdrawal from heat, and trembling. Somewhat more amenable to inhibition and reinforcement are such reactions as winking, sneezing, salivation, and blushing. Still more subject to control are coughing, gasping, weeping, scowling, and wincing. These simple reactions are not generally of great significance for the educator, but they are, of course, quite important for the proper functioning of the body.

Psychologists today question the old idea that the newborn infant inherits unlearned tendencies to action which are more complex than these simple reflexes. There seems to be no sharp dividing line between the reflex (or a series of reflex activities) and the learned reaction to environmental stimuli. A normal, healthy infant will vocalize, but just what form his vocalization will take, and what language it will develop into, depends upon the environment surrounding him. According to Hollingworth, the individual inherits only a vague unrest, not specific tendencies. This vague unrest is allayed by responses, and the nature of these responses, built upon this vague unrest, is determined by the environment. Many of the behaviorist psychologists reject the entire concept of the inheritance of neural patterns and conclude that nothing is inherited except anatomical characteristics which are not definite enough to lead to specific behavior. According to this point of view, it is best to regard behavior at any particular instance as the end result of all previous development. It is generally agreed that the extent to which a specific behavior pattern can be considered inborn (or "instinctive") depends upon the degree to which it is based on biological maturation as contrasted with learning from experience. Indeed, at least from the Gestalt psychologists' point of view, all behavior is determined by the body as a whole, not by any specific neuro-muscular pattern, inherited or acquired. So far as behavior patterns of importance to education are concerned, contemporary psychologists agree, moreover, that what the teacher and parent do, and the natural and social environment as a whole, are the dominant influences.

Manipulation and Vocalization

Manipulation refers to the child's activity of handling objects in order to modify or control them as a means of gaining satisfaction. It involves both reflexes and learned behavior. The desire to touch any object we are attending to is very great, particularly in the young child. "Let Wawie see," says the two-year-old Walter, looking directly at the object, as he stretches out his hands to grasp it. Seeing and manipulating mean for him the same thing. "Do not touch" is plastered over all our museums, unfortunately for the human observers, but fortunately for the precious objects. In teaching, therefore, the more manipulation we can introduce, the easier will the child probably learn. Hence the educational value of teaching by doing, cutting out things, building things, shop work of all kinds, laboratories, apprenticeship, internship. The United States represents a type of civilization which has fostered and rewarded more than others this manipulative tendency of the individual.

All normal infants make vocal noises. Vocalization begins with the cry of the infant at birth. The number of sounds made before anything like speech develops is enormous. Gesell has reported a twenty-four-hour count of the vocal reactions for a six-months-old child. A total of 104 vocal reactions were made, distributed among 64 different sounds. Gradually certain sounds or words or phrases come to be preferred because they obtain results. The child begins to speak the specific language of his environment. If he is in a bi-lingual environment, he begins to speak two languages. One set of sounds brings results when addressed to father and mother, but another set of sounds is needed for children outside the home. In all education we make use of this marvelous ability to vocalize. It is so generally taken for granted that it is not until we are forced to do without it, as in the education of the deaf, that we begin to realize what a great amount of incidental learning the child picks up by means of it.

In all phases of education we should build upon the earliest behavior patterns and original equipment of the individual. Thus we should make use of manipulation as much as possible. We should use the interest in companionship to encourage games and other group activities. Vocalization is generally very well made use of, and it is good that this is so, because much of our thinking depends upon it. The business of education with respect to our earliest basic tendencies is, as Thorndike suggested, to help restrain some of them, to modify others, and to encourage the most desirable.

The Emotions

Emotions may be defined as a general stirred-up state of the whole body, reflected in modified or new feelings, desires, and covert as well as overt patterns of behavior. They may be considered exaggerations of normal reactions, for the state of agitation ordinarily diminishes in due time so that the specific emotions seem to disappear. They are accompanied by definite mental states and by marked physiological action, including increased or restricted glandular activity.

Theories Concerning Emotions. There have been many theories as to the nature and genesis of emotions. The older psychology emphasized the mental aspect, the agitated state of mind. Bodily accompaniments were regarded as consequents of this mental disturbance.

James-Lange Theory. The James-Lange theory challenged this assumption. It is called the James-Lange theory because it was first propounded at about the same time (1884–85) by two scientists independently: William James, the American psychologist, and Carl Lange, the Danish physiologist. This theory maintains that bodily changes are primary, antecedent to the mental state. Instead of the sequence from situation to mental state to bodily expression, the sequence should be from situation to bodily disturbance to mental state. The bodily disturbance is held to be due to instinctive or habitual responses aroused by a specific situation. Perception of these visceral and skeletal changes is the emotion itself. To use James's famous example, we should not say "we meet a bear, are frightened, and then run," but rather "we meet a bear, run, and are frightened." Similarly, we feel sad because we cry, afraid because we tremble. This theory has led to much experimentation by physiologists, most of whom do not believe that the experimental results sustain it.

Cannon-Dana Theory. According to another theory, this one suggested by the physiologists Cannon and Dana (and reinforced by the researches of Bard and others), emotion results from the action and reaction of the cerebral cortex and the diencephalon (a part of the forebrain). When the thalamic processes in the diencephalon are aroused, they lead to discharges in two directions at the same time, into the cortex and into the motor nerves, causing bodily changes. The bodily changes are, therefore, neither consequents nor antecedents of conscious states. They are simply the accompaniments. The essence of the theory, according to Cannon, is that "the peculiar quality of the emotion is added to simple sensation when the thalamic processes are aroused." Recently it has been reported that the amygdala exerts a regulatory influence on the hypothalamus so that, for example, the resulting emotion may become manifest either as rage or calmness. Investigation of brain-wave recordings (made by the electroencephalograph, or EEG) by D. B. Lindsley and others seems to have verified the close relationship between functions of the cerebral cortex and accompanying emotional responses.

Expressions of the Emotions. Among the expressions of the emotions are facial expressions, vascular reactions, respiration changes, gastrointestinal reactions, and the like. Early investigations of emotional reactions cast doubt upon the common assumption that facial manifestations of anger, fear, joy, disgust, hate, and so on are supposed to be distinctive. If we ask observers to judge the emotions depicted by a photo or drawing of the face, we find slight agreement between the judgment of the observer and the conventional expression of an emotion as drawn by an artist or depicted by an actor when photographed. Experiments show that children improve with age in their judgment of facial expression. They learn to recognize conventional modes of expression. But analysis of photographs taken of subjects when emotionally disturbed were shown by Landis to indicate that "there is no pattern of expression which may be said to characterize any situation or emotion." The early studies of facial expression were significant in pointing to the need for careful investigation of popular assumptions about human nature and conduct.

Teachers must bear in mind constantly the important effects of emotions upon the child's behavior. For example, fear, anger, or joy most often lead to increased interest and activity; sorrow, to decreased activity. The use of lie detectors in the investigation of crime illustrates well some of the ways in which the emotions affect the individual's reactions. As soon as a subject taking a lie-detector test hears a question related to his criminal act or knowledge about a crime, marked changes occur in his respiration, blood pressure, and other physiological functions. Psychologists have made extensive use of the lie detector to ascertain and measure emotional states of individuals in a great variety of social situations.

Modifications of the Emotions. Emotions, as they exist in the adult, are not inherited primary reactions, although they may be based on very early reaction patterns. Fear, love, and rage were considered by J. B. Watson to be present at birth and to be reactions to certain types of stimuli. The expression of emotions is modified by our environment, by our training and experience. The stimuli that originally call forth emotional responses in the newborn infant are few. By conditioning, their number is rapidly increased in later stages of development. Conditioning is the process by which a response originally attached to a given stimulus becomes transferred to another stimulus that occurs at the same time as or shortly after the original stimulus. In Watson's classical experiment a child was confronted with a rat, a rabbit, a dog, a mask with hair, etc., and to these the response was reaching and manipulating. When, however, a loud noise (striking a steel bar) was made several times on presentation of the white rat, the child responded by showing fear (shrinking, crying, etc.). Soon the presentation of the white rat alone (without the noise) was sufficient to call forth fear responses. The fear response had been shifted to the white rat. The child had been conditioned to fear the rat. And when the rabbit, the dog, the mask, and similar objects were later presented, the child showed fear responses toward them. Thus the fear spread or was transferred from the rat to similar objects. The child's behavior was modified or conditioned so that a number of stimuli called forth the fear response. Unconditioning is the reverse process and by this means a child's fear for a given stimulus can be changed to another type of response.

Since many of our hates, loves, and fears are probably formed in some such manner early in life, the importance of the pre-school and early school years is apparent. The opportunity to help the child to develop constructive patterns of emotional response which will persist throughout his career has been cited as one of the justifications for the expansion of pre-school education. Some unreasonable antipathies or fears of adults undoubtedly go back to early conditioning. We may "hate" arithmetic or we may "hate" French, because of some events in early school life. And similarly may be explained some of our unreasonable "loves" and "likes."

Emotion and Learning. Emotion has been referred to as a general stirring-up of the individual. It moves him to act (or desist from action) either to gain some desired result or to avoid an undesired one. It can help to sustain or intensify the learner's efforts. Sometimes, strong emotion can impede or inhibit skilled behavior, accurate performance, and clear thinking. Thus, anger may disturb the athlete and destroy some of his skill; fear or embarrassment may cause the lecturer to ramble and to lose the thread of his discourse. In learning, whether motor or verbal, deep emotional states, unless they are kept under control and properly directed, can interfere with the normal on-going of the process. Anxiety about consequences may at times stimulate children to avoid danger or encourage them to prepare for life's contingencies; but excessive fear of the future will more often impede genuine interest, spontaneity, and learning. In creative work, particularly in art or music, emotion has long been thought of as playing a leading role. It does, in the sense of emotional experiences furnishing the motive for creative effort, in furnishing the subjects for portrayal. In production, however, emotion must not be allowed to run wild, for uncontrolled emotion at this stage would undoubtedly interfere with skillful technique. In the appreciation of art by the observer, we have either the unemotional intellectual appreciation of the technique of the artist, or the expression of a mild emotion usually in some conventional form.

The teacher is expected to note the emotional reactions of children and to assist the process of adjustment. Thus, the child who is overdependent, indecisive, or subject to excessive fear needs encouragement, honest praise for successes, and ample opportunities to develop confidence, self-direction, and creativity. Other children, on the other hand, may need guidance in the direction of self-correction, self-discipline, and the assumption of increasing responsibility.

Methods of Behavior Adjustment

Freud and others have suggested how our emotions and behavior patterns develop and function. The desires, wishes, urges, of the individual are the earliest moving forces in his life. At all stages of human development, problems arise which cannot immediately be solved, and it is necessary for us to make adjustments to challenging life situations. Among the principal methods of adjustment are: extroversion, introversion, sublimation, identification, compensation, and rationalization.

Extroversion. From early childhood we have to learn to modify our tendencies to react. They come into sharp conflict with the requirements of our culture. Manipulation must be suppressed with reference to many things. We cannot always strike out when angry, shout or scream when frightened, seize what we desire. Hence the fact of conflict. Freud pointed out that particularly in expression of what he called the sex instinct (he used this term in a very broad sense encompassing basic aspects of human personality), much modification must be made. And when a conflict arises between desires or impulses and the social environment, the child tries to find a solution, often through some form of extrovert behavior, an overt reaction to the situation. If he is angry but does not dare to strike the person who causes the anger, perhaps he will later strike others or let loose his bad temper upon them. Swearing, bullying, playing truant, and many other modes of antisocial behavior may at times be examples of extrovert responses. Knowledge of this mechanism may help us to understand what might otherwise seem to be merely the unreasonable conduct of a child. Perhaps we can then channel his interest and guide his efforts in more useful directions.

Introversion. Here the conflict is resolved by some inner response, such as the play of imagination or daydreaming, the life of fantasy. The introvert retreats within himself and gets revenge upon his opponent by means of imagination. The unsuccessful and despised individual consoles himself with glorious deeds which he accomplishes in his imagination.

Introversion and extroversion are mechanisms of behavior and in themselves are neither good nor bad. Either of them may, however, lead to undesirable types of response. Extroversion may lead to the use of drugs, overeating, or even alcoholism, cruelty, and the like. Introversion may lead to excessive daydreaming, to a withdrawal within oneself, to a refusal to face reality, so that the individual becomes more and more crippled in dealing with the outside world. Fortunately, most people are neither extreme extroverts nor extreme introverts, but *ambiverts*, reacting openly and confidently in some situations, more shyly in others. Teachers can do much to encourage the development of well-adjusted ambivert personality in children through the power of suggestion and example.

Sublimation. If the individual adopts a way around the conflict such that he benefits himself or society, then we say that sublimation has taken place. Sublimation is the turning of unreasoning or less desirable impulses into more desirable channels. If the daydream spurs our ambition and leads to the accomplishment of work, to the creation of a poem or a picture, sublimation has occurred. Sexual impulses are sometimes the most troublesome for young people because drastic adjustments to community standards, as in sublimation, are necessary. The best relationship between boys and girls can usually be achieved through the provision of information and guidance most appropriate to their stage of growth with emphasis upon the goal of cooperation and mutual respect. Through sublimation the child can substitute for some biological urges an interest in creative arts, group activities, and socially approved work for school and community.

Identification. Children look up to and imitate the behavior of those teachers, parents, and other adults who seem to be influential, successful people. They take pride in being close to persons who have achieved power and prestige, including their peers who become leaders, and they try to emulate historical or contemporary public figures. They bask in the glory attached to their heroes, for they themselves long to be respected and admired. The wise teacher helps the child to choose the best models to emulate but to develop his own unique individuality, exercising the right to be "different" while at the same time he shows regard for the opinions, rights, and welfare of others.

Compensation. If the child experiences too many failures, there is danger that he will lose confidence, perhaps even developing a persistent pessimistic attitude, a feeling of inferiority with reference to other people. He may then expect to fail again, avoid taking the initiative, and let others lead the way. Sometimes, however, he may try to cover up this feeling of inferiority by assuming a bold front. To compensate for his shyness, he may become brusque and rude. The child who has a deep-rooted feeling of inferiority must be carefully handled and not be too roughly treated. He must be helped to achieve adequate success and be given well-deserved praise which will foster self-confidence. When he cannot measure up to the accomplishments of his heroes, he must be reassured that he is making satisfactory progress toward a worthwhile goal.

Rationalization. How often we act on impulse or by force of habit, without previous deliberation! We act before we reason why. Yet we pride ourselves upon being reasonable creatures. Consequently, for nearly all our acts, we attempt to find a reasonable motive. This procedure is called rationalization. Frequently we do not know the motive for an act, or, if we do know, we are ashamed of it, because it does not coincide with the ideal we have formed of ourself. We try to find a motive which will not be incompatible with this self-ideal, and in doing so we rationalize, that is, we devise a logical explanation or justification for our conduct. If we earnestly attempt to find the real mainspring of our conduct, then we are not rationalizing. We all rationalize at times and frequently it is of no great moment, but the danger lies in the possibility of forming a habit of self-deception, and under the cloak of rationalization we may then gratify base desires while pretending to ourselves and to others that they are in conformity with our better self.

In the education of children we must beware of fostering this tendency to rationalize. In early childhood many, or perhaps most, acts are not reasoned out carefully beforehand. So, when the child does annoying things, we must not continually belabor him with "Why did you do it?" and insist upon an answer. If we do this, we gradually teach him to find acceptable excuses for his conduct. Better a sharp reprimand or punishment and be done with it. From some adult lecturing and reasoning the child may find suggestions for future rationalizations.

PART TWO

The Learning Process
by John J. Ryan

Chapter 5
Nature and Scope of the Learning Process

Learning and living are coexistent and, in a general sense, there is as little need as there is possibility of defining adequately the one or the other. Learning, deliberate or undeliberate, conscious or subconscious, goes on throughout the life of the organism, resulting in a progressive understanding of, adjustment to, and control of the environment and the organism itself. However, during that period of life referred to as schooling, learning is no longer casual or adventitious. It is largely verbal and demands concentration of effort. It is a race against time toward goals that seem abstract and remote and through media that are mere symbols of realities. Too often the interest and urgency of the life situation are replaced by such extrinsic motivations as grades and the passing of verbal or written tests. Herein lies, in part, the justification for the attempt to analyze and understand learning whether as process or product and to derive principles of guidance for the student.

Three theories of learning prominent in educational literature are the *connectionism* of E. L. Thorndike, the *conditioned response* of J. B. Watson and the behaviorists, and the *insight* theory of the Gestalt psychologists. In a phenomenon so complex and so varied in its manifestations as learning, the proponents of diverse views have little difficulty in finding support for their hypotheses. Most recently indeed, one aspect of the seemingly over-simplified theory of the behaviorists has found fruitful application in the content and arrangement of material or data used in the "programed" instruction of learning machines.

Before the beginning of the present century, E. L. Thorndike (1874–1949) and his followers, in an attempt to establish an objective or experimentally verified theory of learning as a process, had studied the activities of cats and rodents in mazes and other contrived situations where conditions were under relatively complete control. The so-called laws of learning, examined later in this text, resulted from these investigations. At this point it should be noted that conclusions derived from experiments with subhumans are applicable to human behavior only by analogy, with all the limitations attaching to this form of reasoning. In fact, later experiments in the field of human learning forced Thorndike to amend his original conclusions. Furthermore, in the basic studies of human learning the desire for scientific objectivity and control led to the use of nonsense syllables (surely not a life situation) in an effort to avoid or cancel out the effects of association and prior experience.

Connectionism or the "bond" theory of learning states that learning is essentially a process of establishing a bond between a stimulus or situation (S) and a desired response (R). Thus the formula S—R became symbolical of the learning process as a whole and a framework for the planning and interpretation of many experimental investigations. The bond between S and R which constitutes learning is brought about in accordance with three major laws or principles, called *readiness, exercise,* and *effect,* plus a supplementary principle or amendment called *belongingness,* derived from later studies in the learning of humans. These laws are examined later in this text.

The behaviorists, following J. B. Watson (1878–1958), proceeded on the hypothesis that all behavior is learned and controllable, and simply a matter of the repeated association of the factors involved with due regard to recency, order, and intensity. The conditioned response discussed elsewhere in this text represents for them the basis or prototype of all learning. For Thorndike as for most psychologists, it is indeed an important factor in learning but not the fundamental type of learning.

For the Gestalt psychologists, learning is essentially the progressive discovery and relating of elements in any perceived or visualized whole of experience resulting in *insight*. Past related experience is, in this theory, of paramount importance and the mere repetition of any situation is not the operative factor. Considerable experimental evidence in support of this theory has been presented, mainly in the field of perception.

Educational Psychology and Learning

The psychologist tries to discover the elemental facts of the learning process, its physiological basis, and the laws of its operation. His present temper is to reject any explanation which cannot be expressed in terms of natural science (physiology, biology, chemistry, etc.). Within such limits no adequate theory is yet at hand. The educator, however, is primarily concerned with method, and the conditions which favor effective learning. Here, fortunately, he has the assurance of experience and common sense, no less than experimental inquiry, that human learning is facilitated by prior understanding of the material to be assimilated or the goal to be reached, as well as by a judicious use of praise and reproof, and that greater permanence and control are secured by attentive practice and the will to learn. Our knowledge of the learning process in all its phases has been considerably refined, modified, and extended. The functions of praise, reproof, and repetition, for example, have been determined. The process of association or conditioning has been found operative in unsuspected forms of behavior and in a wide range of responses, giving us considerable control over the latter. Innumerable factors ancillary to the learning process, such as motivation, the physiological conditions of learning, the transfer of training, the technique of study, and individual differences have been analyzed. Here the experimental method has contributed much to advancement in educational theory and practice.

Goals in Learning. Since much of the terminology used in the study of learning derives from the analytic approach to the subject found in rational or philosophical psychology, it will be helpful to outline this approach very briefly. Man's psychological experience may be divided into three general categories, namely *cognition* or knowledge, *feeling* or affection, and *volition* or willing. This classification is still valid and useful in that it suggests succinctly the main goals in learning and the scope of learning as an educative process. Those goals are the acquisition of knowledge, the learning of proper values or appreciations, and the development of the will to act, as a habit or tendency. Additionally, it may be observed that this classification offers a perspective from which to view and evaluate the educational system as a whole. The concept of volition, to be sure, though taken for granted in legal and common parlance, is not conspicuous in educational literature, experimental or other. The reason is not far to seek. Volition or will is a concept with philosophical implications not in harmony with the positivistic and analytic approach of modern scientific method. The concept, however, is fundamental and inescapable, whatever its rationale. In current discussions of learning and behavior it appears under some such headings as drive, motivation, effort, and the like, but usually as a response or reaction to stimulation, external or internal, rather than an initiation deriving primarily from the individual himself. Socially desirable behavior, for example, or discipline are best secured, it is thought, by providing the environment or stimulation calculated to evoke such responses, rather than by appealing directly to the will of the individual.

Definitions of Terms. Following are brief definitions of terms frequently occurring in the literature of educational psychology.

Perception. Perception refers to the acquisition of specific knowledge about objects or events directly stimulating the senses at any particular moment. Perceptions or immediate presentations involve cognition (knowledge). In perception, the object is seen or interpreted in the light of pertinent experiences from the past. For the composite of a given sensory experience plus the reinstated or revived past experience, the term *apperception* was suggested by Herbart. Ordinarily all perception involves apperception.

Conception or Generalization. Conception means the acquisition of organized knowledge in the form of concepts or general ideas, which transcend any particular percept. The *percept* refers to an individual or specific situation; the *concept* is general or universal in its reference.

Associative Learning. This aspect of learning corresponds to memory, both as the deliberate recall and recognition of past experience and as habit or automatic memory due to associations. Under the general concept of memory (comprising *learning, retention, recall,* and *recognition*), associative learning is fundamental to all other learning.

Appreciation. In appreciation is involved the acquisition of ideals, attitudes, or dispositions characterized by an emotional tone. This factor is the affective or feeling element in knowledge. An *ideal* is a concept colored by appreciation—a sense of worth or value.

Acquisition of Skill. The educational psychologist regards skills as sensori-motor processes. Writing, reading, musical performance, language acquisition in its vocal aspects, drawing, and the arts generally are essentially a composite of knowledge, appreciation, and appropriate motor reactions developed to the point of automatic response.

Methods of Learning. Methods of learning are investigated from two points of view: the principal types; and the means of guidance. Psychologists distinguish certain modes or types of learning, such as imitation, trial-and-error (or trial-and-success), observation, and insight. They also furnish certain principles of guidance that make for economy and efficiency in learning, with suggestions, for example, on how to study, how to retain, the recitation method, spaced repetition, and the whole-to-part method of learning.

Theories of Learning. The theories of learning developed by educational psychologists may be either explanatory in the scientific sense, or merely descriptive and methodological. An adequate explanation of the learning process would disclose the neural basis of learning and the laws of its operation. Though much is known about the nervous system, psychologists confess inability to explain the relation between structure and function in learning. Nevertheless, the various theories offered, though descriptive and methodological rather than explanatory, have implications as to the nature and functioning of the nervous system. Thus the theory of connectionism, particularly in regard to the law of frequency, often implies acceptance of the neurophysiological conception of resistance at the synapse—a view of learning as the result of neural pathways formed by repeated passage of nerve impulses through the nervous system. The Gestalt theory implies that, since any learning experience is a temporary adjustment of the whole organism, the adjustment is not definitely represented in brain structure; the same parts of the brain function differently under varying stimulus-conditions, and structure does not determine function. Behaviorists, Gestaltists, and other psychologists have contributed many important theories on the transfer of training—how learning acquired in one experience carries over into another—and all such theories have had an impact upon the practical work of modern education.

(The student should note that the psychological terms commonly used represent aspects of the process which have no separate or exact correspondence in reality. All sensori-motor learnings, for example, involve cognition or knowledge in the form of percepts and concepts, just as they imply attention and observation in the acquisition of facility of response. Trial-and-success learning in human beings usually involves some measure of observation and the formulation of hypotheses or suggestions. Appreciations, in the form of concomitant learnings, enter into all types of activity: they are the attitudes, dispositions, and emotional colorings which inevitably attend the general processes of experiencing and learning. Experience is at once cognitive, affective, and conative.)

Important Types or Modes of Learning

The most important types of learning investigated by educational psychologists are the following: observation, insight, and imitation—three interrelated modes of learning; trial-and-success learning; generalization or concept formation; purposeful activity; problem solving; incidental learning; and primary and concomitant learning.

Observation, Insight, and Imitation. *Observation* is but another name for perception characterized by attention. To observe is to attend, and perception is enriched by such attention. Perception can also be enriched by multiple sense appeal. The educational application is that learning should begin with objects, or representations of objects, rather than with symbols. *Insight* is often referred to as the end process of observational activity (which may or may not be preceded by so-called "verbal rehearsal," or mental trial-and-success). Observation means attention to pertinent relations; insight signifies that success has attended this process of mental research. The mental integration by which a problem is more or less suddenly seen in all its relations constitutes insight. *Imitation,* according to some psychologists, is merely uniformity of response of similar organisms to similar situations. It is, therefore, neither conscious nor due to observation. Other psychologists confine it to the blind performance of an activity because one has observed another doing it—the activity already being to some extent within the capacity of the imitator. In this sense, imitation is often limited to the performance of an act regardless of the end to which it leads. To the Gestaltists, however, imitation is always the reproduction of a movement with a configuration involving understanding and aim, though imitation of movements as such, without conscious aim, may be approximated in drill, when mere uniformity of motion is desired. Less technically, imitation is defined as the tendency to repeat the observed actions of others. The tendency is generally inhibited unless the person imitated is deemed superior, or the action itself is deemed worthy of imitation. Imitation may be conscious or unconscious. Wherever models are set up, imitation plays a part; it need never be exact, or mere copy; and instead of destroying initiative or originality it should serve as a stimulus thereto. Through conscious and unconscious imitation the customary behavior and moral codes of his social milieu become ingrained in the child's behavior. Imitation is, therefore, an important moral, intellectual, and social agent in formal education and throughout life.

Trial-and-Success Learning. This type is also known as "learning by selection of the successful variant," and, less accurately, as "trial-and-error" learning. Its characteristic feature is that the perception of relations between means and end is either vague or almost entirely lacking. In this latter sense it is more common among animals, and amounts to selecting, after repeated efforts, the method that has proved successful. Observation of a very elementary kind is always involved, even in animal learning. Ascending the biological scale, observation of pertinent relations increases, and the need of trial-and-success diminishes. But unless there is more or less complete knowledge at the start, the trying out of hypotheses is always present in some degree. In this view, then, trial-and-success learning is purposive. It is learning directed toward a goal; and each step in the process, whether successful or not, is planned. Trial-and-success learning should not be identified with mere random activity in which the correct responses are originally made by chance. When applied to problems capable of yielding general principles, trial-and-error activity results in insight as interpreted by Gestalt psychology.

Generalization or Concept Formation. These two terms represent different aspects of one of the most fundamental processes in learning, i.e., the development of concepts. The educated man has developed well founded concepts of such important factors in life as patriotism, energy, truth, and the like. The concept transcends the particular or individual perceptions from which it is derived. In our concrete experiences of objects, persons, events, etc., of everyday life, we may distinguish, intellectually, two kinds of qualities or characteristics: those peculiar to each situation, and those which it possesses in common with others of its kind or class. When the common or essential element in a number of experiences has been recognized and abstracted from the multitude of individuating or accidental qualities, a concept has been formed: generalization has taken place. The end product of a generalization is a rule, principle, definition, axiom, or scientific law. Experiences thus generalized into concepts become "standards of reference" representing whole classes or kinds of things or events. Transfer of knowledge and adaptability to new situations are thus made possible. Experience with a large number and variety of particular exemplars of a concept or principle helps generalization. In formal instruction generalization is facilitated by having the essential element appear amid a variety of non-essentials. The child who has been led through "dissociation by varying concomitants" (a term used by William James) to realize that the use of x, y, z is not an essential feature in the theory of equations, has been helped to generalize. Thorndike suggested three steps for formal instruction in generalization: *piecemeal examination, varying the concomitants,* and *contrast*.

The Project Method. Three significant results of modern education have been the emphasis placed on *motivation, problem solving* (stressing pupil initiative in planning, organizing and checking, rather than the acquisition of information) and the *project*. Varying definitions refer to the project as (1) a method of teaching and learning, and (2) a principle on which to organize the subject matter of the curriculum. Subject matter so organized results in a series of projects, each involving reference to many traditionally organized topics such as history, geography, arithmetic, and, in addition, whatever else may be needed to conduct the activity in question. To Kilpatrick, whole-hearted purposeful activity on the part of the pupil is the chief characteristic and recommendation of the project. The attitude which the pupil assumes during a project is the very heart of the learning process. Kilpatrick recognizes four types of projects: *producer's, consumer's, problem,* and *drill* projects. The project, no doubt, has its limitations, but carries with it the most desirable and effective type of motivation: interest in the activity for its own sake. Much of the learning resulting from the project is said to be acquired incidentally, but such learning, particularly when followed by a judicious use of the "drill" project is among the most permanent possessions of the pupil.

Problem Solving: Five Phases of Reflective Thought. A major emphasis of modern education is the insistence that the pupil be taught to think—how to solve problems. This emphasis is a reaction against the alleged traditional conception of learning as the accumulation of facts or information. Learning, says Dewey, is learning to think, and, upon its intellectual side, education is the formation of careful and thorough habits of thinking. Reflective thought may be analyzed into five phases, at the extremes of which we recognize a *pre-reflective* or beginning situation, in which there is perplexity or confusion, and at the end a *post-reflective* situation—a feeling of mastery or satisfaction, when the doubt and confusion have been dispelled. In between, as states of thinking, are: (1) *suggestions* of possible solutions; (2) an intellectualization of the difficulty into a *problem* to be solved; (3) the use of one suggestion after another as a leading idea or *hypothesis* to guide observation and the gathering of facts; (4) *reasoning* in the narrow sense of the mental development of the ideas or assumptions; and (5) testing the hypothesis by overt activity. These five phases or functions of thought are not alleged to follow one another in any set order; there is usually considerable overlapping. The student should be familiar with the *five steps in the complete act of thought*, under the headings: activity, problem, data, hypothesis and testing.

Incidental Learning. It is claimed that the alphabet can be taught as effectively *while the child is learning to read*, as it used to be taught by long-continued drill. Experiments by Kilpatrick and Willoughby tend to the conclusion that the products of multiplied numbers are learned best through the process of computing the answers, or through the process of incidental learning attending the actual use of the products. Either of these methods gives the numbers meaning which could not be acquired by memorization alone. Memorization as such is said to be ineffective. In incidental learning the student responds to a total stimulus-pattern involving perceived relations.

There is a place for drill or repetition in learning. Speed of reaction is desirable, and this is largely a matter of automatization, not understanding alone. Sponsors of the project method find it desirable to have drill projects. The issue of incidental learning is an important one. The trend in methodology emphasizes teaching through occupational activities: accordingly, learning is to be largely of the incidental or occasional, and concomitant types.

Primary and Concomitant Learnings. The distinction between primary and concomitant learnings is insisted on by Kilpatrick. Primary learnings are the assigned outcomes or objectives of any particular study or project: e.g., to trace the causes of an existent economic depression. During such activities, the student will have occasion to exercise unprejudiced judgment, accuracy in technique, self-reliance, ability to plan, etc. These are the concomitant learnings. They comprehend all the attitudes, appreciations, and general emotional outcomes which one associates with character or personality. Here the teacher's personal influence on the pupil is most potent. The concomitant learnings, therefore, are alleged to be far more important for that most precious outcome of education, namely, character formation, than the more obvious assigned or primary learnings.

Teaching and Types of Learning

That end-product of the educative process which we call learning may be analyzed into knowledges, skills, attitudes, and appreciations. Though these outcomes form an integrated whole, formal or directed learning may be greatly facilitated by recognition of the fact that all are not equally predominant or attainable as objectives at any particular stage of the learning process. In the traditional curriculum and methodology, different subjects or phases of subjects, as well as different objectives, call for recognition of the modes or types of learning involved. These, in turn, should suggest appropriate selection and organization of material in lesson planning as well as suitable procedures in presentation.

In teaching a foreign language, for example, imitation and association would seem to predominate as the types of learning involved, especially in the early stages. Imitation of a good model and well-motivated repetition with varying concomitants, therefore, are methods to be used. Problem solving, disguised as grammatical analysis, should be long deferred. We learn to think and speak in a new language by thinking and speaking in it correctly and frequently. Lesson planning should here take the form of an exhaustive supply of suitably graded phrases and sentences, close to the experience of the learners. Grammatical and analytical matters when presented later should be embodied in concrete usable contexts. The direction of translation should be rather from the new language and, even then, translation should be used only when there is doubt as to understanding. A joyous, wide-awake manner on the part of the teacher, and the use of daily salutations and oral directions in the new vehicle help to create the desired mental set and atmosphere. Failure to realize that language acquisition is largely a sensori-motor form of learning involving imitation and motivated repetition may well account for the comparative failure of foreign language teaching in our schools. The difficulties associated with Latin and Greek may be due in part to the fact that the teaching rather than the languages is "dead."

On the other hand, where conceptualization predominates, as in mathematics or the natural sciences, imitation and drill play a minor roll, to be used only when automatization or routine responses are desired. The Herbartian methodology is recommended here as a guide to the teacher in preparing his materials for presentation. The predominant type of learning involved is generalization, or conceptualization. The predominant method is problem solving.

A still more challenging situation confronts the teacher who uses modern methods of education. Desired outcomes in the form of attitudes do not automatically emerge from life situations or from problems solved; concomitant learnings are not to be taken for granted. Only by recognition and focalization of the desired outcomes and the types of learning involved can the teacher so adapt his methods as to become an efficient guide.

Chapter 6
Factors That Condition Learning

Learning is now regarded as essentially an active process; it is not a passive absorption of knowledge, not the mere reading of books or listening to lectures with the object of reproducing what has been read or heard. True learning is an enrichment of experience. Some consequences of this view are found in the emphasis now laid on <u>activity programs, learning by doing, direct contact with objects, the project method, self-activity, the life situation</u> in the school, etc., rather than on "book learning" or "being told."

More technically, learning is defined as modification through experience, <u>the acquisition of behavior patterns,</u> the modification and coordination of the responses of the organism, and so forth. Such definitions reflect the physiological or objective bias of modern psychology. However inadequate, they are useful in that they bring to light and stress the fact that in learning there is an organism in interaction with its environment, being stimulated by and responding to that environment, and that learning, intelligence, and insight exhibit themselves in greater control of or adaptation to the environment.

Three Factors Condition Learning

Three factors are involved in the learning process. It is the <u>activity</u> of an <u>organism</u> in interaction with its <u>environment</u>. <u>Activity</u> or movement is brought about by <u>motivating</u> the learner.

Motivation is the *psychological factor* in learning. The response of the organism is dependent on the sensitivity of the sensory receptors (visual, auditory, etc.), the condition of the effectors, and the general tone of the organism. Defects of vision, hearing, and the malfunctioning of the glands affect learning directly; and here also must be considered the influences of age and maturation, drugs, and fatigue. Conditions of temperature and ventilation are extremely important, and insofar as they directly affect the organism, forming the milieu in which it is active, they may be classed with purely internal conditions as the *physiological factor* in learning. The third or *environmental* factor represents that management or arrangement of the total environment which experience and psychological analysis demonstrate to be most favorable to the learning process as a whole.

The Psychological Factor: Motivation

For the psychologist, the terms incentive, interest, drive, and purpose stress various aspects of motivation. Motivation is the very heart of the learning process. Adequate motivation not only sets in motion the activity which results in learning, but also sustains and directs it. Reflection, interest, effort, all the outcomes most desired by the teacher and most valuable to the pupil, spring into being with adequate motivation. The average pupil works below his maximum capacity: his achievement quotient (A. Q.) is rarely 100, because of lack of adequate incentive to learn.

Two kinds of motivation are commonly recognized: *intrinsic* and *extrinsic*.

Intrinsic Motivation. This most effective type of drive is secured by making the subject matter significant or meaningful to the learner. The learning carries its own reward; interest is within the activity, and binds the pupil to his work. Meaningful subject matter often depends upon the number of associations successfully discerned by the learner, the form, organization, and pattern into which he organizes it (a factor stressed by J. S. Bruner in the 1960's), and a positive emotional tone which helps to sustain intrinsic interest in the material. The educational application is to begin at the point of contact, and within the range of interest and capacity of the pupil. The project method (wholehearted purposeful activity), the occupational activities in a social medium (characteristic of contemporary education), the apperception concept in the Herbartian methodology, are all attempts to create and utilize intrinsic motivation.

Extrinsic Motivation. Learning must often proceed in the absence of intrinsic motivation. Intellectual immaturity and lack of sensitivity to ultimate consequences and ideals may stand in the way of intrinsic appeal. Extrinsic motivation, however, is so called only because it is external to the learning activity itself; it is not in any sense artificial; it must be built upon the foundation of some existing natural response or tendency; it must be intrinsic to the nature of the individual. Psychology has always recognized the existence of such drives as mastery or dominance, emulation or rivalry, desire for social approval, curiosity, construction, etc. Psychologists disagree whether such tendencies are inherited or acquired, or partly one and partly the other. These drives are the chief sources of spontaneous attention and painless effort. They are enormous resources of potential energy at the disposal of learner and teacher, and they await only judicious employment and wise direction.

Some of the more common forms of extrinsic motivation may be summarized briefly as follows:

Praise and Blame. These incentives are most effective when they come from persons held in esteem by the learner. Limited experimental evidence tends to show that praise stimulates average and inferior children, but has less effect on those of superior intelligence. Reproof is felt most by superior children; but girls seem more susceptible to praise than do boys. Some studies indicate, however, that regardless of age, sex, or initial ability, praise is the most effective of the incentives tested. Reproof seems to decline in effectiveness, for all students. Among experimenters on this factor, Chase in 1932 reported praise to be less effective than blame with young children, but Hurlock's studies in the 1920's led to the general conclusion, still accepted by contemporary investigators, that praise is the more effective stimulus in motivating both immediate and long-continued tasks.

Rivalry. Rivalry between individuals is the least desirable type in that it may tend to breed resentment, jealousy, and an excessively competitive spirit. Rivalry between groups stimulates, but needs control. Self-rivalry, or rivalry in the form of competition with one's past record, is the most valuable type. Graphs of progress and objective standardized tests are of great instrumental value here. It is true that experimental researches have shown rivalry to be a powerful motivating influence. (Leuba's experiments in the 1930's indicated an increase of 47 per cent in the achievement of school children with the introduction of the rivalry element. The work of the superior upper fourth of the group increased 34 per cent, that of the lowest fourth 71 per cent. Maller's studies showed group rivalry to be less effective than individual rivalry.) However, the emotional and social consequences of rivalry must be considered, and the experimental data must be interpreted and utilized with caution.

Rewards and Punishment. These are more concrete expressions of praise and blame. They are, perhaps, the least desirable forms of motivation. Punishment that is too severe, or inflicted when the reason for punishment is not clear and acknowledged, may breed resentment, antagonism, and desire to avoid the form of learning to which it is attached. Rewards, in the form of money, exemptions, and the like, have been shown experimentally to be powerful incentives; but they are hardly ideal forms of motivation. On the intrinsic side, moreover, the joy of beholding a task well done is the best reward and incentive; while punishment by natural consequences (of failure due to lack of effort) carries its own moral.

Observation of child behavior and experimental studies show that individuals tend to repeat forms of behavior which have previously led to satisfying results. A sense of accomplishment may sometimes be induced by an artificial or even unjustified reward, but it is far better grounded if based on the pupil's awareness of real success in learning. The rewarding nature of "felt" progress helps to explain the stimulating effects of progress charts and similar evidence of educational achievement. There is a close relationship between rewards and the next form of extrinsic motivation, knowledge of progress.

Knowledge of Progress. Self-display or elation and a feeling of creativeness are the incentives operative here. A concomitant realization of progress stimulates further effort. The use of graphs, curves of work, and other records of progress is invaluable, especially for younger children. Opportunities for successful accomplishment should be provided, because too frequent failures dishearten pupils and develop a sense of frustration. Work should, therefore, be definite in aim, within the capacity and interest of the pupil, but difficult enough to challenge effort in the accomplishment. The use of the teaching machine with its immediate detection of errors and knowledge of results (feedback) has special advantages from this point of view.

Experiments by Judd in 1905 were among the first to demonstrate that practice without awareness of results had no effect on certain types of learning. For example, Judd found that such practice did not improve the learner's judgments concerning the lengths of lines. Correction of errors supplemented by knowledge of progress did improve the learner's judgments. Thorndike's experiments (reported in 1935) showed similar results in the case of both mental and motor behavior. His experiments with nonsense words seemed to indicate that imperfect learning, under conditions of self-direction, is risky in that it may strengthen incorrect responses. The experimental studies of C. L. Stacey with meaningful material in 1945 led to the contrary conclusion, however, that allowing the learner to discover facts for himself, noting his own errors and progress, is more effective than requiring him to accept ready-made decisions and explanations. More experimentation is needed in order to clarify the complicated processes whereby knowledge of progress influences growth and attainment.

Other Sources of Motivation. These include desire for social approval, the urge to mastery or dominance, to excel, to overcome opposition, to acquire, the sex and parental impulses. To repress ruthlessly such urges is to try to denature the individual; but to allow free and unrestrained outlet is equally disastrous. Natural impulses in themselves are neither good nor bad: they become so to the extent that they are directed into desirable or undesirable channels of action. Management may take the form of redirection or sublimation. It is the part of wisdom to provide outlets that are not merely escape valves, but positive opportunities for achievement. Pictorial art, sculpture, music, literature, etc., are largely expressions of natural drives colored with an emotional tone and given intelligent direction.

The Psychological Basis of Motivation. The psychological factor in all its varied forms is based ultimately on a sense of well-being and satisfaction. This satisfaction results from or accompanies anticipation of successful accomplishment of a task that is attractive in itself, a duty well done (with its consequent relief from tension), or negatively, the avoidance of painful or undesirable consequences. Such experiences tend to impress themselves, and so to be remembered and learned. The popular maxim is "nothing succeeds like success"; and the principle involved is more ambitiously, if less accurately, formulated in the so-called *law of effect*. This law is also expressed as the principle of reinforcement, as, for instance, when his knowledge of success motivates the learner to repeat a learning experience or to take the next step.

Motivation in Contemporary Education. The forms of motivation we have described are not all acceptable to contemporary education. A fundamental thesis of the contemporary school is that education should take place in and through the life situation, that is, through occupational activities true to life and carried out in that spirit of cooperation and responsibility necessary for human beings banded together in a community. Traditional education emphasized the competitive and acquisitive motives, in consonance with a social order which revered individualism and regarded accumulation of wealth as a criterion of successful living. Contemporary education stresses cooperation and sharing, in consonance with its ideal of democracy, a sharing of interests within and among the various groups which constitute the larger society of mankind. Exaggerated competition is no longer to be encouraged. Yet marks, grades, scholarship contests, honor rolls, and the like are still too often considered reputable incentives in an effort to stimulate intellectual endeavor; the dominating influences of the social order from which we are trying to emerge are thus perpetuated, and the school becomes a stumbling block in the path of progress. It is the claim of the proponents of modern education that not only are external or individualistic incentives undesirable as forms of motivation, but they are also unnecessary. Many contemporary schools have successfully subordinated them to social values.

The Physiological Factor

Learning depends on the sensory apparatus, which makes perception possible, and the general tone or condition of the organism.

The Organism and Perception. Throughout the organism, internal to it as well as on the surface, there is a complex organization of sensory receptors which receive and record, in some undefined fashion, the impressions made by internal and external stimulation. To the five important senses recognized by tradition, modern science has added the kinaesthetic, posture, pressure, pain and other senses, largely refinements of the sense of touch. Whatever the number, the aptness of Milton's poetic reference to *sight, hearing, taste, smell,* and *touch,* as the "five gateways of knowledge" remains. All knowledge is based on sense perception. The loss of or defect in any sense means that knowledge and learning are impoverished by so much. Perception means, etymologically, to grasp thoroughly (*percipere*). To grasp thoroughly (on the perceptual level) signifies to react in all possible ways, by sight, touch, etc. This fact is well expressed in the pedagogical dictum, "multiple sense appeal." Perception is not merely the visual, auditory, or other image of an object present to the senses; it involves cognition or the consciousness of a number of facts associated with the object perceived. These facts are derived from past experience with the object, or with related objects. In this sense, it may be said that every act of perception involves *apperception*. It is important, therefore, to examine the organic factors which condition perception, for perception is the foundation of all higher forms of knowledge.

Organic Defects. Sensory defects are obvious adverse factors affecting the learning process. These defects (discussed above, pp. 35 f.) include visual and auditory deficiencies, focal infections, and glandular disturbances. Defects of vision may easily pass unobserved for long periods; they may cause headaches, nausea, and a disinclination to study, often attributed to laziness. The importance of properly printed textbooks, lighting, and posture relative to light is now generally recognized. Estimates of the prevalence of auditory defects range from 3 per cent seriously deaf to 10 to 20 per cent who do not possess entirely normal hearing. Focal infections of the palatine and pharyngeal tonsils, ears, appendix, teeth, and sinuses are common causes of irritability, headaches, and emotional as well as physical maladjustments. Adenoids are the enlarged masses of tissue in the pharyngeal tonsils which may cause mouth breathing and lower vitality. Common glandular disturbances, especially those affecting the thyroid and pituitary glands, may retard growth and mental development and cause muscular and nervous disturbances. Such organic defects often become serious long-lasting obstacles to the learning process.

Fatigue. Muscular, sensory, and mental fatigue are differentiated. Muscular and sensory are conveniently designated as bodily (muscle) fatigue; mental or neural fatigue is generally referred to the central nervous system. Physiologically, fatigue is attributable to the presence of toxic waste products resulting from activity, to the lack of oxygen, and other causes. The chief effect on the learning process is the accompanying set or disposition against sustained intellectual activity. Experimental evidence shows that mental fatigue is extremely difficult to produce. Prolonged mental work may be engaged in with little loss of efficiency, provided adequate stimulation be present. What is called mental fatigue is attributable to *ennui* or *boredom,* and the latter to lack of interest in the subject, poor teaching methods, etc. The remedy is change of method or change of subject, particularly in the case of young children. So-called nervous or mental breakdowns are attributed to worry, malnutrition, or some organic deficiency, rarely to excessive mental work. Eyestrain, posture, and atmospheric conditions are important contributing factors to what is called mental fatigue.

In regard to *sex differences,* there is some evidence that during the secondary school years in particular, girls are more susceptible to strain and anxiety than the majority of boys. School work should be adjusted accordingly. Boys not only have greater resistance physiologically, but being less conscientious as a rule, acquire a degree of immunity to fatigue by giving up work that requires too much scholastic effort.

Time of Day and Learning. Experimental studies by Winch, Gates, Heck, and many others indicate that there is little variation in efficiency throughout the school day. Lessened interest, boredom, restlessness, and poor ventilation (according to Heck) account for any decrease in capacity. Improved teaching methods may, therefore, prove to be the remedy. Studies of progress of evening school pupils show losses of efficiency varying from one to six per cent only. Undue stimulation may, however, account for these results, so that normally such stimulation and greater effort must be used to secure results comparable to work done during the early part of the day.

Atmospheric and Other Conditions. The optimum atmospheric conditions are 68° F., 50 per cent relative humidity, 45 cubic feet of outside air per person per minute. According to experimental evidence, a hot stagnant air condition, undue noise, etc., need not retard the learning process, provided adequate stimulation be present. The experiments, however, covered comparatively short periods of time, and showed merely that when work is undertaken with a will physical discomforts can be overcome. Normally such discomforts are distracting and do not favor the proper mental set or disposition to learn.

Drugs: Alcohol, Caffeine, Tobacco. The experimental evidence about consequences for learning is inconclusive and conflicting. Temporary stimulation in the case of students using such drugs may help tide over a brief period of intense effort, but, in general, prolonged indulgence is, in the long run, unfavorable to the learning process and dangerous to the physical health of the individual.

The Effects of Age on Learning. As indicated in Chapter 2, growth is most rapid in childhood, begins to slow down in adolescence, and reaches a maximum in early manhood and maintains that level of mental power with slight diminution in the forties and fifties. See Figure 1. The maxim "You can't teach an old dog new tricks" is only a half truth, although more effort and application may be required in old age than in youth for the acquisition of a new language or trade. Adults between twenty and forty years of age seem to learn a foreign language more rapidly than young children do. In evaluating the effects of age on learning, the following factors must be taken into account: the age of maximum mental growth (the age at which the Mental Age reaches its limit); the interests, motivation, and apperceptive background present at the ages compared; and the plasticity and general responsiveness of the nervous system.

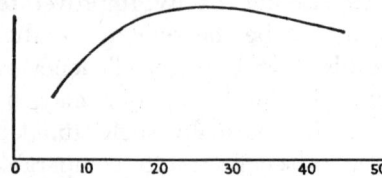

Fig. 1. The general form of the curve of ability to learn in relation to age.[1]

The following conclusions are widely accepted on the basis of the theoretical considerations, apart from any experimental evidence:

1. Activity, fundamental to all learning, has greater directness and control at the later age-period: there is less waste of energy.

2. Attention, interest, and motivation are more likely to be present at middle age, when there is the will to learn.

3. Perceptual learning is distinctly in favor of the mature person because a richer apperceptive background of experience is brought to bear on the learning.

4. Problem solving is easier for the same reason, as is also the memoriter learning of organized material.

5. In the case of nonsense or unorganized material, the difficulty of motivation and lack of receptivity for such material may militate against the mature person, but more efficient methods of study will largely compensate for these factors.

6. In sensori-motor or skill subjects, to begin in youth and to continue through adulthood often makes for greater permanence and excellence, particularly in the case of language. It is probable that a greater amount of practice rather than the age factor accounts in large measure for this difference.

---

[1] From Thorndike *et al.*, *Adult Learning*, 1928. Used by permission of the Macmillan Co.

The Environmental Factor

Environmental factors consist of all changes in the learner's surroundings which stimulate and influence his reactions and growth. Environmental stimuli include changes in physical conditions and objects, communication and other relationships with parents, peers, teachers, and various persons active in community institutions. The learner learns much arithmetic from experience with the neighborhood storekeeper, reading skills from the local newspaper, moral lessons from people in the home, school, and church. A great variety of natural and human resources affect his physical and psychological progress.

Thus, a bleak natural and cultural environment usually constitutes a severely adverse influence upon his behavior, whereas rich natural, cultural, and social surroundings in home and community stimulate interest, enthusiasm, and achievement. The earliest physical environment of the unborn infant, within the mother's womb, is known to have a profound effect upon his physical and psychological development. The constant interaction thereafter, during each period of his lifetime, between his inherited equipment and innumerable environmental influences molds his attitudes, habits, capacities, and behavior.

Method in Learning

For the student, method in learning resolves itself into the question of how to study. The objective here is economy of time and effort in the mastery of material and in the retention of what has been mastered.

How to Study. Insofar as the *physiological factor* is concerned, maximum results accrue when one is free from fatigue of any kind, physically fit in general, moderately comfortable, and subjected to no undue environmental distractions. On the *psychological* side, optimum results are secured when the material has meaning and assumes its proper place in the apperceptive mass (experiential background) of the learner, when there is a definite purpose or aim, and the outcome is seen to be worthwhile. Corresponding to the *environmental factor,* we have a large number of maxims as to method of attack, distribution of time, etc. Among the latter maxims, the following recommendations have the authority of experimental investigation:

1. *Whole to Part Method.* This means that the general nature of the material should be apprehended first, at the level of the learner's insight. This method is in accordance with the Gestalt principle that learning proceeds from the whole to its parts and not *vice versa.*

2. *Whole versus Part Method.* In memorizing a poem of reasonable length, it is best to do so as a whole rather than by parts. What a reasonable length is, depends on the possibility of securing a central idea or unit of thought which may act as a focal or reference point for related material. Where the material is too long, the mediating method (discussed below) should be used. The part method has proved most fruitful in the learning of nonverbal material, such as skills, typewriting, and handwriting, and in the learning of meaningless material, such as nonsense syllables. The whole method is not valid here because there is no logical unity or continuity in the material. Yet the whole method is operative to this extent, that spatial *position* and *order* assume a coherence or whole which enables the learner to retain the material.

3. *The Mediating Method.* The whole method, strictly interpreted, proves cumbersome and even wasteful in material of great length and varying difficulty. If all the material receives the same time, the middle and more difficult portions of a long speech or poem are not so well learned as the beginning and end. Such disadvantages are remediable by the mediating method. This method, applicable to long vocabulary material, as well as to more logical wholes, proceeds from whole to part as before, but allows the marking off of more difficult or unfamiliar parts for more intensive study. It is still the whole method; and the learner must never lose sight of the relation of the parts to the whole, nor concentrate on the former to the exclusion of the latter.

4. *The Recitation Method.* When time allows, this method is always of value and for all kinds of material. It simply means checking up on one's self by being one's own inquisitor, from time to time. The outstanding advantages are (a) weak connec-

tions are discerned and made the object of concentrated attention; (b) a general feeling of accomplishment stimulates to further effort; (c) errors due to wrong first impressions are soon detected and eliminated before they become established; and (d) since the material is learned as it is to be used, little transfer is necessary in the later reproduction. Experimental evidence indicates that about three-fifths of the period of study may, with profit, be devoted to recitation. It has also been found that the recitation method of study is better for (a) both immediate and delayed recall, and (b) both sense and nonsense material.

5. *Length of Practice Periods.* The maximum period of productive study, as found by experimentation on memorization, typewriting, arithmetical operations, and archery, is 20-30 minutes. Periods of more than 30 minutes of concentrated study are relatively unproductive. It is probable that such a recommendation cannot be made for history and subjects that may demand an initial warming-up process. Interest in a subject, likewise, may extend the limit beyond which the law of diminishing returns would begin to operate.

6. *Distribution of Practice Periods.* Distributed efforts are favored. The experimental evidence is entirely against continuous study over a long period. Suppose 120 minutes are available for study. Ten minutes twice a day, for six days gives better results than 20 minutes once a day, for six days; and this latter method is in turn far more productive than one 120-minute period. In the case of delayed recall of meaningful material, the distributed study method gives relatively greater return.

7. *To Counteract Forgetting, Overlearn.* The Ebbinghaus and Radosavljevich studies on the retention of material or the rate of forgetting show that after material (nonsense syllables) is learned to the point of one (Ebbinghaus) or two (Radosavljevich) correct reproductions, forgetting sets in immediately and is most rapid in the early stages. To counteract this factor, reviews should begin on the next day at the latest (especially for the very young) and take place at comparatively frequent intervals. The periods between practice may be gradually lengthened and continued until overlearning is assured. Overlearning, in general, is necessary for delayed recall.

8. *Cramming.* This is the attempt to acquire control, usually

for the purpose of immediate reproduction, of a relatively large amount of material in a comparatively short time. Cramming, therefore, may not be confined to a few days or weeks before an examination; it may cover weeks or months of study. A Summer School course of six weeks may be tantamount to a cramming process in the case of certain subjects. Certain types of examinations and certain life situations may justify cramming; but where real permanence is desired cramming is of little value. Learning is a product of maturation, of enlargement of meaning and apperceptive mass, of assimiliation. For such an outcome time is necessary.

9. *Speed of Learning in Relation to Retention.* There is a popular saying that "quick learning means quick forgetting," that there is a negative correlation between quickness of acquiring a habit and its retention. The experimental evidence is not conclusive enough to reject the generalization altogether. With meaningless material the popular view is correct: those who learn quickest forget quickest. With all other material those who learn quickest forget the least. Again, those who learn quickest make more use of the *whole method* than the slower individuals, and retain the best when the material is *logical* in character.

10. *Retroactive Inhibition.* When learning is in process, neural patterns are formed whose elements are dynamically associated or interrelated. Such interrelation may be the result of repetitive rhythmic sequence, contiguity in space or time, intensity of stimulation and, on a "higher" or more psychological and complex level, logical structure or "belongingness" of the constituent parts. Whatever the principle of coherence involved, remembrance is, in this view, the revival in whole or in part of a pattern of associated impressions, by the stimulation of any part thereof. Now the patterns formed, for example, in the learning of the Romance languages will obviously have many elements in common and if those subjects are studied in too close a sequence, particularly in the early stages, confusion or conflict of patterns is likely to result. The interference thus caused is known as *retroactive inhibition* and is found not only in verbal learnings but in those that involve muscular adjustments such as typing, piano practice, and even the grosser muscular movements used in tennis, handball, and the like. The alternation of learnings needed to avoid

retroactive inhibition may well fit in with a schedule of practice periods based on spaced learning, discussed above.

General Conclusions on Method. The advantage of studying when one is in a mood for study needs no emphasis. In its application to teaching, this major principle of *readiness* savors less of a truism: it found a place in the first explicit and scientific formulation of teaching method originated by Herbart (*d.* 1841) and elaborated by his followers in the five Herbartian steps, viz., preparation, presentation, comparison or association, generalization, and application. It is obviously unwise, moreover, to await the pleasure of a mood; it may be at least invited by going through the motions of study. It is obvious also that learning should proceed in the way in which the material is to be reproduced later; the need for transfer will thus be largely eliminated. To prepare an oration by reading it over silently is an example of a violation of this principle.

Method in general, though amenable to psychological laws of wide application, is, nevertheless, largely an individual matter. The idiosyncrasies of the learner may require that he subscribe to no method or procedure derived from experimental inquiry in which, perhaps, all the factors operative were not known or under complete control. In the case of older pupils, in particular, ingrained habits should be taken into account. In fine, the results of experimentation on method or motivation in learning should be accepted with great caution. In educational psychology, it is rarely possible to lay down laws or generalizations that hold true for all individuals or all situations, with the possible exception of the fundamental psychological principles dealing with understanding and intrinsic motivation.

Memory

Whatever is thoroughly learned, and reviewed or used at intervals, is remembered. Learning or modification of some kind is fundamental to memory, but in the latter term psychologists recognize, in addition to the primary factor of learning, the three additional factors: *retention, recall,* and *recognition*. The division is justified on other than introspective or a priori grounds: disorders and abnormalities are found to occur in one or more of the four factors while the others remain comparatively undisturbed. In what is known as "Korsakoff Psychosis," for example, a mental disturbance caused by chronic alcoholism, learnings acquired before the onset of the disease remain unimpaired, but new learnings meet with resistance. Disorders of retention result from injuries to certain portions of the brain. Recovery from accidents may never be entirely complete; commonplace things known and remembered previously are no longer retained because the brain substance has been removed or damaged. Disorders of *recall* occur in hysteria and emotional shock; while disorders of *recognition*, conspicuous in the case of certain mental afflictions, are unknown in normal life. Paramnesia (a feeling of familiarity in a situation not previously encountered) emphasizes recognition on the positive side. The new situation may have elements similar to those of some past experience which, being revived momentarily, causes the feeling of familiarity.

Improvement of Memory. The problem that memory presents for the student of education lies chiefly in the question as to whether memory is capable of being improved. Insofar as memory is a function of the organism, it is obvious that, like intellectual capacity and learning in general, it is limited by the inherited structure of the organism. By improvement of memory, therefore, we must understand simply improvement in the technique of learning and methods of memorizing.

Mechanical Memory: Mnemonic Devices. The use of mnemonic devices, sometimes referred to as mechanical memory, is recommended only for items of information which do not lend themselves to meaningful associations. The number of days in each month may well be remembered by "Thirty days hath September . . ."; a rule for spelling by "I before E, except after C . . ."; and the colors of the spectrum by "Roy G. Biv." Such devices are not entirely arbitrary; they are effective to the extent that they approximate a meaningful or related whole, capable of recall by other than the brute force of memory. "Roy G. Biv," for example, however lowly as a mnemonic device, is a far more reasonable and commendable aid than the nonsensical "Vibgyor." Devices invented by the student himself to fit the situation are usually the most effective.

Logical Memory. In logical memory the material is remembered because of the relationships growing out of the partial data presented. Obviously, meaning and understanding are essential elements. It is probable that all memory is dependent on some kind of organization of material, rhythmic or space-time organization being used when no other is available. In so-called rote association or rote learning, organization of the rhythmic kind and a slight interplay of meaning are probably involved. It is this principle of logical memory that underlies the "whole to part" method of learning.

Memory Systems. So-called memory systems may, on analysis, be resolved into (a) the use of artificial aids to learning, and (b) the use of recognized psychological factors such as attentive repetition, immediate review after first impressions, spaced repetition, and the laws of learning. Insofar as they incorporate the latter factors, memory systems are valid, but they can claim no prerogative in this respect. Insofar as they rely on artificial aids (and this seems to be their unique feature) such systems have no more validity than that attaching to mnemonic devices. In general, they may exaggerate all the weak features of the nonsensical mnemonic.

Laws of Association. Traditional psychology from the time of Aristotle has recognized the fact that in the presence of a given stimulus or situation there is a tendency to recall past experiences which (1) are similar to the present situation (*law of similarity*); (2) are in contrast with the present situation (*law of contrast*); or (3) have been connected with the present situation in space or time sequence (*law of contiguity*). Secondary laws of *recency*, *vividness*, and *frequency* have been used to supplement these primary laws of association. There is a consensus of opinion that these three primary laws are fundamentally one, viz., contiguity. Contrast has been reduced to similarity because contrasting experiences must have an element of similarity to furnish a basis for comparison. A dwarf recalls a giant because they are alike in being at the extremes of height. Contiguity in space and time are effective only when there is a connected experience involving both. They are, therefore, aspects of the one law, contiguity of experience. Similarity and contiguity remain. Similarity implies the existence of elements common to two situations otherwise unlike. The common elements, however, are tied by contiguity to the unlike elements; and the whole pattern is reinstated by the factor of contiguity. *Contiguity of experience*, therefore, remains as the fundamental factor in association.

Modern Applications of Association. Traditional laws referred to the association of ideas; and this concept was the cornerstone of the British School of Associationism. The term, association, is still in use, but refers to overt responses; objective psychology rejects the vague concept, *association of ideas*. Thorndike's *law of associative shifting* and the *conditioned response* of the behaviorists are examples of the old theory in a new setting. According to Thorndike, the learner may associate any response of which he is capable with any situation to which he is sensitive. The physiologists and behaviorists have shown us that visceral and glandular responses, such as salivation and emotional reactions, may be transferred from "natural" to "artificial" stimuli. The process of transferring is called conditioning, and the resultant is called a *conditioned response*. The one factor that appears as a *conditio sine qua non* of all new connections or learnings is the traditionally recognized *law of contiguity*. But is mere contiguity enough? The Gestalt theory seems to give us additional insight into the matter.

Association in the Gestalt Theory. The hypothesis of the Gestalt psychology is that all mental phenomena have a structure or pattern. The problem of association, approached from this standpoint, is not to explain how ideas or any other occurrences are associated, for they never existed otherwise than as part of a totality or configuration. Ideas, events, etc., do not come in isolation; they are always part of some definite context or pattern by virtue of which alone they have meaning and significance. According to this theory, one sentence of a poem serves to stimulate recall of another sentence, because the whole poem is thus being partially reinstated as a unit. Still, contiguity remains as a factor not to be disposed of, for contiguity of experience is an essential element in the formation of the pattern itself.

Chapter 7
Laws and Theories of Learning

Laws and principles of learning are attempts to state the more fundamental conditions favorable to the learning process. (In our classification, therefore, laws of learning are statements or theories of method rather than explanations of the process or the goal in learning.) There is an increasing tendency among writers of texts in education to omit academic discussions of laws of learning. This departure has probably been influenced by (1) the early preoccupation of investigators with animal learning, the implicit assumption that human learning differs therefrom only in degree, and the consequent inadequacy of the theories propounded; (2) the seeming triteness or artificiality of the problems investigated; (3) the lack of harmony among interpretations by the different "schools"; (4) the conviction that the conditions of learning are specific, not general, and hence are not amenable to formulation in laws of universal application. It would, however, be unwise for students of education to ignore salient points in the more important theories, or to neglect educational suggestions which not infrequently result.

Thorndike's Three Major Laws: Five Minor Laws

E. L. Thorndike is credited with the first explicit formulation of what are now termed the major laws of learning. The laws are said to have been the outgrowth originally of experiments in the field of animal psychology. Later experiments with human subjects, and the pressure of criticism, caused Thorndike to modify his initial interpretations of the major principles called *readiness, exercise*, and *effect*, and to add a quality or psychological factor, termed *belongingness*.[1]

Readiness. *When a bond is ready to act, to act gives satisfaction, and not to act gives annoyance. When a bond which is not ready to act is made to act, annoyance is caused.* A child who is eager to do something but is restrained, is annoyed. He is pleased if allowed to express himself, and annoyed if compelled to do something distasteful, or for which he is not in the mood.

Exercise. (Equivalent terms are frequency, practice, repetition, use and disuse). *The more a given response is connected with a certain situation, the more likely it is to be made to that situation.* Or negatively, by disuse, *when a modifiable connection is not made between a situation and a response, over a period of time, the strength of that connection is decreased.* More briefly, other things being equal, *exercise strengthens and lack of exercise weakens the bond between situation and response.* "Other things being equal" refers chiefly to the consequences (pleasure-pain) of the response, recognized in the law of effect. Subsidiary factors affecting exercise are *intensity of the stimulus* (on the subjective side, this amounts to attention), and *recency of the stimulus* (the more recent the connection, the easier is the recall).

Effect. *Satisfying results strengthen and discomfort weakens the bond between situation and response.* This fact, according to Thorndike, is the fundamental law of teaching and learning.

Minor Laws. Thorndike formulated five minor or secondary laws which amplify and extend his major laws of learning: (1) *the law of multiple response to the same external situation,* stating that learning can involve several possible responses and much more than a one-to-one relationship between stimulus and response because "the connection is often a compound of several

---

[1] The term *bond*, occurring so frequently in the formulation and discussion of the laws, may be interpreted as *link, relation, tendency,* between stimulus situation and response. The term represents, in fact, an unexplained and undefined assumption. The term *belongingness* seems to represent the capacity for association between two or more events or factors, and obviously is dependent on the apperceptive basis of the learner. The paired stimuli "twin-22" possess the quality of *belongingness;* "twin-75" are without it. Unless a belongingness of some kind, of meaningful connection, rhythm, etc., exists between two events in temporal sequence, repetition does not result in learning, that is, in connecting the two.

connections each having possibly a different degree of strength"; (2) *the law of attitude, set, or disposition*, stating that the attitude of the learner and the kind of situation to which he responds affect the "vigor and duration of each connection . . . as well as the number of times it is made"; (3) *the law of partial activity*, stating that the learner notes many aspects of a situation but selects those with which he will cope by means of specific responses; (4) *the law of assimilation or analogy*, stating that reaction patterns to meet one situation can be applied by the learner to similar situations because "of the connections to be studied in man's learning an enormous majority begin and end with some state of affairs within the man's own brain"; and (5) *the law of associative shifting*, stating a principle of conditioning that what is learned at one time or from one situation—the bonds thus formed—can be applied by the learner (within the limits of his capacity) at another time or to a new but similar or associated situation.[2]

Thorndike's Theory of the Nature of Learning. The laws of learning are expressed in terms of method but are based on the physiological theory that learning is the result of modifiability in the paths of neural conduction. Explanations of even such forms of learning as abstraction and generalization demand of the neurons only growth, excitability, conductivity, and modifiability. The mind is the connection system of man; and learning is the process of connecting. The situation-response formula is adequate to cover learning of any sort, and the really influential factors in learning are readiness of the neurons, sequence in time, belongingness, and satisfying consequences. Thorndike admitted the difficulties confronting the explanation of human nature as a neural connection-system. But he believed that this connection-theory, inadequate as it is, constituted nevertheless the most fruitful and scientific theory yet formulated. It is not so naive as the theory of the extreme behaviorist, who limits human responses to activities of muscles and glands. It is not so speculative and mystical as the theory of the Gestaltist.

---

[2] Based on E. L. Thorndike, "The Psychology of Learning," in his *Educational Psychology* (New York: Columbia University Press, 1913), Vol. II, pp. 1–5, 54–56.

Evaluation of the Laws of Learning

The majority of psychologists no longer accept the laws, in their naive form, as adequate explanations of the conditions under which learning takes place. The laws are rough generalizations which at first sight seem to fit in with our experience, but on analysis are found to ignore the really operative factors in learning. The law of repetition, for example, brings us no further than the maxim *repetitio est mater studiorum* or the trite "practice makes perfect." Obviously, too, many factors which common experience shows to be operative potently in learning find no place in the laws. Purposiveness and the influence of the emotions will occur to the reader. Purposiveness would seem to be the great driving force in learning surmounting in importance such factors as pleasure and pain as well as repetition; and purposiveness may not be assumed as obvious in any alleged explanation of learning or any statement of its conditions.

The Law of Exercise.[3] Consider the law of exercise. Practice makes perfect; repetition strengthens connections. But sheer repetition does not result in improvement or strengthening of connections or in the learning of a response. Practice makes perfect only if and when intention, attention, and observation go along with it; and in proportion to the degree in which these are lacking, practice is of no avail. Now these factors are utterly alien to the intent of the law and the psychological theory basic to it. In brief, numerous other factors are operative in addition to mere repetition; and these are claimed by many to be the influential conditions. Again, a single vivid emotional experience is sufficient to make a lasting impression. Repetition, therefore, is not a necessary factor. This fact is particularly evident when we are learning material which has meaning for us.

The Synaptic Resistance Theory and Repetition. A physiological theory of learning, in terms of synaptic resistance, has long seemed to give plausibility to repetition as a causal factor in learning. The theory states that learning is the process of forming

---

[3] In his work, *The Fundamentals of Learning,* Thorndike recognized the inadequacy of frequency as a cause of learning.

neural connections in the nervous system by breaking down the resistance at the synapses. Learning is the establishing of preferential routes or pathways of least resistance; and this process could, quite plausibly, be attributed to repetition. This assumption, however, is a form of the trace theory of learning, and is no longer acceptable to the majority of experimental psychologists. The findings of Lashley, Franz, Cameron and others show that learning cannot be explained in terms of either neural conduction or neural integration.

The Law of Effect. Reinforcement Principle. The law states that when pleasant or satisfying consequences follow or attend a response, the latter tends to be repeated. When painful or annoying consequences attend a response, it tends to be eliminated. Behavioristic psychology has been disposed to reject this law, because of the subjective or purely psychical element involved. Objective psychology cannot accept as explanations subjective factors such as feelings of pleasure or pain. The tendency, therefore, has been to stress repetition and recency as the causal conditions. Other psychologists have objected that pleasure and pain, if they follow an activity, would, on the recurrence of the activity, have to change their position in the sequence: they would have to precede the activity in order to be considered as causal factors. This difficulty has prompted explanations in terms of conditioning; and interesting theories of "positive" and "negative" conditioning and higher orders of conditioning have been suggested to explain the mechanism of the process.

At first sight, it would seem a truism to say that annoying consequences bring about avoidance of the activity which caused them. To say, however, that we do not learn or remember such activities, because of those consequences, is a conclusion not warranted by the premises. Experimental evidence, if any be needed, tends to prove that painful consequences are most effective in "stamping in" responses. In conclusion, it may be said that here again, as in the law of exercise, we have a loose generalization expressing, probably, not causal but contributing or symptomatic factors in the learning process.

Present Status of the Laws of Learning. Since their first explicit formulation, the laws of learning, particularly the laws of frequency and effect, have aroused spirited discussion and opposition. They have been criticized adversely by psychologists so fundamentally opposed to one another as the behaviorists and the Gestalt school. The behaviorists deny the law of effect (considered most fundamental by Thorndike) and declare frequency to be the principle of selection in trial-and-success learning, and the effective factor in all forms of retention. Thorndike concluded that frequency as such is utterly inadequate as an explanation of learning. Frequency does, he said, play some part in learning, but it may at times be of no consequence whatever.

The Gestalt school objects to the very formulation of the problem of learning implied by Thorndike in the three laws. Thorndike's basic position is called connectionism. To the connectionist, learning consists essentially in the attaching or connecting of a response R to a stimulus S (S—R) which did not originally call forth that response. The explanation of the learning process is the explanation of how this connection is established, or how it may be facilitated. Learning, then, is the organization of independent units of behavior, and the entire concept is often referred to as *psychological atomism*. To the Gestaltist, on the contrary, there is no building up process to be explained or facilitated. The organization is already given in the act of perception. Perception and learning consist in the discovery of the relations already existent among the elements of a perceived whole of experience. The consequences of the Gestalt theory are serious and far-reaching in their effect on educational practice. Since discovery is regarded as the essence of learning, learning must be achieved through creative work. Where drill methods are relied upon, or wrong motivation (pleasure or pain) used, the child may learn, but he does so in spite of such methods, and his progress is seriously retarded. Thorndike's answer to the Gestalt viewpoint is, in general, that the tendency is unjustified that treats all or most of the constituents of perceptions and thought as mystic totals unified by subjective forces apart from the laws of connection-forming. In addition to the experimental evidence which they offer in favor of their theory, the Gestaltists allege that Thorndike was not himself immune to the charge of mysticism. Had he not, *malgré lui*, introduced a new principle of *belonging*, which cannot be explained in the terms of his theory?

Thorndike's Emendations of His Laws

As a result of numerous experiments especially designed to test the adequacy of the laws of frequency and effect, and dealing for the most part with the learning of humans, Thorndike made some important emendations of those laws.

Readiness. In regard to this law, no thorough investigation has been made, and little that is new has been discovered. "Learning may consist in changing the readiness of connections as truly as in changing their strength," and "much of learning consists in making certain responses more available, or more easily summonable." [4]

Frequency. Exercise or sequence are no longer considered major factors in the learning process. Thorndike concluded that repeated occurrence of a situation does not assure learning. It was difficult for Thorndike to discard repetition of response as a real conditioning factor, because his theory is largely a quantitative affair. It is even more difficult for the behaviorists. So-called insight or understanding plays no part in their theories. It is evident that repetition does function in learning, but mainly to this extent, that it furnishes additional opportunities for growth in understanding, or, if we may use the terminology of the Gestalt theory, it provides the stimulation for that maturation which is learning.

Effect. The general principle of satisfiers and annoyers has been retained, but many conditioning factors have been introduced. Thorndike protested that he could not accept the law as originally formulated: its suggestion that the action of annoyers is the opposite of that of satisfiers in all respects is misleading. There are important differences; and moreover, the intimacy of association is conditioned by the facts of belonging in general, attentiveness to the situation, response, and satisfier. Belongingness is not only needed to supplement both frequency and effect but the latter laws often sink into insignificance by comparison.[5] If objection was made that the principle is mystical, the answer of Thorndike was that it has a physical basis, and a neural equiv-

---

[4] E. L. Thorndike, *Fundamentals of Learning*, p. 329. Used by permission of Teachers College, Columbia University.
[5] *Ibid.*, p. 274.

alent in the form of temporally uninterrupted conduction from one locus to another. However, the truth of the fact of belonging is entirely independent of this physiological explanation. An objection was made that if satisfying after-effects strengthen connections, whereas annoying after-effects weaken them, we ought to remember satisfying and forget annoying experiences—whereas, in fact, we remember annoying experiences equally or nearly as well. Thorndike replied that the law of effect would not cause us to recall experiences that were pleasant and forget experiences that were painful, but only to remember experiences that were pleasant to remember, and forget experiences that were painful to remember. The fact remains, however, that we do remember experiences that are painful to remember; and no adequate explanation seems to be found in the law of effect. Thorndike realized the difficulty: owing to certain perverse tendencies, the contemplation of painful facts may even be accompanied by subtle and morbid satisfaction. Such explanations are found helpful to his interpretation. It is evident from Thorndike's defense of the law as a whole that it must be interpreted carefully and with great limitations.

The Conditioned Response Theory

The conditioned response is a physiological theory which many psychologists, notably the behaviorists, have relied on as a more or less adequate explanation of many phases of the learning process. The fundamental concept at the basis of connectionism, namely, that learning is the linking of a response to a stimulus, is evident again. The human organism, in common with other organisms, has an original fund of responses, tendencies, or reactions which are set in motion by the presentation of the appropriate stimuli. Salivation, for example, is the natural response of a hungry dog to the sight of meat. In the case of infants, fear and withdrawal are natural responses to loud noise. Such reactions are not learned; they are innate. But if another or artificial stimulus be presented along with, or shortly before, the natural stimulus, and if this association be repeated a number of times, the presentation of the artificial stimulus alone (the ringing of a bell, let us say) will ultimately cause the response to occur. The natural response, therefore, has been transferred to an artificial stimulus; and the animal is said to have been conditioned. Learning, in its elementary and fundamental form, is essentially the modification of all natural responses, and their transference to artificial stimuli. When natural and artificial stimuli are presented together in the formation of a conditioned reflex, the latter is called a *simultaneous conditioned response*. When the artificial stimulus precedes the natural stimulus by several minutes, the response is called a *delayed conditioned response*. If just a few moments elapse between the artificial and natural stimuli, the result is known as a *trace reflex*. Note that, in the case of animals, no conditioning occurs when the natural stimulus is presented prior to the artificial stimulus.

The foregoing is a simple statement of Pavlov's conditioned response experiment. The variations of this experiment, however, have been numerous and complex, especially in the field of the emotions. The experiment has become a cornerstone of objective psychology. The conditioned response theory has been advanced to explain many of our fears, repugnances, and otherwise unexplained reactions to people, places, and things generally. Such conditioning, it is said, often takes place in childhood, and though the real causes are unknown to us, or forgotten, the effects remain. Thus it is said that certain fears, e.g. the child's fear of the dark or of certain animals, are not natural: they are cases of conditioning.

Comment on the Conditioned Response Theory. At first glance, the theory seems to be an extension and refinement, in physiological terminology, of the traditional law of "association by contiguity of experience" (the law that things experienced together tend to recall one another). There are, however, two important differences: the association theory spoke of ideas, images, and percepts; the present theory is in terms of responses. Again, mere contemporaneity and sequence seem to characterize conditioning (at least to many behaviorists); the association theory demands that its elements form a connected whole of experience. Because of its simplicity and physiological context, apparently needing no assumptions of a mental or psychical nature, the conditioned response theory at once commends itself to those who demand an objective and definitely physiological basis of learning. Such a basis, however, is not yet established. The neurophysiological theory associated in the past with conditioning is now generally admitted to have been inadequate, even erroneous; and since the experiments of Franz, Lashley, and Coghill, behaviorists have been wary of binding themselves to any definite neural basis of learning. The conditioned response theory, therefore, is not put forward as an *explanation* of learning; it merely states the conditions of learning; and in the last analysis, we are told, the fundamental factors in habit formation, the conditions that must be present if learning is to occur, are but two: *unconditioned* (or well-established conditioned) *responses* and *time*. A certain amount of frequency, or duration of time, is required to permit the effective factors to operate. The space of time (recency) separating the two stimuli or responses to be connected must not be too great for the backward or forward spread of association.

B. F. Skinner has distinguished between two types of conditioning: the classical or *respondent* and the instrumental or *operant* types. The respondent type involves direct response to specific stimuli, typical of Pavlov's experimental techniques and represented generally in reflex actions. The operant type is more variable and only indirectly associated with a specific stimulus; the organism takes time to interpret stimuli as cues which affect its emotional tone and result in complex voluntary reactions.

The experiments of Pavlov, in their simplest form, dealt with learning of the associative or memory type, but the theory has been considerably elaborated into ascending "orders" of conditioning, to explain the higher thought and reasoning processes, and even voluntary activity. At this point most psychologists demur. While conditioning gives a plausible account of the conditions of specific learnings, particularly those involving emotional reactions, its adequacy in the case of complex thought processes is widely questioned. To the educator, in particular, it is of no apparent value in describing the higher stages of learning. In the last analysis, therefore, the educational psychologist must be eclectic in his attitude. There seem to be room and need for *readiness, repetition* with *belonging, effect, configuration, conditioning,* and perhaps still more important factors, at present ostracized by scientific psychology, to explain and facilitate the learning process in all its complexities.

The Trend Toward an Organismic or Totality Theory. This trend on the part of experimental psychology may be gauged from the following excerpts: "The neural theory of learning is based upon the questionable assumption that the nervous system is the seat of the mind, and therefore a controlling mechanism for the organism's behavior. A specification of this assumption is that certain acts are localized in particular places in the nervous system at particular synapses. An overwhelming series of facts has been recently accumulating to dissipate this localization theory." Again, "It is highly improbable that learning can be looked upon as merely a phenomenon of neural conduction and integration. Even the biological coordination of responses is not merely the organization of neural patterns. It involves as well the muscular, circulatory, and all the other systems."[6]

Advocates of a more liberalized conditioned response theory join in the trend toward the organismic or totality theory of response. The behavior of any animal is a total integration, they say, in which we can merely recognize and name occasional details. Behavior and learning are thus not to be described in terms of a limited number of identifiable elementary reflexes or responses. The very process of conditioning mingles responses to form new combinations, and involves many parts of the nervous system. A conditioning stimulus may fail to elicit the expected response, not only because of fatigue, or because the stimulus happens to be below the threshold, but because it has become associated with other responses in the total integrated reaction. Much repetition is usually needed before a habit becomes localized in a limited number of muscles; it then functions as a more specific response, without attention.

Gestalt Criticism of the Conditioned Response Theory

Gestalt psychologists regard learning as a process of directing activities toward some end or goal. In this process the essential

---

[6] From J. R. Kantor, *A Survey of the Science of Psychology*, p. 255. Used by permission of Principia Press.

feature is the relating or combining of the elements involved. The S—R theory (reaction hypothesis), it is said, makes no mention of this relating of one element in a situation to another, and no conditioning is produced unless this essential factor be present. For example, the easiest way to condition fears in young children is to let them *observe* the emotional reactions of their parents. There is no mechanical conditioning of the emotions. Children do not fear snakes, because they do not know, or have not been told, that they are dangerous. When an infant comes to fear an animal because the sight of it is accompanied by a loud noise or other unpleasant factors, it is because he thinks the animal means or causes the noise. This relating or connecting together of elements into a totality is necessary for so-called conditioning or learning.

Learning Curves

The progress made in certain forms of learning extending over a comparatively long period of time may, to a degree, be represented graphically by means of a practice or learning curve.

Insofar as human learning is concerned, learning curves are confined almost entirely to the sensori-motor types of learning, the acquisition of such skills as typewriting and telegraphy, and the learning (memorizing) and retention (or forgetting) of practice material like nonsense syllables. Such material is divisible into units and capable of quantitative expression.

Limitations of Learning Curves. Exact quantitative expression is basic to all curves. Curves of improvement in or acquisition of knowledge, appreciations, etc., are unreliable, because the determination of exact units in such material is practically impossible. For this reason, we have no reliable curves for the learning of languages, history, geography, and ordinary school subjects in general. Even if objective tests, scales, and other refined instruments of measuring knowledge should enable us to approximate the skill curves, the results would be far from representative or typical. The results would be abstractions which could not take into account the multiplicity and variety of interests and incentives operative in the individual life situation. Composite curves, in particular, which bring together the achievements of many individuals, and which are so frequently used in experimental studies of motivation, transfer, etc., disregard individual learnings and other differences peculiar to the situations in which learning takes place. Furthermore, curves of learning which presume to show progress made per unit of time presuppose that the material to be learned is of the same degree of difficulty throughout. This rarely happens. We need, therefore, curves based on different mathematical reasoning. Such curves would take into consideration individual variations in the task.

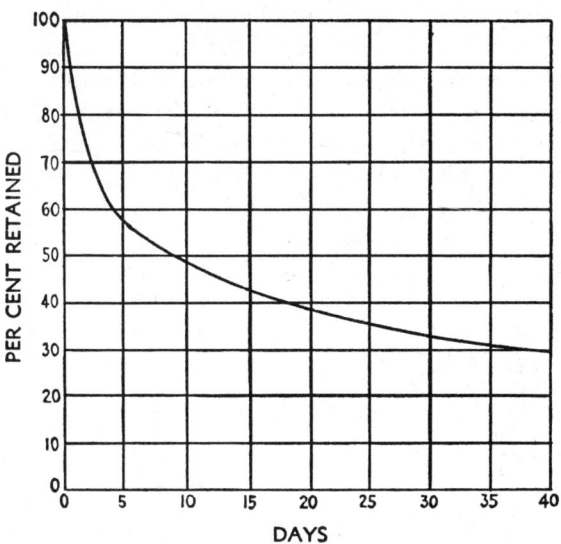

Fig. 2. Typical curve of retention for meaningful material.[7]

Types of Curves. Improvement in the acquisition of a skill may, when graphically represented, take the form of (1) *a straight line*, showing constant rate of improvement (seldom found); (2) *a convex curve*, where the initial rate gradually diminishes, and the curve becomes a straight line, or plateau (logarithmic type, and most frequently found); (3) *a concave curve*, where the initial rate gradually increases; and (4) *a combination of types* (2) *and* (3), with intervening plateaus.

---

[7] From A. J. Jordan, *Educational Psychology*, rev. ed., 1933. Used by permission of Henry Holt & Co.

The most common type of curve is exponential or logarithmic. In this curve, improvement gradually diminishes in relation to time, somewhat as follows:

Time in Minutes	Achievement
1	1
2	2
4	3
8	4
16	5

The logarithmic curve seems to obey the law of diminishing returns. It is probable that curves of knowledge, appreciations, etc., would not generally conform to this type, but rather, in the early stages at least, to the concave (3) form. The reason is that each accretion of knowledge adds to the "apperceptive mass" and acting accumulatively, makes further progress more rapid by giving greater control. There would, no doubt, be many plateaus and irregularities in such curves.

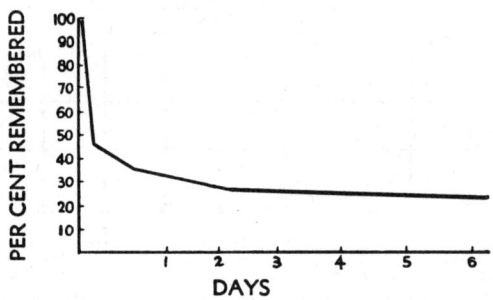

Fig. 3. Curve of forgetting.[8]

Uses of Curves: Significance of Plateaus. Though curves do not give us specific information about any learning process, they are extremely useful as rough generalizations of the rate of progress, the regularity or irregularity of progress, and the relation of progress to increasing difficulty of material. These generalizations may hold even for knowledge subjects. An outstanding contribution to the theory of the learning process, resulting from a study

---

[8] From H. Ebbinghaus, *Memory*, 1913. Used by permission of Teachers College, Columbia University.

of such curves, is the discovery of plateaus by Bryan and Harter. (See Fig. 4.)

Plateaus have been explained as due to (1) a more difficult stage in the learning process; (2) the loss of interest, or boredom; and (3) the reaching of higher stages in the *hierarchy of*

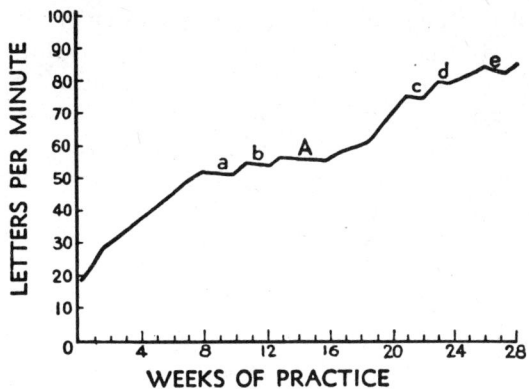

Fig. 4. Curve showing typical plateaus (Bryan & Harter).[9] A marks a major plateau; a, b, c, d, e, minor plateaus.

habits, of which all learning, according to Bryan and Harter, is composed. In telegraphy, the basic habit is the "letter habit." Upon the letter habit the "word habit" is built; and following and depending upon the latter is the "phrase habit." A plateau appears when a higher stage in the hierarchy is being attempted before the necessary lower stage is perfected. Experimental evidence does not support the conclusion that plateaus are inevitable in all forms of learning, though many psychologists accept the theory of the hierarchical nature of all habits, and incline to believe that all three causes of plateaus are operative. A Gestalt explanation attributes plateaus to failure to construct a satisfactory configuration through requisite mental processes and muscle activities. However nearly perfect the letter habit may become, when a higher stage is attempted a plateau may appear which is

---

[9] From R. H. Wheeler and F. T. Perkins, *Principles of Mental Development* (adapted from Bryan and Harter). Used by permission of Thomas Y. Crowell Company.

due not to any imperfectly learned letter habit, but to the fact that words are not simply composites of letters, but exhibit their own *gestalten*. The learner is thus presented with a new problem at each stage in the entire process.

The Physiological Limit in Learning. Learning curves have drawn attention to the fact that the capacity of the individual in any phase of learning is limited by the potentiality of his organism. The speed of performance in any subject, such as typewriting, depends upon the neuro-muscular mechanism and the general control of the responses. In knowledge subjects, too, one is limited by one's inborn capacity, which is supposed, for the average individual, to reach the maximum between fifteen and twenty-five years of age. This latter limitation applies primarily to the ability to perceive relations, not to the amount of knowledge one acquires, though there is obviously a relation between the two.

The concept of physiological limit is of immediate interest only in connection with the skill subjects. Few persons reach this limit, though it is probable that many approach it more closely in skills than in knowledge subjects. The ratio of actual to theoretical physiological limit is for each person a measure of his achievement (A. Q.).

Learning Ability and Intelligence: Constancy of Learning. Among the many definitions of intelligence we find "the ability to learn" and "the ability to solve problems." Experimental investigation, however, indicates that learning ability and intelligence, though so closely related as to serve as indices, the one of the other, are not to be identified. If we define intelligence as the ability to respond to complex situations (as presented in intelligence tests), ability to learn must be restricted to specific situations demanding a greater focalization of attention, an integration of responses, and the mechanization of the latter through repetition. Indeed, as learning proceeds, the responses become more or less automatic.

Related to the foregoing is the question whether learning ability is constant for all types of material. The theory of constancy of learning is generally rejected. Capacity to learn varies with differences in the material and in the conditions of learning.

Chapter 8
Transfer of Training: Subject Matter

The problem of transfer of training affects directly both the content and method of all formal schooling. The modern curriculum, following the traditional method, is composed largely of differentiated and compartmentalized subjects of study. The answer given to the question of formal discipline and its correlate, transfer of training, will determine the subjects of the curriculum and the form of motivation to be used in learning those subjects.

Historical Outline of the Problem

Formal discipline, in the historical sense of the term, is not to be confused with transfer of training; the latter is a much narrower concept. If the question be asked: Do modern psychologists as a whole accept the original theory of formal discipline? the answer is No. Do they accept transfer of training? Yes. Is there unanimity regarding this latter question? No. They disagree as to the *conditions* under which transfer takes place, the *amount* of transfer, and *what* it is that transfers. Some of the views on this latter point amount to a modified as opposed to an absolute form of mental or formal discipline.

General Faculties. Formal discipline is alleged to have found its psychological justification in the faculty theory of mind. Two faculty theories of mind are to be distinguished. In the faculty theory generally criticized by contemporary psychologists the mind is viewed as composed of an aggregate of faculties or powers, each one working more or less independently of the others. Such faculties are memory, reasoning, discrimination, judgment, will, imagination, and the like. The theory is that since these powers are used and needed in all situations of life, it should be the concern of education to train such powers rather than to teach specific subject matter of immediate utilitarian value. According to faculty psychology, subject matter of social value will be learned outside the school, and learned all the better for the general faculty training that has been received. Modern psychology, however, not only discarded the theory of mind as a working hypothesis but, largely as a result of its dependence on neurophysiology to explain mental processes, abandoned the view that general functions of any kind exist. In a word, it proclaimed that we have no general memory power, for example, but specific memories, and specific learnings, each with its correlative "neural pattern." There is no possibility, therefore, of general training of any kind. This view has been considerably modified by recent investigations in the field of animal learning.

Organismic Unity. The second faculty theory is stated in ancient Greek literature; it is still accepted by those who hold the mind to be a substantial entity. To the Greeks the mind was a unitary whole which expressed itself in the activities of judging, reasoning, remembering, etc. Those powers were not considered distinct in the sense of being isolated from one another. Intelligence, will, memory, and the like were distinguished from one another, but only as distinct modes of activity. We might compare this theory to a theory in modern psychology which insists that all activities are organismic, that totality is the keynote of reaction, that the organism responds as a whole and to wholes of experience.

Whatever its ultimate basis, formal discipline simply means that the faculties of the mind, such as reasoning will, attention, perception, etc., may be trained or influenced by the study of special subject matter.

There is evidence of belief in formal discipline as early as

Plato. In the *Republic,* Bk. VII, we find the following: ". . . even the dull, if they have had an arithmetical training, although they may derive no other benefit from it, always become much sharper than they would otherwise have been." And again "the inhabitants of your fair city . . . should learn geometry, by all means." Its indirect effects are not small, and "we know, of course, that the man who has studied geometry will be wholly and entirely superior to the man who has not, with respect to the better apprehension of all subjects."

Whether through the influence of the Greeks or not, the belief in the indirect effects of training in *certain subjects* persisted. Francis Bacon, in his essay, *Of Studies,* writes: "Nay, there is no stone or impediment in the wit but may be wrought out by fit studies; like as diseases of the body may have appropriate exercises. . . . So, if a man's wit be wandering, let him study mathematics; for, in demonstrations, if his wit be called away never so little, he must begin again. If his wit be not apt to distinguish or find differences, let him study the schoolmen; for they are splitters of hairs."

In the middle of the nineteenth century we find Huxley and Spencer clamoring for recognition of natural science in the curriculum on the ground of its utilitarian value. But when science did gain recognition it was mainly on the ground that it, too, was a disciplinary subject, as well as the classics. The function of formal schooling was considered to be that of giving an all-round intellectual and disciplinary training, not to cater to utilitarian subjects which could be acquired in life situations or in professional schools.

The Issue in Modern Education: Transfer of Training

Three forces may be recognized as instrumental in the rejection of the formal discipline theory insofar as it affected the educational curriculum. *First,* with the advance of the natural and social sciences, a great body of useful and necessary subject matter accumulated and had to be recognized. *Second,* the faculty theory of mind, as already stated, was questioned and largely rejected. A *third factor,* especially influential both in establishing the specific-bond or specific-habit psychology and in the rejection of formal discipline was the interpretation given to a multitude of experiments on transfer of training.

On the whole, it may be said, the possibility of general training, in the sense of training for adaptability, is again recognized as being not only consistent with the most advanced views of the nature of brain activity, but also confirmed by the experimental evidence which has been alleged to deny it. The old theory, however, has not been revived in its naive form: new and conditioning elements have entered; and it is this new version that is properly referred to as transfer of training. Of the old theory this remains: habits, dispositions, attitudes or ideals of attention, accuracy, neatness, fairmindedness, suspension of judgment, promptness, and a host of other qualities may be developed, provided certain conditions regarding method of teaching, etc., be fulfilled. It is to be noted also that the classics and mathematics hold no monopoly in regard to the content of such training. Furthermore, no longer is mention made of *faculties* of attention, discrimination, etc., but rather attitudes, or ideals; and, in the aims of contemporary education, the stress is on socially desirable qualities and the "scientific method."

The Experimental Evidence on the Transfer Problem

Experimental investigation began with William James's experiment on memory training (1890). The results of ninety-nine experiments reported between 1890 and 1928 are admirably presented in summary form in Figure 5.

Experimental evidence is entirely in favor of the transfer theory. Yet the idea long persisted that the experiments in transfer had completely discredited the formal discipline theory. Two reasons put forward to explain this extraordinary situation are: the influence of the prevailing specific-habit psychology, and the general desire to oust from the curricula those subjects which were claimed to embody the formal discipline theory and which might prove too difficult for the large unselected groups that now enter our high schools and colleges. Social and scientific studies facilitated revision of the traditional curriculum.

Transfer of Training 121

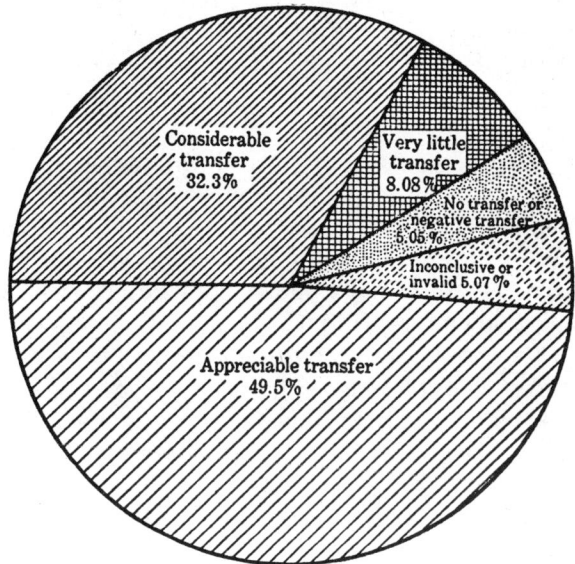

Fig. 5. Orata's interpretation of the findings of 99 "transfer" experiments.[1]

Apart from the favorable evidence resulting from the experimental investigations, it would seem that the latter are frequently open to the objection that they make a travesty of the real issue or, at least, tend to narrow the problem beyond recognition. To practice, for example, the perception of certain letters in certain words in order to determine whether this transfers to, that is aids, the perception of different letters in other words; or again, to ascertain whether memorizing nonsense syllables helps in the memorizing of verse, prose, etc., is, to say the least, a dubious way of testing either formal discipline or the narrower concept of transfer. It is a dubious procedure, because training which consists largely or entirely of prolonged practice of a mechanical

---

[1] From W. C. Bagley, *Education, Crime, and Social Progress*, 1931. Used by permission of The Macmillan Company.

nature is not discipline in any adequate sense of the term. Discipline, in the theory in question, implies understanding, and understanding deals with units of thought, relationships, and meanings.

Four Theories of Transfer

The theories which follow embody (1) the conditions under which transfer may take place (the *how* of transfer); (2) *what* it is that transfers; and (3) by implication, the *amount* of transfer.

Identical Elements (Thorndike). Identities of *substance* or *content*, of *procedure, mood* or *attitude* are necessary for transfer. Experiments such as those by B. J. Staner (1956) and L. Postman (1962) showed, respectively, that similarity in content correlates highly with the degree of transfer, and that dissimilarity in content produces negative transfer.

Generalization of Experience (Judd). The subject does not matter very much. The method of teaching or study and the degree of self-activity aroused in the pupil are all-important. Material presented in such a way as to lead the pupil to disregard the elements peculiar to the situation, and to abstract the general or essential, assures transfer. The real problem of transfer amounts to this: "How does the education which the pupil receives in school affect his subsequent thinking and conduct?" Education is training *how to think, how to generalize, how to be scientific.* Numerous corroborative experiments have been completed. For example, experiments by I. Maltzman *et al.* (1956) showed that methods of solving problems tend to persist and to be applied to new problems in preference to alternative, more efficient methods. An experiment by A. R. Entwisle and W. H. Huggins (1964) showed interference with learning and performance of tasks (negative transfer) when two very similar methods of problem solving were presented to learners who thereafter intermingled parts of both methods incorrectly.

Ideals of Procedure. *Ideals* of *procedure, neatness,* etc., when *consciously* striven for and given an emotional tone, transfer. Generalization *plus appreciation.*

Configuration. *Insight into the configuration of a perceived* *situation* is fundamental to transfer. This may mean, at times, a positive avoidance of identical elements, and a concentration on the relations within a whole situation.

Criticism of Theories

The status of transfer theory in contemporary education is reflected in the following criticisms of the preceding hypotheses.

Identical Elements. Many psychologists consider this theory to be, in effect, a denial of transfer, especially in regard to identities of substance or content. Nor does it improve the position to substitute *similar* for *identical*. To recognize *porter* (to carry, in French) because one has already met *portare* (in Latin) cannot be called transfer in any adequate sense of the term. It would seem that the study of Latin is often mistakenly justified on this ground, viz., its etymological value in the Romance languages and in English. It is obvious that a limited period devoted to etymology, and specifically to Greek and Latin root words, would dispose of the entire dispute about the classics if this were their only or main justification. The theory of identical elements is consistent with Thorndike's general theory of learning. For Thorndike, as for the behaviorists, learning is the establishing of new connections in the nervous system. These connections whether in the form of conditioned reflexes or S—R bonds are, in the last analysis, largely specific situations; and any theory of learning or transfer based on either will be characterized and limited by the fact that like responses will be made only to like stimuli. This specific-response theory has given foundation to such a dictum as "We learn what we practice, and nothing more." Thorndike, therefore, seemed committed to the terminology and the theory of "identical elements." What was called transfer by him, therefore, is simply repetition, in a new situation, of behavior which was previously learned. The difficulty remains and is even increased when the theory is extended to embrace identities of procedure, mood, or attitude.

Generalization of Experience. In this theory, method of teaching or study is the most important factor; subject matter is of relatively little consequence. If the theory be true, the formal disciplinarian who relies on the classics or mathematics may have to surrender his position, but he may rest assured that his objectives will, nevertheless, be realized. The advocate of the generalization theory agrees that the function of education is to discipline, to train intelligence, to inculcate the scientific method, to assist pupils to abstract the general and essential from the particular and accidental in their experiences. But this means training in attention, observation, discrimination, reasoning, etc. And if it be true that almost any subject will serve as a training ground, the advocates of the socially useful and scientific studies may have their demands fulfilled. The social studies, in any event, may properly lay claim to a place in the curriculum on the ground of being absolutely indispensable. What is to be said, however, of the claim that the desired procedure or disciplinary values may be derived regardless of the relational or structural values of the subject?

Content versus Procedure Value. Though present in all stages of the educative process, the problem of transfer becomes especially acute during the secondary school period. In order that he may take his place as a useful citizen in our complex social order, particularly in a democratic community, the student must become thoroughly acquainted with the social sciences, and the so-called English subjects. All agree, however, that mere information is not enough; certain ideals, and habits or attitudes of mind are equally, if not more, important. Those *procedure values*, as they are called, comprehend such attitudes as accuracy, self-reliance, concentration, fairmindedness, the spirit of inquiry, suspension of judgment in the presence of doubtful data, and a logical approach to problems. As opposed to content values which are largely specific, procedure values are probably of wide application. It is the opinion of some few educators (and, be it noted, experimental inquiry has pronounced no reliable decision on the question) that the subjects which are socially useful in content lack the structural qualities which make for procedure value. Inaccuracy, inexactness, faulty generalizations are brought home to the student with telling force in mathematics, the exact sciences, Latin, and the inflectional languages generally. The student, in his study of the social sciences, may be told about the desirability of certain habits of mind, but he will not achieve them until he sees the need for them. The theory of generalization then, insofar as it relies on method alone, simply disregards the fact that the social studies are largely speculative, inexact, and lacking in the structure and precision of the disciplinary subjects. Thus the argument runs. The reply is made, however, that the social sciences are open to radical improvements in organization and presentation. Such improvements may, in part at least, overcome the alleged handicap.

Ideals of Procedure, etc. This was a theoretical formulation by W. C. Bagley which has received some experimental support from the findings of Squire and Ruediger, and may be considered a special form of the generalization theory. According to Bagley *appreciation*—a recognition of the *worth* or *value* of the generalized controls—must characterize the generalization. Generalization itself will not tell the whole story. To insure transfer, therefore, the attitude in question must be raised to the plane of an ideal and given an emotional tone.

Gestalt Theory. The underlying assumption in this aspect of the Gestalt hypothesis is that a psychological or experienced whole is more than the mere sum of its parts; it may even stand in opposition to some of its parts. It is necessary, therefore, to abandon the notion that identical elements are the central factors. When a person (or animal) learns to respond to a given situation the operative factor is insight into the configuration as an integral whole. Köhler found that the more intelligent apes solved their problems *suddenly*, after a period of groping; they had seen the total situation in all its relations.

A simple experiment, moreover, demonstrates the fact that identical elements may even stand in the way of transfer, and so may interfere with learning or the solution of a problem. Let an animal be trained in the usual way to select the brighter of two colors in order to reach its food. The position of the brighter colored box, let us call it *bb*, is varied until the animal is thoroughly conditioned to respond to *bb*, as such, not merely to its position. Let us call the less bright color *b*. When training has been completed, substitute for the color *b* a color *bbb*, brighter still than the original *bb*. Now, if transfer takes place in response to identical elements or factors in the new situation, the animal ought to choose the color *bb*, since nothing can be more identical with itself than the same color. As a matter of fact, four stupid hens, some apes, and a child, all trained under similar circumstances, responded in every instance to the new and brighter color *bbb*. Their choice was determined by the relationship (brighter color), the configuration or pattern; they avoided the identical element in the two situations. The inference is that unless a task is carried out with insight or understanding of the configuration as a whole, the effects of training may not be transferred, and that such insight into relations is the real means of securing general training.

It is obvious that this theory emphasizes another aspect of the generalization concept. The greater the meaning an experience has for an individual, the richer his conceptualization, and the deeper his understanding, the greater are the transfer possibilities. Meaning consists in the perception of relations within and without a present experience. This explains also the experimental finding of Thorndike that the amount of transfer is positively correlated with the intelligence of the learner.

Summary of Conclusions on Transfer of Training

Our conclusions on transfer of training may be summarized briefly as follows:

1. The theory of identical elements seems to deny transfer in any worthwhile sense of the term. It denies, therefore, the possibility of generalization and training for adaptability. The theory of identical elements is consistent with the general theory of learning which lies behind it; but the theory of learning as specific-habit or specific-bond formation is now regarded by many as untenable. The evidence from neurophysiology tends to the conclusion that in learning, dynamic patterns are operative, rather than connections over particular synapses.

2. Experimental evidence, heretofore widely interpreted as denying the possibility of formal discipline and general transfer, offers no conclusive evidence against the one theory and is entirely favorable to the other. The few experiments which showed

little or no transfer dealt with specific habit situations and mechanical processes not amenable to generalization. So-called transfer in such instances depends on the existence of identical elements and their recognition as such by the learner. The transfer value of any subject, therefore, depends not alone on its content, but also on the extent of the pupil's reaction thereto. The amount of transfer, particularly with pupils of mediocre ability, is appreciably increased by directing their attention to the applications of their existing knowledge.

3. Since intelligence and insight into the meaning and possible relations of subject matter make for greater transfer, subject matter should be adapted to the intellectual level of the learner. From this point of view mere rote learning is obviously of little value, and subjects in which the pupil is interested offer the greatest opportunities for transfer.

4. Desirable attitudes, dispositions, methods of attack, ideals of accuracy, neatness, honesty, and the social virtues generally may be inculcated and generalized so as to be of wide application, provided such traits are made a conscious aim in the mind of the pupil. The effectiveness of attitudes is greatly increased if they are given an emotional coloring and their intrinsic value is pointed out to the learner.

5. The reality of transfer may be deduced *a priori* from the phenomenon of apperception: new situations are spontaneously interpreted in the light of pertinent or related past experience.

In brief, it may well be that here, as in the analysis of learning, the various theories emphasize partial aspects of a complex experience to the full explanation of which each contributes a necessary share. If we do not insist on a strict definition and use of the terms "identical" and "transfer," we can grant that the theory of identical elements satisfactorily explains transfer on the perceptual and specific-habit level, in which specific reactions and skills function in response to identical stimuli. Language study, in some of its aspects, motor reactions, and the elementary tools of knowledge are examples of transfer at this stage of learning. Since less of intellectual effort and initiative are needed as routine habits become established, the theory is a useful guide to curriculum construction and methodology in the elementary school. Primary learnings should emphasize typical life situations and life problems, both in content and approach.

To explain the transfer of concepts and abstractions operative in the more difficult studies we need the generalization or configuration theories which stress essentials and relationships as against incidental or concomitant elements. To claim that such transfer may be explained by an extension of the theory of identical elements is not only inconsistent with the psychology behind the theory but goes beyond the original intent of the latter, and the value of the term "identical" becomes lost in its very indefiniteness. Finally, the theory of ideals is particularly apt and is needed to explain transfer on the level of social and moral attitudes. The fact that a person is found to be reliable, unprejudiced, charitable, etc., in one sphere of activities, and strangely lacking in these traits in another, may well be explained (insofar as it can be, apart from the important element of volition) by the fact that such desirable character traits have not been cultivated as ideals which bind and ought to function in all situations. The value of this theory in character formation should be obvious.

The Transfer Problem in Contemporary Education

In the curriculum of contemporary education, occupational activities which typify present social life and social problems take the place of the more or less unrelated subjects and other vicarious experiences of the traditional scheme. Contemporary education seeks to develop desirable attitudes; and the school environment must be so arranged that the way of life cultivated in the school will continue in the larger life outside the school.

Since the transfer problem centers largely around the choice of certain subjects of study, the elimination of the traditional curriculum would seem *ipso facto* to eliminate the problem itself. The remaining problem would be to choose for the pupils those occupational activities which are most typical of life, which offer the greatest opportunities for enrichment of experience and the practice of the social virtues. The habits thus formed might be expected to function in the larger social environment and assist in a reconstruction of the social pattern. Indeed, would not the situations in school and in life be "identical elements" involving no need of transfer? A growing insight into the real needs of our times should eventuate in a comprehension of the basic conflicts and problems that arise in religion, in government, in economics, and in private and social conduct. It is claimed, however, that to assume such a position would be to repeat the errors of the formal discipline theory. To provide opportunities for participation in social life with its need for cooperation, sense of responsibility, consideration for others, etc., is only the initial step. A new philosophy of life must be developed: our conception of the universe must be reconstructed. The problems that confront us, religious, economic, public, or private must be seen and resolved in the light of the scientific method.

Modern education thus demands a training that is as general in its objectives as formal discipline ever attempted, and as specific in its methods as the modern theory of identical elements demands. A life situation in the school is not enough; the pupil's attention must be directed deliberately to the basic conflicts and problems of life. And he must study those problems in the light of one supreme, and only one, principle of solution, the scientific method. There is urgent need, it is said, for the steadying factor of scientific method amid the multitude of studies, materials, and principles with which the schools are deluged.

It would seem, then, that the contemporary school adopts the position of W. C. Bagley, namely, that generalizations must be made into ideals to insure transfer. This view is a modified form of formal discipline. The means and the methods of arriving at the objectives may be different; but the ends—certain dispositions, attitudes, or habits of thought, that are to work in all situations, in the solution of all problems—are very much the same.

Selection and Arrangement of Material in Learning

The learning process in the formal school is affected not only by the method of study on the part of the student, but also by the nature of the material to be learned, and the form in which it is presented. It is the province of philosophy to set the ends or aims of the educative process; it is the duty of educational psychology to find the most efficient means of reaching those ends. Educational psychology may initiate changes suggested by an examination of the psychological processes themselves: the new theories of transfer of training are examples of such revisions of traditional methods of study and teaching.

General Principles of Method and Selection of Material. The *psychological method* of approach is now widely sponsored in preference to the *logical method*, for young children and all who are beginning a difficult study. Thus, the teaching of science or geography should begin at the point of contact, where interest centers, and proceed as a development motivated mainly by socially desirable objectives.

Selection and arrangement of material, in such subjects as spelling, reading, arithmetic, etc., should be guided by the factor of utility, and the life situation. This principle means that the child should learn to spell the words he will need, and practice the kind of reading he will use, viz., quick, silent reading, with comprehension, of ordinary newspaper, magazine, and similar material. The material selected for reading should as far as possible be appropriate to the age and interests of the children. It is claimed, for example, that adolescent boys and girls show a preference for adventure and fiction stories, respectively. Here is a form of motivation ready-made. By judicious selection of readings along those lines, a lifelong taste for good reading may be developed. By presenting material that is of formal or structural value, but lacking in interest, a repugnance to literature may be developed, especially among pupils of mediocre ability.

Method and Material in Modern Education. Contemporary education is strongly socio-economic in its objectives and methodology. The present division of the curriculum into more or less isolated departments of knowledge would disappear, as now organized, under the radical revision demanded; and occupational activities carried on in a social setting would take their place. Education, in the eyes of the new theory, does not consist in burdening the minds of young people with more or less isolated bits of information, but in the practical formation of moral and intellectual attitudes requisite for social purposes. Subject matter is incidental to some purposeful activity; books, lectures, pictures, etc., may be needed and used but only as sources of information and reference, when there is a felt need. The teacher's role is to select or suggest representative projects from life situations, and help the pupil to a realization of all the bearings of the activity and its incidence in the life of the community.

Subject matter is what one needs to know in order to do what one has an interest in doing. What is method? Method is the same, according to Dewey, in all subject matter, because method is identical with the stages of thinking—the method of knowing, in any educative process. Five steps appear in the essentials of method: *experience, problem, data, hypothesis, testing.* The first essential for all learning is that the pupil have an intrinsic interest in an active experience. The most important traits that should characterize the individual in his use of the general or scientific method are: (1) directness or whole-souled attack without concern for side issues; (2) open-mindedness, welcoming all suggestions or information; (3) single-mindedness, or absorption in the subject for its own sake, not merely enjoying it for extrinsic reasons; and (4) responsibility, considering in advance all the implications of a situation, and accepting the consequences.

The Froebel and Montessori Methods. "The senses are the five gateways of knowledge." They are the prime source and basis of learning. The first task of education, therefore, is to analyze sense activity, to discover the ways and means by which such activity, particularly in early childhood, is stimulated, refined and guided toward the most fruitful outcomes. In one form or another the basic principle of sense activity underlies the play activities of the kindergarten of Froebel (1782–1852), the planned exercises of Montessori (1870–1952), and the "purposeful activity program" of Dewey and his followers. This common principle, however, is neither interpreted nor applied in the same way in each system. In the Froebelian method activities and objects are selected for their alleged symbolic, rather than their social or didactic, value. In the Montessori system the senses are regarded as tendencies or potentialities to be trained by activities devised and arranged to result in the "complete unfolding of the child's individuality." This sense training, moreover, is intended to be formal or disciplinary in nature: "It is exactly in the repetition of the exercises that the education of the senses consists; their aim is not that the child shall *know* colors, forms, and the different qualities of objects, but that he refine his senses through an exercise of attention, of comparison, of judgment. The exercises are true intellectual gymnastics. Such gymnastics, reasonably directed by means of various devices, aid in the formation of the intellect, just as physical exercises fortify the general health and quicken the growth of the body." [2]

In modern education activities are not selected or arranged in accordance with any preconceptions as to the nature of mind or the senses. The activities result from the child's contact with normal social situations or projects within the range of his interest and intellectual grasp.

Insofar as any methodology discounts, in the early stages of education, the bookish or purely verbal methods of traditional education and brings the child into direct, meaningful contact with objects and situations of his environment, it is a move in the right direction. However, when learning situations are so arranged or manipulated as to avoid difficulties, prevent errors, or save time in arriving at outcomes, their educational value is so far lessened. Intellectual outcomes must, as completely as possible, be the child's own, arrived at by manipulating crude materials. Prearranged situations too often, as in the Montessori System, embody adult knowledge and so deny the child the opportunity of discovering it for himself. They are a form of telling, and telling is not teaching. "The notion that a pupil operating with [material already subjected to the perfective work of mind as in books and occupations arranged to avoid trial and error] will somehow absorb the intelligence that went originally to its shaping is fallacious. Only by starting with crude material and subjecting it to purposeful handling will he [the pupil] gain the intelligence embodied in finished material." [3]

It goes without saying that the belief in formal or disciplinary training expressed in the Froebel and Montessori methods is in conflict with the views of most modern educators.

Learning on Secondary and Higher Levels. The view that true

---

[2] Maria Montessori, *The Montessori Method* (New York: Schocken Books, 1964), p. 360.
[3] John Dewey, *Democracy and Education* (New York: Free Press, 1966), p. 198.

learning takes place only when the outcomes of activities, of direct contact with the raw materials of experience, are intellectualized and integrated into a system of meanings, has important implications for method on the more advanced levels of learning. In the physical and biological sciences, crude materials are of course available and generally are used in forms demanded by the theory. In other areas of the curriculum we must often be satisfied with "raw material" in the form of content and meanings embodied in the symbolic forms of language or mathematics. In the social sciences, moreover, available material in such form may often be "cooked" rather than raw, distant from its source, and the danger that it may remain, for the student, as something given and on the level of mere information, rather than knowledge, is increased, if the method of communication be that of the lecture. As a routine method of instruction, lecturing is time-consuming and conducive to undue dependence on teacher-telling. Classroom periods are generally most efficiently conducted and most fruitful when devoted to discussion of assigned readings, when students and teachers may express opinions or evaluations informed by previous study.

Audio-Visual Aids in Learning. The *Orbis Pictus* or illustrated world of John Amos Comenius (1592–1670) marks a milestone in the development of the textbook as a teaching aid. The learning principle involved in this and later improvements is that of multiple sense appeal.

Teaching involves communicating: learning is reacting. Beginning with the spoken word, followed by the written manuscript and the printed text, the simple art of communication has, in recent times, grown into a complex and formidable array of scientific devices delivering auditory and visual stimuli that rival life itself, in the home, the church, the school, the library, and the market place. Tele-lectures or lectures from a distant source to groups or classes multiply, for good or ill, the reach and influence of a single voice. Educational television, by open or closed circuits, subsidized by civic, professional, or commercial interests, is now being used by those interested in promotion or propaganda. Even computer-based teaching systems are being planned and, since new devices call for new methods and new skills, teachers must be specially trained to employ such devices with economy and profit. This multiplication and refinement of visual and auditory stimuli bombarding the modern learner makes it more important than ever before to keep in mind what is involved in the learning process.

While it is generally agreed that great possibilities lie ahead for the new teaching aids, it will take time, much experimentation, and much field work before conclusive generalizations can be made, not only on the educative values or consequences of such devices in general, but on the peculiar and proper places to be assigned to each type.

Learning is reacting. The final test of the effectiveness of any mode of communication is the extent to which reactions, internal or external, are stimulated, and which indicate that the desired changes have taken place. Such reactions vary from the relatively simple sensori-motor or habit-forming responses to those on the conceptual or ideational level of integrated knowledge. The effectiveness of teaching devices on the sensori-motor, habit-forming, or largely drill subjects seems to be already assured, and the teaching of such subjects as typewriting and stenography has been facilitated and with great economy in terms of teacher personnel.

On the conceptual level of learning, however, much remains unresolved. The most advanced scientific medium of communication is, in essence, simply a more economical, speedy, and generally more effective means of providing information, stimulating sense activity or even mental reactions. It may be considered petty to object that information so easily acquired may result in superficiality and, in controversial areas, facilitate indoctrination, but the fact is that only the assimilation and integration of information into conceptual wholes can be truly educative, and this is a matter of time, thought, and circumstance. The teaching-learning complex or process, therefore, on the conceptual levels seems to comprise three stages: preparation, presentation or communication, and follow-up, and the very effectiveness and variety of the media now available in the middle stage demand that preparation and follow-up be all the more thorough.

Autoinstruction: Programed Learning. Self-teaching devices in the form of texts or manuals which enable a pupil to progress in the drill or learning of a subject with the minimum of teacher assistance have been available for many decades. Acceptance of such teaching aids has been relatively slow and grudging but within the last decade or so impetus has been given to their development by the greatly increased student population, the interest of industrial managers in mechanizing the instruction of employees, and a rather belated realization by teachers that much time-consuming and boring routine work could be safely entrusted to learning machines.

Teaching machines developed during recent years, considered as vehicles of instruction or drill, are designed to point and supplement a manual or text and, in particular, to enable the pupil to dispense to a considerable degree with teacher assistance and checking. Professionally, the content or "program" inserted in the apparatus has received much attention from students of education in an effort to bring the entire procedure into conformity with recognized principles of the learning process.

In educational literature, at the moment, discussion centers around three types of "programming": *linear* or *vertical; branching*, horizontal or *intrinsic;* and *adjunct.* Linear, proposed by B. F. Skinner,[4] and based mainly on his extensive experiments with animal learning, leads the student by means of a very gradual and carefully graded sequence of steps to a predetermined end or conclusion. Skinner's theory, being largely a matter of association by contiguity in time, calls for the avoidance of wrong answers, and pains are taken, even at the risk of boredom, to insure that the responses are correct; for if wrong responses should appear later and have become reinforced, they may be mistaken as correct and "learned." Reinforcement is all-important and, to be effective, must occur immediately after each step or answer is completed. In linear "programed" learning, since the student becomes aware of his success on completing each answer, the satisfaction derived from such awareness provides the necessary reinforcement. There are, of course, many kinds of reinforcement in human learning, such as praise, rewards, privileges. For programed learning knowledge of results is the most practicable. In general, the conditions or principles underlying linear pro-

---

[4] B. F. Skinner, "Teaching machines." *Science,* 128 (1958):969–77.

gramed learning seem very similar to those basic to Thorndike's law of effect and learning as a conditioned response.

Branching programing, sponsored by N. A. Crowder,[5] consists of a sequence or series of multiple-choice questions, enclosed in frames. If the answer selected in a frame is correct, the student proceeds to the next frame; if incorrect he is referred to another frame or text which shows him the consequences of his wrong choice and refers him back to the frame to begin again. Wrong responses, therefore, are not only expected but utilized and, in this respect, are more educative and representative of the life situation.

Adjunct programs, as the name indicates, are intended as adjuncts or supplements to selected texts or treatises of substantial content. Their aim is to diagnose, evaluate, extend, or otherwise develop the implications of such texts.[6]

The advantage, above all others, claimed for programed instruction is that it makes provision for individual differences among pupils. However, it does not follow that it is suitable for all individuals. Since the program, in a manner of speaking, reduces a learning sequence to the lowest common denominator, it is not unlikely to prove too boring for the brighter students and still not easy enough for the dull. Some programs, indeed, try to allow for the former contingency by instructing the learner to skip known steps. Programed learning has proved very effective and economical in training courses conducted by commercial and industrial organizations. Such students are, to be sure, more mature and more highly motivated and job analysis makes it possible to select the specific learnings that lend themselves to the step-by-step development demanded by the program method.

To summarize, in the opinion of many educators the machine as a vehicle of instruction has proved its claim to be considered, not as a rival, but as a welcome assistant in the very arduous and complex work of teaching. It still needs and deserves to receive every possible encouragement and active assistance from

---

[5] N. A. Crowder, "On the differences between linear and intrinsic programming." *Phi Delta Kappan,* 44 (1963):250–54.

[6] S. L. Pressey, "A puncture of the huge 'programing' boom?" *Teachers College Rec.,* 65 (1964):413–18.

the rank and file of the profession. Much remains to be done in the way of defining and selecting the types of learning and segments of subject matter to which machine teaching lends itself for use in the school classroom or laboratory. The continued improvement of the machine as a gadget or apparatus may be safely left to the manufacturers; that of the programs, the better half, is in the hands of professional educators or experts. Perhaps the most effective use of the innovation would result from a reorganized administrative system in which the present lock-step classification and instruction by grades would be replaced by one which allowed and encouraged pupils to proceed, in their academic learnings, each at his own pace and with a minimum of group aggregations or classes. The vision of a classroom with thirty pupils seated before thirty machines must give place to that of a laboratory or workshop in which learning machines of various types are available and used as the most effective aids to certain aspects of the learning process.

Brief Evaluation of Contemporary Methodology and Material. As to method, contemporary education is psychologically in a strong position insofar as motivation is concerned. The primary condition of real learning, viz., activity stimulated by an interest in what one is doing, is the very essence of the method; the motivation is intrinsic and strong. The project method, an example, though not the only expression, of contemporary education, has had dubious success in the past. Its alleged failure, wherever it did fail, may be due to inadequate support, or inadequate handling in the media in which it has been tried. Again, it may be that it is not suited to all types of learning, nor to pupils of all ages or abilities.

As to subject matter—since all subject matter is incidental to the activity or occupation in hand, it is probable that much of value to the pupil will be left untouched. Occupational activities, considered either as the manipulation of material things or the solution of social problems, do not exhaust all the possibilities of worthwhile knowledge. Reading and study may well be carried on for their own sake, with no reference to their incidence in a social situation; and intellectual or emotional activity, in general, may well expend itself with profit on issues that have but the remotest social references.

PART THREE

Tests and Measurements
by Paul V. West

Chapter 9
Measurement—Basic Definitions and Principles

The term "measurement" refers to the process of ascertaining the extent, duration, or quantity of something. Everyone has had some experience with measurement. Many of our concepts of the world about us, such as duration of time, distance, area, height, weight, and number, are based on measurement.

Evaluation and Measurement

Often the evaluation of education depends upon careful measurements which enable us to judge the abilities and accomplishments of children and teachers. Measurements are thus instruments or tools of evaluation. It is true that there are some phenomena which are not subject to measurement, such as intimate human relationships or aesthetic reactions. William A. McCall asserted that "whatever exists, exists to some degree" and, further, that "whatever exists to some degree can be measured." The latter statement should be qualified by adding the conditional clause, "if an appropriate measuring instrument can be devised and applied." In all aspects of evaluation, excepting those which directly involve human observation or judgment, measurement requires the use of some kind of more or less elaborate device or instrument. Tests are the principal instruments of measurement in the evaluation of education.

The Measure

A measure is the unit, symbol, or value in which the measurement is expressed to indicate the amount of that which is being measured. Measures which originate in numerical form are called *variables*. This term is a mathematical one which refers to the number of things in a type or class of things; it does not refer to change or variation. Measurements which originate as subjective judgments (for example, by the teacher concerning pupils' achievements) are sometimes designated as *assigned values*.[1] The teacher may assign a value of "good" to an examination paper and later give it a value of "4," but this evaluation does not make the measure a variable.

Measures obtained by measuring an object itself are *direct* measures, as in ascertaining the height or the weight of a person. When the object cannot be measured in this way, the information desired may sometimes be obtained by measuring certain forces, functions, effects, or characteristics which the object manifests. Measures thus derived are called *indirect*. Common measures of this type are those describing electric currents. Special instruments have been devised to measure emotional states by recording measures of blood pressure, pulse, and rate of breathing.

The degree of accuracy of a measure is highly significant. A measure that is strictly accurate or correct, neither more nor less than the true value, is known as an *exact* or *precise* measure. We use this type of measure when we count things as units or individuals, not when we count them by groups (such as by dozens, in which individual units may differ in some ways from one another). All other measures are *approximate*, approaching precision more or less closely. Judgments are subjective and, by their very nature, rough estimates or approximations. Objective measures depend for their accuracy on the procedure used and the susceptibility of the object to measurement.

The Scale

Measurements are accomplished through the use of scales that are adapted to particular needs and purposes. A *scale* is a grad-

---

[1] An older term not so widely used today is "attributes."

uated series of potential measures, progressing from low to high values or from high to low values by steps or degrees. The amount or size of any object of measurement is denoted in terms of the units which indicate the steps on the scale.

As a rule, the steps on a scale appear to be of even size, as in the ordinary foot rule, but in some scales they appear to be very unequal, however they may be interpreted. It is also true that steps which appear to be of equal size may not be at all equal or even comparable. While a person six feet tall is definitely twice the height of a person three feet tall, a temperature of 60° F. is not twice as warm as one of 30° F.

Four types of scales are commonly recognized. In the *nominal* type, the scale steps and indices are rather arbitrarily assigned, with no assumption being made that the steps are equal in value. Measures that are subjective in origin (assigned values, or attributes) are associated with such scales. Thus, a teacher may rate a pupil assignment "fair" on a five-step scale, with possible ratings of very poor, poor, fair, good, and very good.

In the *ordinal* scale, the indices are whole units such as those obtained by counting. Here there is an assumption of precision and equality of steps. This type of scale would be used in assigning a pupil a score of 17 on a test in spelling.

Although equal mathematical units may be given as indices in the *interval* type of scale, it is understood that the accurate measure will fall somewhere between these points. Therefore, all values that are located along the scale are approximations. The steps may or may not be equal. This type of scale can be used in finding and recording such measures as height, weight, and age.

The *ratio* scale is one that is established on the basis of a mathematical relationship between each step and the preceding step. It tells us what percentage one measure is of another, assuming a lower limit of zero. A person three feet tall is 50 per cent as tall as one who is six feet tall. One would use this scale in recording the accumulations of a principal investment with interest compounded at a given rate during certain periods of time. The steps are regarded as equal in value, although they do not appear so, and all values are approximations. Geometric and logarithmic scales are of this type.

A scale may be *standardized*, in the sense that it is accurately predetermined, established, and authorized, as a point of reference. A model of a physical scale may be constructed from which copies may be made or with which objects may be compared, as in the case of the metric bar kept in a sealed vault in Paris. Scales that do not refer to physical objects may be standardized by the use of rigidly prescribed procedures, and published for information and comparison. In contrast, a scale may be *unstandardized,* being merely relative to the particular object of measurement, at the time and under the conditions then existing. A teacher-made test given to a class would result in scores arranged on a scale of this type.

Characteristics of Good Measurements

The principal criteria for judging the quality of measuring instruments, such as scales and tests, are reliability, validity, and usability.

Reliability. A prime requirement of any measurement is *reliability.* A measure or a set of measures can be called reliable if it is dependably accurate and consistently equivalent in repeated measurements.

The accuracy of any obtained measure depends upon many factors. As before noted, a measure collected in terms of whole units is precise. It would be called *discrete.*

Many, if not most, measures are *continuous* in the sense that the scales used in their derivation are infinitely divisible. Any such measure, even though it may approach the theoretically correct (or perfect) measure by infinitesimal degrees, can be identical with that ideal measure only by chance. For this reason, measurements generally provide only approximate values.

Continuous measures are always marked by a *possible error.* Technically, the sign $\doteq$, meaning "approximately equal," should be used with such measures, or at least kept in mind in dealing with them. One may measure his own height and record it as 71 inches, but it really is approximately 71 inches, and it is also understood that the measure 71 is really $71 \pm .5$ inches, since the measurement was made to the nearest inch. One should be able to infer from context what is the possible error of a measure. It is evident that recording ages to the nearest month will yield more accurate measures than if they were taken to the nearest year.

The accuracy of a measure depends greatly upon the definiteness of the object of measurement. Objects that are plainly seen and counted should yield precise measures. Objects which have definitely marked limits may be measured with fairly high accuracy, but if these limits are hazy and ill-defined or irregular, inaccuracies will surely occur. When the measurement relates to an intangible object which has no definite form, real accuracy is indeed difficult to achieve.

The attitude of the one doing the measuring is highly significant. Complete objectivity and open-mindedness are essential as an assurance of accuracy. One may be inattentive, or so prejudiced in favor of a certain possible outcome that he subconsciously directs the procedures to this end.

Great care should be used, both in the handling of procedures in collecting data and in the treatment of the measures. The reader will find it an enlightening experience to undertake the task of measuring the length of a table with a foot rule, then repeating the process a number of times and comparing the measures. With intensive care and practice, accuracy will be found to increase. Also, adequate training is needed in the interpretation of measures.

Validity. Good measures are also marked by *validity*. A measure is said to be valid when it actually measures what it is purported to measure. If a teacher were to grade a pupil assignment as "superior" because the pupil was an excellent penman, the grade would not be a valid index of the pupil's knowledge of subject matter or of composition ability. While it is relatively easy to test reliability in most situations with various techniques now available, this is not the case with validity. Great care and good logic are required in determining the criterion or standard of validity in a particular situation and in adhering to it.

Usability. A good measurement is one that is *usable*, in the sense that it fills a practical need, is not extraneous to the material or situation or a duplication of data already at hand. The procedures to be employed should not be so complex that they cannot be adequately mastered by those who are to do the measuring.

Difficulties in Measuring Mental Abilities and Attitudes

The measurement of mental abilities, attitudes, and functions, with which the psychologist and educator are concerned, is much more difficult than the measurement of physical objects. Nevertheless, rapid progress has been made in overcoming many of the difficulties by devising procedures and specialized measuring instruments, namely, *tests*. Among the difficulties encountered in mental measurements are the intangibility of mental traits, their complexity, their non-quantitative nature, and the lack of an absolute scale.

Intangibility. Mental traits are not objects that are perceptible to the senses and that occupy space. It is impossible to apply a physical scale to the mind and thus discover the amount or quality of a person's knowledge or thought processes. Although direct measurements are not possible, indirect procedures have been very fruitful. An individual's behavior in reaction to life situations is generally observable, and much of it is measurable. Therefore, all measurements that are made in the investigation of mental abilities are measurements of behavior.

Psychologists now generally prefer to speak of "measuring behavior" rather than "measuring mental ability." However, the procedures employed in such measurement rest upon the assumption or inference that there is a true correspondence between a person's behavior and the mental processes underlying this behavior. A teacher may wish to measure the extent and accuracy of a pupil's knowledge of how to spell a certain list of words. The only way by which such a measure can be secured is by having the pupil attempt to spell these words, either orally or by writing. Similarly, the actual performance of pupils will provide more or less satisfactory measures of ability in most school subjects.

What has been said here regarding mental abilities applies also to the measurement of emotions and feelings. Such measurement similarly often depends upon assumptions or inferences based upon the analysis of behavior, but emotional states can sometimes be measured more directly by means of instruments which record changes in heartbeat, rate of respiration, and blood pressure.

Complexity. Both the mental life and the emotional states, as well as the behavior and physiological associates, are so complex that great care must always be used in planning and interpreting measurements in these areas.

Under the impression that elementary mental states would be relatively simple and more susceptible to testing, psychologists early centered their attention on singling out and measuring certain specific aspects of mental activity, such as memory, imagery, perception, alertness, and sensory acuity. The task of developing techniques and procedures that would insure the isolation of each such trait was not only formidable; it was impossible. No one of these traits is really elemental, for each one, in practice, is an actual melding of various traits. Even the relatively simple trait of reaction time is really a complex of perception, attention, memory in the form of habit, and other characteristics.

Attention then came to be centered on measuring general mental abilities, knowledges, skills, and attitudes, without making any effort to identify the particular traits that were involved. This approach has proved to be more productive. However, in using this procedure, it must be recognized that obtained measures may not be valid. A person's failure to respond in a certain way on a test may be attributable to any of many extraneous factors, such as a temporary distraction or an emotional reaction, rather than to any lack of ability.

A superior measure secured on any test almost surely indicates a superior ability or status in the trait being tested, but an inferior mark or measure may be to a greater or smaller degree the result of many factors that are unrelated to the particular trait or traits that the test is designed to measure. Two persons of the same level of ability take the same test. The one who is lazy and inattentive will certainly receive a lower score than the one who is alert and observant. Therefore, constant care must be exerted, not only in devising and administering tests but also in interpreting results.

Non-quantitative Nature. Even though the various aspects of mental and emotional life are not physical objects that are directly subject to measurement, it is safe to assume that they differ in amounts for different individuals, or for the same individual on different occasions. Each child makes some progress in school subjects, such as arithmetic, from one year to the next, and his knowledge of these subjects can be compared with that of other children progressing at different rates. The teacher's marks on report cards represent her estimates of pupil mastery and progress in school subjects. Similar progress undoubtedly takes place in the areas of mental and emotional growth.

The basic difficulty in assigning a measure that indicates quantity to mental traits, which have no dimensions, is overcome by using tests that provide a variety of possible responses in specific areas, scoring each item of the response as right or wrong, and adding these scores to give a total measure. The scores are objective, and yield a measure of the particular behavior being investigated. They also provide a basis for inferences regarding the amount of the mental ability or abilities underlying and responsible for the behavior.

Attitudes are apparently even less quantitative than mental traits. An investigator might ask a person to tell how he feels about various situations or people, but this procedure would yield results that would be thoroughly subjective, unreliable, and probably not at all valid. Instead, the examiner now obtains more objectivity by having the person react to a large number of diverse items, among which are certain ones that will indicate attitudes, but will be presented in disguised form.

An individual may be asked to rank a list of items in terms of approval or disapproval, or simply to accept or reject them. In such ways the person's attitudes may be measured on a scale, as in the case of the social distance scale. For example, one might be asked to indicate whether or not he would accept members of another race as citizens, as neighbors, as friends, as members of his family, and so on. While such procedures may not prove the actual existence of relevant feelings and attitudes, they do provide valuable insights into the person's behavior, and these are found to be of practical value.

Lack of an Absolute Scale. As has been noted previously, the scales used in the physical sciences exist independently of the investigator and of the object of measurement, and are generally applicable. A child living in Tokyo who is five feet tall is the same height as a New York City child who is five feet tall. In contrast, scales used in measuring mental traits and behavior are always relative to the individual or the group being measured. A score made by a rural child on a certain test does not carry the same significance as an identical score on the same test made by a city child. Also, while physical scales are usually composed of equal mathematical units, so that a distance of four feet, for example, is twice that of two feet, scales used in measuring mental ability cannot be so interpreted.

Standardization of Measurements

To overcome the difficulties in measuring mental abilities, adjustments in measurements are made by the process of *standardization*. The first step in this process is carefully to select the group to which the measures and conclusions will apply. This group is called the *universe*. It might consist of all pupils at the sixth-grade level in the public schools of the United States.

Since it would be practically impossible to secure the measures of all of these pupils, *samples* must be taken from the universe, so as to represent the universe. These are *random samples*, meaning that every individual in the universe has the same chance as any other individual of being selected for the samples.

Enough individuals must be included in such samples to provide good representation of the universe, and yet not so many as to make the measuring process inefficient.

A thorough analysis of the universe should be made, in order to discover the composition of the whole, and approximately the proportion of cases found in each of the subgroups that compose it. Samples to be tested should be so selected as to represent the subgroups in the universe and to have about the same proportion to the total random sample as the subgroups have to the universe of which they are a part. If one-fifth of the universe are rural pupils, then one-fifth of the random sample should consist of rural pupils. Picture the universe as a circle 50 inches in diameter. Let it take the form of a pie-chart, with segments $A = 1/4$, $B = 1/3$, $C = 1/6$, and so on. Now picture another pie chart, one inch in diameter, but otherwise a duplicate of the first one, to represent the random sample.

In the process of standardizing educational tests, the subject matter which is to compose the body of a proposed test must be carefully selected so that it accurately represents in some detail the material actually taught in the universe. This material must be suited to the age and grade levels of the pupils to be tested. Directions for the proper administration of the test must be developed. The test must be so planned that responses may be secured which can be scored accurately and objectively.

Before the test is given to the various sample groups, there must be adequate preliminary administration of the test to other groups for the purpose of securing information that will help in revising the directions and test items, as needed, and in establishing the reliability and validity of the test.

After this refinement, the test is administered to the samples that compose the random sample, and the scores made on the test are accumulated, organized, and treated statistically so that a true scale may be made. It is now possible to establish norms. A *norm* is a test score or range of values which is used to represent the theoretical status of the members of the universe, as inferred from the random sample tested, and which might reasonably be expected from the individual members of the universe. Not only are norms established for the entire universe; various norms for subgroups, such as for certain ages or groups, for example, may be determined.

A norm is not an ideal score, beyond the reach of most of the group, nor is it one which any individual or group may be expected to exceed. It is anticipated that, for definite reasons, some persons and groups will make scores that are above or below the stated norms. Norms are not absolute and final, but are in need of revision from time to time. They also need careful interpretation. They are helpful indices of the relative status of pupils, and are significant aids in guidance.

Purposes in the Use of Tests

There are those who deplore the testing movement and see little if any value in the use of tests. An honest appraisal of practical testing reveals many worthwhile achievements through their use.

Descriptive and Predictive Values. Whether the test results are to be used for descriptive or predictive ends is determined by the purpose in mind of the person administering the test.

Descriptive tests and measurements are designed to reveal the characteristics of a given individual or group of individuals at a given time and under certain conditions. For example, the results of a spelling test might indicate that the members of a class taken as a whole are below the norm in spelling.

In contrast, a test or other measurement is *predictive* in nature when it is used to draw conclusions regarding the object of measurement as it would be under other conditions or at other times, or relative to other individuals or groups. Here we enter the territory of inferences that are more or less hazardous.

Diagnostic Values. A test is *diagnostic* if it reveals certain points or areas of weakness or strength in the specific ability or abilities which the test measures in the individual or group. Practically every test can have some diagnostic significance, especially when it is carefully interpreted. Thus, a General Intelligence Test may disclose a child's weakness in reasoning, or his strength in certain types of observation or imagery. However, compared with general tests of this kind, tests which are designed specifically to yield diagnostic information are much more fruitful. Describing a pupil's status as low or high in arithmetic skills is a diagnosis, but the further step of showing why he has this status is more helpful.

Diagnosis may be used with groups as well as with individuals. In this way, it might be discovered that an entire class, or a majority of a class, may not have attained the mastery of certain number combinations.

With a good diagnosis of an individual or class at hand, a teacher can intelligently plan her next steps in instruction. (See discussion of the practical aspects of diagnostic tests, page 168.)

Motivation. The key to effective learning is *motivation,* and testing may be used as a potent instrument to this end. A pupil will generally be moved to put forth his best efforts if he competes with his own records or with the records of others, as evidenced by test results. The diagnostic test is of special value along this line, for the pupil thereby knows definitely what he needs to do.

Teachers are also motivated to work toward certain standards of achievement. The standing of individual pupils and of classes on tests is a matter of pride or of shame, and these are strong incentives. The diagnostic test is especially helpful to a teacher. Rapid advancement of pupils is found possible when the teacher is working for specific goals. Sometimes the task of overcoming the revealed deficiencies calls for a good deal of ingenuity. It always offers a challenge.

The use of tests in the classroom provides an opportunity for close cooperation of teacher and pupil, as they work together to improve school work. The teacher wisely informs the pupils of their standing on all tests and secures their enthusiastic teamwork.

Administrative Aid. The superintendents, principals, and supervisors in school systems are largely concerned with educational procedures and accomplishments. Tests make it possible for them to have at hand real evidence of the actual achievement of schools, grades, or classes, or their relative status. No longer is it necessary to make snap judgments based on general impressions. Test results make it possible to introduce remedial work when and where it is needed.

This aspect of testing brings the topic of teacher evaluation to the front. Great caution must be used at this point. Some teachers may be thus discovered to be in definite need of help in their teaching methods, but others may be doing the best possible work, although with no outstanding results because of the nature of the groups they teach, or the conditions governing the situation. Thus, a school superintendent may discover that all of the classes in a certain school are deficient in reading, but he will not blame the teachers when he also notes the generally lower standing of these pupils in an intelligence test.

Classification of Pupils. It is generally recognized that the time-honored procedure of teaching relatively large classes made up of pupils of wide ranges of ability and knowledge is very wasteful. Superior pupils will surely be neglected because it is necessary to give so much attention to those who, for one reason or another, are behind in their work. The materials and methods of instruction are, in most cases, so greatly simplified to meet the needs of those of lower ability that they fail to offer a challenge to superior students.

The practice of organizing pupils into homogeneous groups therefore renders the task of education and specific instruction easier and more effective. School systems sometimes provide for individual instruction and progress. In such situations, grouping does not enter the picture. This practice is not feasible in most communities, but even where it is not done, pupils should be promoted only when there is evidence of their individual competence.

It has been the practice in many school systems to group pupils into superior, average, and slow classes according to mental ability, as determined by tests. Those in the superior group are provided with an enriched curriculum, while those of average ability are taught the regular course of study with assignments of average difficulty, and the lower-ranked pupils are presented the minimum essentials of subject matter that are within their capacity to learn. Although theoretically sound, this procedure must be used with caution. It requires an unwarranted faith in the accuracy of intelligence tests, and calls for a labeling of pupils as to their degree of intelligence, a socially obnoxious process. Efforts to disguise the real classification do not succeed for long.

For these and other reasons some schools and school systems prefer to use the results of general achievement tests of school subjects as a basis of classification. The mastery of subject matter is the immediate concern, and there are many factors besides intelligence that are involved in the success or failure of pupils. It would be absurd to place a child in the sixth grade on the basis of intelligence alone when he has not advanced beyond the fourth grade in his knowledge of school subjects. It would be equally absurd to retard a pupil in his school progress, or to place him in an inferior group only because he happened to receive a relatively low score on an intelligence test.

A method of classification of pupils which is very logical and effective is one that is rarely used. It is based on diagnosis of instructional needs as revealed by diagnostic tests or by other analytical processes. For example, in a class in English composition, pupils might be organized into several groups, one being concerned with the use of adjectives, another with the construction of paragraphs, and another with the writing of introductions. As pupils master their particular weakness, they may be transferred to another group with a view to overcoming other deficiencies. This procedure is a close approach to individual instruction, for the pupils in each of the groups are being directed with one purpose and aim. Homogeneous grouping of this kind is especially adapted to skill subjects, but careful diagnosis will make it useful in the teaching of other subjects, such as history.

Common sense dictates the use of all possible information about the pupils, including the judgment of teachers, in any system of classification. Furthermore, any system should be flexible. One should never act on the assumption that test results give absolute proof. Instead of making a rigid and final classification, those who are responsible should arrive at only a tentative grouping, and feel free at any time to transfer pupils from one group to another as the quality of their work indicates the need.

When homogeneous grouping has been achieved by any method, it is still true that each group will be made up of pupils who are widely variant in their specific abilities. In a group made up of pupils of relatively low mental ability, for example, some pupils will be found who are energetic, ambitious, and attentive, while some in the group composed of those of higher intelligence will be lacking in such significant traits. Therefore, teachers and others concerned will need to give constant attention to the adjustment of individual pupils in the various groups.

Types of Tests

Tests have been developed to measure many, if not most, of the aspects of human behavior, and have been applied in the areas where any specific behavior is considered significant in the analysis of mental life or in the guidance of individuals and groups. Only a brief presentation of the various types can be given here. (For a discussion of their use and interpretation, see Chapter 10.)

Tests of Emotional States. Most of the tests of this type are carried on in the psychological laboratory with refined apparatus.

They are of special interest to school psychologists. Since emotions are not subject to direct measurement, direct measures are taken of bodily states that are the accompaniments of emotions. It is now recognized that some emotions of which we are conscious may be stimulated, intensified, or manifested by physical reactions. Accordingly, measurements are made of steadiness, muscular fatigue, reaction time, brain waves, and other phenomena. (Psychologists have made use of the so-called "lie detector" test and apparatus in this way.)

Tests of Attitudes and Appreciations. These are usually pencil and paper tests of the indirect type. Their use and interpretation rest on the assumption that one's response to a hypothetical situation presented by the test will be a reliable and valid index of his actual attitude when faced with a similar situation in life. Although no absolute conclusions can be drawn, the test results may prove to be of definite help in analyzing a person's behavior, especially when taken in connection with other available data.

Tests of Specific Abilities. Although there is no such thing as a completely specific ability, since all mental abilities are greatly intermingled, valuable tests are made of those compounds of abilities we call specific. Thus, a test of perception, even though it must involve such other abilities as attentive power, interest, memory, and sensory acuity, is of value in estimating and analyzing a person's behavior when he is required to perceive a stimulus or situation. A child of rather low mentality was given tests of visual and auditory imagery and found to have a relatively high score. Further analysis led to the discovery that the child possessed a marked talent in music and drawing.

Tests of General Mental Ability. Intelligence tests fall into this category. They are necessarily limited to measuring the knowledge and skills that a person has previously acquired. The basic assumption is here made that an individual's mastery of certain materials that are presented to him is a reliable index of his basic mental ability.

The first test of this type, the Binet Test, was devised as a result of the observation of many children. Detailed records were kept of their activities and the mental tasks they normally performed, as well as the knowledges that they had acquired at various ages and stages of their development. It was noted that the children who were manifestly mentally retarded were inferior to the others in terms of the items noted above, and that bright children were superior in these respects.

Eventually the test was organized and expressed in terms of ages. A group of test items prepared for children six years of age would be more difficult than another group to be used with five-year-old children. A child seven years old might receive a score on the test of four years eight months, indicating that he is retarded two years four months.

Tests of general mental ability must be thoroughly standardized to have any true significance. They must also be administered and interpreted by persons who have been thoroughly trained in this field.

Tests of Educational Achievement. Tests of achievement fall within the scope of educational rather than psychological measurement. Although intelligence enters the picture, it is not singled out for measurement. The content of these tests may consist of any subject matter of the school curriculum that is susceptible to testing.

Achievement tests are rather definitely limited in scope to factual knowledges and mental skills which pupils are supposed to master at certain levels of development. Test items are selected that are representative of the material that is actually taught at the specific grade level for which the test is adapted, and in the geographical area that is covered by the test.

Sometimes speed records are important and should be provided for, as in testing arithmetic, reading, and typewriting. The measurement of ability to originate ideas and to organize and handle them in a logical manner is not readily susceptible to measurement, but progress is being made along these lines.

Tests of this type are better adapted to elementary school levels than to those of the secondary school and college, because the subject matter is there more fixed and universal and less stress is placed on highly complex courses and rational processes.

Standardized achievement tests are available for use in school surveys and to provide analyses of the status and needs of school systems. However, tests of achievement may be constructed and used in any local situation without reference to a larger universe, extensive subject matter content, or norms.

Diagnostic Tests. The purpose of the diagnostic test is to discover the specific weaknesses or strengths of individuals or groups. Many of the achievement tests will yield diagnostic information if a careful analysis is made of the scores made on the specific items of the tests, but it is a decided advantage to use tests that are especially designed to provide this information. Teachers may construct their own tests of this type after receiving adequate training.

Aptitude Tests as Prognostic Tests. Aptitude tests are designed to secure information regarding a person's special and general abilities, skills, knowledges, and interests which will assist him in making a wise vocational choice or other line of activity. For example, if a young man desires to become an airplane pilot, the examiner gives him tests of sense of balance, depth perception, visual and auditory acuity, quickness of reaction, general intelligence, and other abilities.

In this type of test, the major stress is placed on *prognosis* or *prediction*. The whole situation, including the one taking the test, the vocation or vocations involved, and the test process itself, is so complex that the prognosis is rarely as accurate a determinant as is desired. There are so many factors incorporated in success on the job and future development in it that all cannot be taken into account or be given the proper weight. It is certain that the prognosis is improved in accuracy when provision is made for adequate analyses of personality and character.

This type of test yields better predictions of what an individual should not do than of what he should do. For example, a high school student may express a desire to become an electrical engineer, and he may be given a prognostic test. The test results may indicate that he has little or no command of basic mathematical knowledges and skills that are essential to a successful career in that field of engineering. Another student may be found to be notably superior in mathematics and science, but this evidence merely indicates that he might succeed well in a number of vocations. Much more data would be needed before a recommendation as to the choice of a career could be made.

Some Test Adaptations

Any of the types of tests here presented may be adapted to suit certain purposes, chiefly through the modification of the form or application of each test.

Individual or Group. The *individual test* is devised for administration to one individual at a time. The Binet Intelligence Test, and others following this pattern, are of this sort. The *group test* is one that is given to a group of persons at a time. The saving of time, and of expense, by the use of a group test is evident. It would have been impossible to have developed testing programs covering wide areas, as has been done, without the use of group tests. However, the individual test provides greater reliability. Better rapport is obtained between the examiner and the one being tested. In addition, in using the individual test, the examiner may readily observe how the individual reacts as he takes the test. This qualitative analysis makes possible a more revealing interpretation of test results than would be the case if only test scores were available.

Verbal and Non-verbal. The *verbal* form of test, which is by far the most common, involves the use of oral or written directions and includes material consisting of written or printed words. The responses to the test items are also usually written. The *non-verbal* test eliminates reading and writing. The directions may be spoken by the examiner but, as required, for example, in testing persons who are deaf or who do not know the language, directions may be given by the use of gestures and demonstrations. The test content is usually made up of objects or pictures, and responses are made by checking in some way, as in pointing out what is missing from a picture, or by designating which pictures are related in a specified way.

Some forms of the non-verbal tests are called *performance* tests. They are required in testing certain types of persons such as young children, persons unfamiliar with the language, illiterates, the deaf, or the mentally retarded. They are sometimes used in modified form in vocational and aptitude testing, and may be employed in any testing program.

The Power Test. Most tests are *timed tests*. They are constructed with the items in mixed order in terms of their difficulty, and are administered with the object of discovering how much of the test can be covered by a person in a given time. The *power test* is so planned that the items steadily increase in difficulty throughout the test. Development of this test necessitates a preliminary administration of many potential test items to large random samples of the population and a thorough analysis of the results in order to find the proportion of individuals responding correctly to each item. The finally completed test is given with a view to discovering how far a person can go in the test successfully during an extended period with plenty of time available.

The Test Battery. A test may be a *single test* designed to measure a specific area of knowledge, such as a test of arithmetical knowledge or skill. When a number of tests of this kind are administered during a certain period, they are termed a *test battery*. Most standardized tests that are used in the survey of schools or school systems are batteries, consisting as they do of tests in a number of school subjects; some batteries consist of or include intelligence tests.

Brief Chronology of Test Development

A thorough presentation of this topic would require many pages. Only those items which have had a marked influence on measurement programs will be noted here.

1879 First psychological laboratory established at Leipzig, Germany, by Wundt. Beginning of experimental and test investigations in the field of psychology by Ebbinghaus in Germany.
1890 Start of testing of students of Columbia College, New York, along psychological lines by Cattell and Farrand.
1896 Psychology clinic established at the University of Pennsylvania.
1897 Completion test developed by Ebbinghaus. A spelling test constructed by Rice, and his arguments for such objective tests, met with ridicule.

1904 First text including a treatment of the subject of testing written by E. L. Thorndike.
1905 First intelligence test developed by Binet in France for children.
1908 Revision of the Binet Test. Arithmetical Reasoning Test by Stone.
1909 Arithmetic Computation Test by Courtis. Handwriting Scale by Thorndike.
1911 Revision of the Binet Test in terms of Mental Ages. Handwriting Scale by Ayres.
1912 English Composition Scale by Hillegas. Researches by Kelly, Starch, Elliott, et al., showing the unreliability of teachers' marks on traditional examinations.
1913 The Buckingham Spelling Scale.
1916 Stanford-Binet Revision of the Binet Test by Terman, as adapted for use in the United States. Rapid development of tests in spelling, reading, arithmetic, and other subjects from this time on.
1917 Preliminary work on group intelligence tests by Thorndike, Pintner, Otis, and Miller.
1918 Development of Army Alpha (verbal) and Army Beta (non-verbal) Tests and their application to millions of soldiers in World War I. Otis Group Intelligence Test.
1920 Terman Group Test of Mental Ability. McCall-Thorndike Reading Test.
1922 Stanford Achievement Tests by Kelly, Ruch, and Terman.
1930 Cooperative Test Service established by the American Council on Education. Beginning of period when greater stress placed on the questioning of procedures and steps taken to refine tests. An extension of testing to include interests, attitudes, social relationships, and other areas.
1937 Revision of Stanford-Binet Test.
1940 Survey revealed over 4,000 standardized and semi-standardized tests extant. Interest in tests on the college level taken by the American Council on Education. Wechsler's Adult Intelligence Scale. World War II activities. Clinical and prognostic tests developed.
1942 Testing of college students, results forwarded by the College Entrance Examination Board.

1945 New emphasis on application and refinement of statistical procedures. Otis Primary Abilities Test based on factor analysis. Research on secondary-school level especially, stimulated by Westinghouse Talent Search. Merit Scholarship Qualification Test.
1949 Wechsler's Intelligence Scale for Children.
1955 Revision of Wechsler's Adult Intelligence Scale.
1959 American College Testing Program for those not using the College Entrance Examination Board tests.
1960 Revision of Stanford-Binet Test.
1963 Preliminary trials of Scholastic Aptitude Tests. More emphasis on use of tests for guidance in the secondary school, both on the junior high and senior high levels.

Chapter 10
Applications of Measurement

Even in the early stages of the development of civilization, some kind of testing was practiced. Initiation ceremonies provided tests of endurance, heroism, skill in hunting and warfare, and knowledge of tribal customs. A satisfactory standing on these tests was regarded as an index of a person's fitness to take on the responsibilities of adulthood. The tests were informal and competitive.

The Formal Test

As systems of education evolved, it was found necessary to devise examinations to determine the readiness of pupils to advance. When a teacher had few pupils in charge, recitations proved to be an adequate index of fitness, but with larger classes some kind of detailed examination was required. Although the elimination of such tests has occasionally been proposed, it is recognized that there must be some means of determining the pupils' mastery of school subjects. Schools cannot place their stamp of approval on the promotion and graduation of pupils without some definite assurance of their preparedness for the step.

Criticism of the Formal Test. Examinations given at the end of a semester or a year of school work came to be regarded as major crises in the life of the pupils. These tests were the chief, or perhaps the sole, criteria of promotion. The penalty for failure was usually the severe one of compelling the pupil to repeat the work of the period and to endure, in school and at home, the humiliation of defeat.

In the early part of the twentieth century, scientific investigations revealed the marked unreliability of traditional examinations. Researches carried on by Starch, Elliott, Kelly, and others demonstrated clearly that the grades given by teachers to the test papers were not accurate criteria of the pupils' abilities. It was found that teachers differed widely from each other in the marks they assigned to the same term paper. They were also inconsistent, for they would assign different grades to test papers that were presented to them for a second rating. Even tests of strictly factual materials were rated differently by teachers, for some would take into account evidence of neatness and others would not.

New Movement in Testing. As a result of these investigations, it was realized that in such a critical matter there should be a more reliable means of evaluating the work of pupils than was supplied by the traditional testing procedures. Two important changes gradually took place. The first development came when standardized tests were constructed for many subjects of the curriculum. These provided objective scoring, and therefore were generally reliable. Two teachers could now score the same papers and find themselves in perfect agreement. There could no longer be any suspicion of partiality or other extraneous factors which might affect the grading. The second significant development came when objective tests were designed for use as teaching and diagnostic aids by which the specific needs of individual pupils could be discovered as a guide to remedial instruction. This procedure requires rather frequent testing of smaller units of subject matter than is the case with standardized tests.

Interpretation of Test Results. In the earlier traditional testing programs, there was a general tendency to take the test results too seriously as a decisive guide in the grading of an individual pupil or group of pupils. This tendency has given way to a more wholesome attitude. In the first place, tests are now much more inclusive and comprehensive, telling a more complete story. Secondly, tests are now properly regarded as devices which will throw valuable light on the behavior and ability of an individual, but which, in themselves, do not tell the whole story about his competence.

Test scores are now taken as just one index of a person's status. It is also recognized that several carefully selected tests will yield more information than one and that such data coupled with facts collected from other sources will provide a sound basis for a preliminary and temporary estimate of a person's status or ability.

New Attitudes Toward Testing. With these progressive changes, there has come about a much better attitude toward testing and testing programs, at least in most school situations. School administrators and supervisors have become aware of the value of testing as a means of discovering the strong and weak points in the work of the schools, grades, and classes. They are less likely to judge the efficiency of teachers unfairly than was formerly the case, because the true facts are so readily revealed by a variety of tests.

Teachers, whether on their own initiative or in cooperation with their superiors, undertake testing with enthusiasm, for the tests are easy to give and score and help the teachers to discover the needs of their pupils. Pupils can now face the examinations with little or no fear, and tend to regard them as an interesting game or contest. They wish to know their test scores and thus to learn in what respects they excel or fail, so that they can decide where they need to apply their efforts. Parents also evidence a genuine interest in tests and test results. In general, modern tests are proving to be vital motivations in all phases of the educational process.

Preparation for Testing

Many teachers and others called upon to engage in a testing program assume that they will have a very easy task. However, it cannot be too strongly emphasized that special training is needed for this work. Otherwise, the test results will fail to give an accurate picture and facts will be distorted. Tests are too often administered and interpreted by those who are not really qualified to do so.

Standardized Tests. The art of administering and interpreting standardized tests should be learned under the guidance of someone who is an expert in this undertaking. Not everyone possesses a personality or manner which fits him adequately for establishing rapport with the persons being tested. This factor is especially important when the individual test is used. But with proper training, one may learn the correct approach.

The mechanics of planning and organizing a test session, and of preparing the groups or individuals for testing, require careful attention. Precautions should be taken so that there will be no distraction of any kind during the testing period. Individuals should be comfortably seated, with good light and ventilation. More than one sharpened pencil should be provided for each person, so that if one breaks another will be available.

The directions for administering the test should be followed exactly. Complete attention of all persons should be secured while the directions are given, both the general directions and the directions for each part of the test. It is preferable for the examiner to memorize the directions so they will not be given hesitantly and with errors. Directions should be given slowly and with emphasis.

Any specified time limit on the test or on any part of it should be strictly adhered to because any change in this factor would affect the scores. The examiner should use a stop watch or at least a watch with a second hand and should say "Start!" and "Stop!" clearly and emphatically, not in a low voice or a drawl. Care should be taken to see that each person starts and stops the test as directed.

Great care is necessary in the handling of test papers. To avoid mixing papers, identify each test and each unattached sheet by entering on it such information as the name of the pupil, school, grade, and class. The scoring of the papers and the interpretation of the measures must follow accurately the methods prescribed in the manual accompanying the test, so that the examiner makes no erroneous inferences as to what the test as a whole or any part signifies. It is probable that a fair knowledge of statistical methods will be required for a comprehensive grasp of these procedures.

Local Teacher-made Tests. A great deal of care should be taken in the use of objective unstandardized tests. (The construction of such tests will be discussed later in this chapter.) They should be administered with the same attention to details as were noted above in regard to giving standardized tests. The scoring methods should be carefully devised and adhered to.

Interpretation of Standardized Tests

The explanations and discussion below will generally apply to most tests that are available. There is no assurance, however, that all points of information and comments will be applicable to every test.

Intelligence Tests. The score made on an intelligence test may be directly expressed in terms of *mental age* (M.A.), as in the Binet Test, or in terms of a point score which may then be transmuted into mental age by the use of tables that indicate the mental age equivalent for every possible score on the test.

Mental age indicates the stage of development of a person in mental ability in comparison with and as determined by the average age of the persons in the universe who make the same score. For example, a score of 68 on a test means nothing in and of itself, but if the M.A. equivalent of this score were 123 months, or 10 years 3 months, it would take on meaning. If the child were nine years old, or twelve years old, the measure would be even more meaningful.

Another term commonly used in treating the results of an intelligence test is the *intelligence quotient* (I.Q.). This value indicates the relation that the M.A. bears to the *chronological age* (C.A.), expressed in terms of per cent. It is computed by dividing the M.A. by the C.A. and multiplying the quotient by 100, so that the I.Q. is expressed in terms of units. A child who is 135 months of age is found to have a mental age of 123 months, so his I.Q. is $\frac{123}{135} \times 100$, or 91. This value indicates that the child's mental ability is about 91 per cent of what might normally be expected of a child of that age. There have been many proposed categories of mental ability distributed along the scale of possible I.Q.'s, such as: 70 and below, mentally retarded, and 130 and above, very bright; but such classifications must not be taken too seriously. The I.Q. has little significance beyond the chronological age of fifteen or sixteen years, as the ratio no longer holds true.

Achievement Tests. There are also various ways of interpreting the results of *achievement tests*. The *educational age* (E.A.) of an individual refers to the position he holds on the age scale as determined by the age of the average child in the universe making the same score on a test battery composed of a number of subject tests. If an achievement test in reading were given, one would refer to *reading age* (R.A.), and so on with other school subjects, as *spelling age* (S.A.) or *arithmetic age* (A.A.)

The *educational quotient* (E.Q.) has the same connotation as the I.Q. and is computed in the same way: $\text{E.Q.} = \frac{\text{E.A.}}{\text{C.A.}}$. If a pupil is 146 months old and has an educational age of 186 months, his E.Q. is $\frac{186}{146} \times 100$, or 127, indicating that his general educational achievement level is about 27 per cent above what might normally be expected on his age level. Similarly, one might compute the *reading quotient* (R.Q.) or the quotient for any other school subject.

Another term that is frequently used in analyzing the results of achievement tests is *grade score* (G.S.), which may be used in connection with a test battery or a subject test. This value is found, as was the case with M.A. and E.A., by reference to tables giving equivalent values for the possible scores on a test. The value signifies on what grade level the individual really belongs when the score he makes on a test is compared with the grade level of those in the universe making the same score. A child in the middle of the sixth grade (6.5) might be found to have a G.S. of 5.2, indicating that he is then actually capable only of achievement markedly below the level of his grade placement. The term applies to various subjects of the curriculum as well as to general placement.

Other Interpretations. There is an increasing tendency in recent years to disregard some or all of the terms noted above as aids to the interpretation of the measures secured by testing, and to use other indices. One of the most common is that of per cents, in some form. Thus, one might say that a child had a percentile score of 93, meaning that 93 per cent of his test group fell below him in the scale of measures. Or, in referring to the universe, the child with this score might be found to have a percentile score of 76, meaning that 76 per cent of the norm group received lower scores than he did. Or, grouping the per cent scores, one may speak of a pupil being in the sixth percentile group (60% to 70%) or in the upper quartile (75% to 100%). (These and other statistical procedures will be presented in some detail in Chapter 11.)

Cautions. Just one test, however well administered, will not yield an absolute value of a score, age, or quotient for any person, for no test is perfectly reliable or valid. Examiners are sometimes misled by the factual appearance of a number into believing that it has precision. No two tests of the same ability will yield results that are identical or nearly alike, except by accident. This is also true of the results obtained by repeating the same test or by giving an equivalent form of a test.

A better and more dependable conclusion may be reached by administering two or more tests and finding the average score or other index, or at least by supplementing the information thus gained with other available data. A pupil in Grade IV was found to have a very low I.Q. It was then discovered that she had a marked deficiency in reading because of inadequate instruction in the preceding grade. As this defect was corrected, the I.Q. rose to a normal value. We should never dogmatically assert that an individual has a certain M.A., E.A., I.Q., or E.Q., but merely recognize these as values supplied by one or more particular tests which are helpful indications in forming judgments and conclusions when properly used.

Diagnostic Tests

Pupils do not learn lessons or subjects as a whole, but progress to the extent of their mastery of specific elements of subject matter. Some will be found to be deficient in their knowledge of one or more particular items, while another pupil will manifest different lacks.

The Need for Diagnosis. A mere test of a subject as a whole, as in a standardized subject test, will not reveal the strengths or weaknesses of individual pupils. Neither will teaching detect or overcome deficiencies unless special efforts are made to this end, and with measuring instruments that are appropriate to the purpose. As a direct result of giving a diagnostic arithmetic test to her pupils a teacher discovered that many of the pupils did not know how to deal with zero combinations, the mastery of which had been taken for granted.

Diagnosis, followed by remedial instruction, helps to prevent the fixing of wrong habits. It necessitates a fairly thorough awareness of each child's knowledge and ability. It also stresses the constant mastery of subject matter with a view to the prevention of failure. The work of instruction is thereby made more interesting and meaningful. If the children are informed about their own strengths and weaknesses, they will be definitely motivated in their school work, for they will then have specific goals and will enjoy their studies more as they succeed.

Procedures in Diagnosis. Diagnostic analysis can be carried on with standardized tests or with local teacher-made tests, but the major reliance must be placed on the latter, since standardized tests can be used only infrequently. Diagnosis is difficult to execute with the standardized subject achievement test; therefore the standardized diagnostic test which is available for a number of school subjects is preferable. Tests of this type sometimes provide for a repetition of test items in different form so that deficiencies may be more readily detected. They also deal with the various basic elements of the topic measured. One advantage of the local test is that it may be made to apply to the current topics of study, such as long division, or the adjective in composition.

For effective analysis of test results, it would be advisable to make a tabulation or chart, as in Figure 6. At the left of each row is the pupil, here identified by number. The items are numbered in order in the top head row. A mark drawn in any coordinate indicates what item was incorrectly answered by that particular pupil. The total errors made on the test by each pupil are indicated at the right and the total of wrong answers to each item of the test are given at the bottom. You will note that the chart is here condensed by omitting part of it. As you look at this

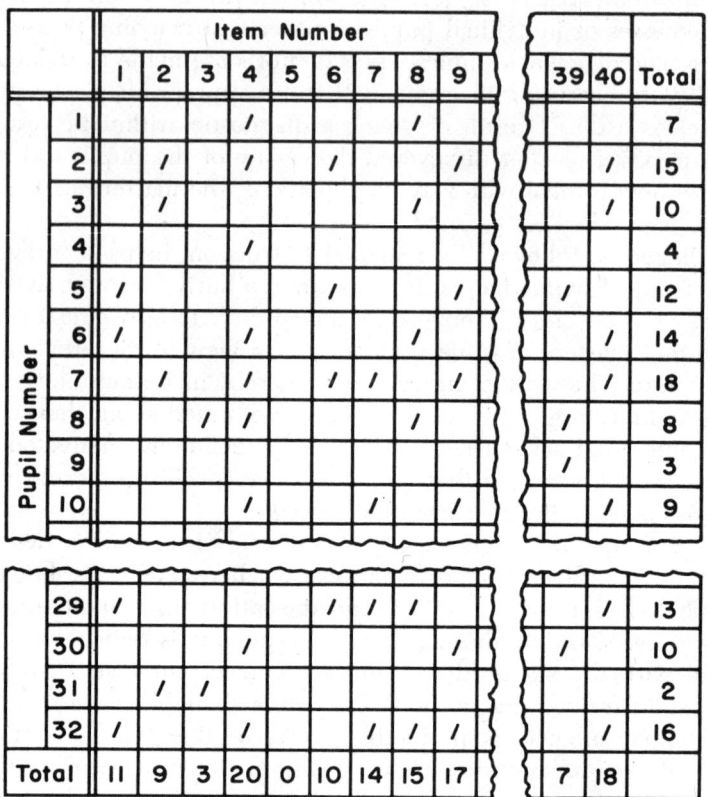

Fig. 6. A diagnostic chart.

figure, you can see at a glance that Item Number 3 was easy, having been missed by only three pupils, while Item Number 4 was difficult, having been missed by more than one-half of the class. One can also readily note which pupils are superior and which ones are inferior on the test, and find the items which are responsible for a low mark.

Such knowledge will serve as an essential and effective guide in the review of and further instruction in the subject. It may also provide for the homogeneous grouping of pupils according to needs, as previously discussed. A test of this type may be made and given to a class before the first lessons of a topic have started, to discover what instruction is needed and where the emphasis should be placed. There would be little use of spending time in teaching and drilling on a spelling list of 25 words if only a few of the words were spelled incorrectly on such a pre-test.

The Local Teacher-made Test

There is a definite need for more frequent testing than is possible with the use of standardized tests. Attention must ever be given to evaluating the progress of pupils and making instruction more efficient. It is also true that standardized tests seldom cover the material that is receiving local emphasis. The only way to secure adequate and accurate information about the work of the pupils is by the use of tests made by the teacher. Therefore, the teachers at all levels of the educational system, even in college, should learn the art of making good tests, for much depends upon them.

When a teacher is teaching the same class or the same subject, year after year, a test made this year covering a certain topic or area can be preserved and used in succeeding years. In this way a great deal of labor may be saved, even if revisions are found to be advisable.

As will be noted, the emphasis throughout this treatment is on objectivity of tests. There are many patterns or forms for such tests, ranging from very simple to very complex types. The patterns that are presented here for the guidance of the teacher in preparing his own tests are those commonly used in standardized tests.

The reader is urged to consult the *Encyclopedia of Educational Research* (edited by W. S. Monroe), especially the article "Tests, Achievement." Here will be found an excellent presentation of the strengths and weaknesses of the various forms and types of objective tests, as well as cautions governing their construction. Another valuable reference is *Tests in Print* by Buros *et al.*, which presents in detail the many diverse types of test items selected from standardized tests that have been used. (The material in these references is not included here because of lack of space.)

The Oral or the Written Test. The oral test falls mostly in the area of the classroom recitation, though it is sometimes used by examiners who desire to study the personality of an individual or who are called upon to test individuals who for some reason cannot express themselves in writing. The written examination relates mostly to the formal examination given at certain times to establish ratings, but it may also be employed as a form of recitation. A combination of the two types is sometimes used, as, for example, when a pupil writes a solution of a problem in mathematics on the blackboard and at the same time tells why he followed the various steps.

These types of tests have always been a very important feature of school work and will remain so. Every recitation a pupil is called upon to make and every answer the pupil gives in response to the teacher's inquiry is a test. It is probable that a teacher's eventual rating of a pupil is determined largely by the pupil's responses in recitations. The improvement of these types of testing is greatly needed.

There are two broad divisions of the oral and the written test. One is the controlled-response test in which specific facts are required in the answer, as in the question, "What was the date of the Boston Tea Party?" or "What does the text state are the five chief causes of the American Revolution?" This kind of test is definitely objective and any response can be graded accurately. The greatest objection to it from an educational point of view is that it calls for only a parrot-like response from memory, but this is not a bad feature unless it is carried to extremes.

The free-response type of test is one that calls for responses that are based on reasoning, judgment, imagination, or other functions not directly related to memory. Here one enters the area of the essay test which has characterized many of the formal examinations of the past. Here also one faces the problem of subjectivity in grading responses. The question may be asked, one not even suggested by the pupils' textbook, "Do you believe the Revolutionary War could have been avoided? Justify your answer." There is a growing demand for this kind of testing, but the problem of grading remains.

The customary procedure in rating responses to such an inquiry is that of making a judgment based on a general impression.

Grading may be made more objective by deciding before the question is asked what a practically perfect answer would be and planning a system of point credits, such as: manner (1), presentation (1), accuracy of facts (2), fitness of facts (2), thoroughness (3), organization (2). In this way pupils would be rated on a point scale and two or more teachers would more nearly agree in scoring. Never ask a question which permits a very long response which cannot be assigned a definite value, such as "Discuss the American Revolution."

Teachers who are determined to make the entire recitation and testing process more accurate and meaningful sometimes make use of sheets of paper with two rows following each pupil's name. For any given day, the point value of the question asked is recorded on the upper row, and the points earned by the pupil are marked on the lower row. Some questions may be of the controlled-response type, others of the free-response type. By a procedure such as this, testing and grading are placed on a sounder basis.

It has been customary practice, in administering the essay test, or any other free-response test, to ask ten questions, each having a value of 10 points. This is not a logical procedure. The questions are certain to be of unequal value, and the 100 points given to perfect answers to every question cannot be thought of as a 100 per cent grade, for tests themselves vary widely as to difficulty. One item may receive 12 points of value and another 4. The point values on a test may come to any amount, not necessarily 100. Point scores may be transmuted into grades by the use of statistical procedures. (See pages 189–93, 212.)

It is certain that the oral recitation and daily written tests will remain the chief basis for the grading of learners on all levels of the educational system, and it is indeed important that they be made as accurate as possible when used as measuring instruments.

The Short-Answer or Completion Test. This form of test is one which calls for a specific answer and is therefore a controlled-response test. The oral or written test discussed in the preceding section may be given this form. It is especially suitable for testing the pupil's knowledge of definite facts and his ability to recall them.

In most instances blank spaces are provided in which the answer is to be written. One should avoid making the blank space small because the desired response is short, for the space would then suggest a short answer. In preparing the test, care should be taken to make clear what response is required by providing a definite cue. If an item were written "Columbus discovered America in _____," any of a number of correct responses might be written in the space, such as "a ship," or "the Santa Maria." The item should be written "Columbus discovered America in the year _____." Compare thus the question "What did Columbus really discover in the year 1492?" with "What land did Columbus discover. . . ?"

Two or more spaces may be provided for one item, as "Water is composed of the two elements _____ and _____." Either response may be placed in either space unless the instructions specify "in alphabetical order." All questions calling for the solution of mathematical problems, such as $7 + 8 = $ __, or $x = 3y + 5$, are completion tests; this is the type of test most frequently encountered in the daily life of the school and in the task of measurement as well.

Many adaptations of the completion test may be found. For example, pupils may be given a map of the United States having numbers on it at the sites of various cities. The pupils are asked to identify the cities indicated by the numbers on the map. In the same way the various parts of a machine may be identified. It is best practice in such items to treat only one topic at a time, such as cities, mountains, rivers, parts, or functions. In this way, confusion is avoided.

The Alternate-Response, or True-False, Test. In this type of test, the person is asked to indicate in some way whether a given statement is true or false, or whether or not it belongs in a stated category. A choice between alternatives is required. A pupil may be asked to write "True" or "False," or "T" or "F," after the statement, but to avoid illegibilities, it is better to have the pupil simply make a check mark in the space after the T or F already printed after the statement. The same method would apply to "Yes" or "No" or any other designation.

This type of test has been criticized because it presents wrong answers to pupils, but that is not a marked fault, if immediate steps are taken to emphasize the right answer. The chief defect is its unreliability, since there is an even chance that the correct answer to any item may be obtained by guessing. Theoretically, one could answer at least one-half of the items correctly if he put the responses down at random. Consequently, some have been reluctant to use this type of test, even though it is a very easy test to construct.

Efforts have been made to overcome its unreliability. One procedure, much used, is to find the score on a test by subtracting the number of wrong answers from the number of right answers using the formula $R - W =$ Score. Negative values would be counted as zero. The assumption is here made that the guesses that happen to be right will actually balance the ones that are wrong. The formula may penalize the pupil who does not guess. Even if it were proved that the formula is true in the long run, there can be no assurance that it is true for a particular group of test papers or for a relatively small number of items on a given test.

Better test results have sometimes been obtained by asking the pupils being tested to indicate after each item whether they were guessing (G), fairly confident (F), or certain (C). In scoring the test, each item that is correctly answered would receive the mark of 4 if the "C" were used, 3 if the "F" were indicated, and a 2 if the "G" were reported. Thus, for a wrong answer, the values for the item would be 0 for "C," 1 for "F," and 2 for "G."

Another method of improving the test results is to make some adaptations. The pupil may be required to underline a word or term in the statement that makes it wrong, in case he so marks it. For example, a test item might be "Water is composed of oxygen and nitrogen. R____ W____" If the individual marked this statement wrong, then he must underline "nitrogen" to receive credit. Or the completion-test form may be added to each item, as "Water is composed of oxygen and nitrogen. R____ W____ _____" Here the pupil must, in addition to underlining the wrong word, write on the blank at the end the word that makes the statement correct. Of course, the blanks would have to be provided for all items so that no cue would be given as to which ones are wrong.

Special care must be taken to avoid ambiguity or uncertainty as to what is meant. Also, there should not be any terms in an item that will serve as cues to the correct answer. Such words as "never" and "always" should generally be avoided, as in the item, "Standardized tests are always scored only by experts." This type of test, especially in its simpler form, should be used only with a large number of items, perhaps 100 or more, so there will be a good chance for right and wrong guesses to cancel each other out.

The cross-out test may be considered a variety of the true-false test. Here one simply crosses out any term which makes the statement wrong.

The Multiple-Choice Test. The multiple-choice form is really an extension of the alternate-response test. As a rule, a partial statement is made and three or more possible conclusions are offered, and the pupil is asked to check the conclusion that is correct. Thus, an item might read, "One of the elements of which water is composed is (1) nitrogen ___, (2) hydrogen ___, (3) chlorine ___." Here again the problem of unreliability because of guessing arises. Sometimes this is taken into account in scoring the test by using the R-W technique. If three choices are given, the formula is Score $= R - \frac{1}{2}W$; if four choices are given it is Score $= R - \frac{1}{3}W$; and so on. A much better procedure is to modify the test form. The items may be made more complex by providing five, or more than five, possible choices and stating in the directions that none, one, or more correct completions follow. For example, the item itself might be:

Water is composed of the following element(s):	chlorine	___
	oxygen	___
	nitrogen	___
	ozone	___
	hydrogen	___

In this instance, substitutions might be made for one or both of the elements, leaving one or no spaces to be checked. Another variation would be to add the completion test procedure by placing one or more spaces at the right on which the pupil being tested is to write any words or terms that will make the statement complete and accurate. Thus, the question may be:

The names of the Great Lakes are:
Niagara _____ _____
Michigan _____ _____
Oneida _____ _____
Champlain _____ _____
Huron _____ _____

Questions of this type call for free response and recall, instead of mere recognition.

This type of test is difficult to construct and requires some ingenuity. But effort expended in making a test in this form, especially as adapted, is definitely rewarding, for when well made, it is an objective and reliable test and one well fitted to varieties of situations. For example, the completions might be numbered and so refer to numbers on a map, for which names must be identified or added. The method may be used in the definition of words, especially for homonyms, or words having a variety of meanings. It could also be used for spelling tests.

Matching, or Paired-Associates, Test. In the matching test, two lists are given, and the pupil is asked to indicate which item on one of the lists is in a stated way associated with each of the items on the other list. One of these lists may be organized in some kind of order—alphabetical or chronological, for example—but the other must be presented in a thoroughly mixed order, so that the position of an item will give no cue as to the right answer. A test item might treat of explorers of North America thus:

A	B
_____ Cartier	a. Mexico
_____ Clark	b. Pacific Coast
_____ Cook	c. Florida
_____ Coronado	d. The Great Lakes
_____ Cortez	e. Northwestern United States
_____ DeSoto	f. Canada
_____ Hudson	g. Mississippi River
_____ Lewis	h. Southwestern United States

The instructions would be: place any letter or letters in front of the names of explorers in list A that will identify the region or regions that were the chief area of their exploration. There is no assurance that every item in list A will receive a letter or that every item of list B will be noted. The directions make it possible that any item of list A may receive more than one letter. The test may be made more complex by providing spaces after the names of list A or list B or both in which may be written the word (or words) in that list not given but which has an associate that is stated in the other list.

This type of test is highly objective and reliable, as well as valid. It is also relatively easy to construct, and has the virtue of covering much information in a small space. It is well adapted to testing in the fields of geography, history, and science, or in any area in which categories that can be associated exist.

In constructing this type of test, care must be taken that no cues to the correct pairing occur. Each list should be homogeneous. For example, a list might contain the names of rivers and rivers only. The test should not be at all complex when used with younger children, being limited to from three to five pairs.

Combinations of the Various Types of Tests. As suggested and also illustrated in the preceding discussion, it is advantageous on occasion to modify the basic form of a given type of test by combining various types. This procedure is desirable for higher grades and levels of education, for the pupils are then ready to handle the more complex concepts. Care must always be taken not to make any one test too long for young children. While there might be 100 items in an alternate-response test given to pupils in the eighth grade, a test of only 25 items in a test of this type would be suitable for pupils in the third grade.

In constructing the test, do not intermingle different types of items. If there are two or more parts in the test, each part will consist of only one type of question (the form and complexity will vary among the parts), with one set of directions. This procedure will prevent confusion. Thus, Part A of the test might be true-false, Part B completion, and so on.

Practical Considerations. Fortunate indeed is the teacher who has available a duplicating apparatus that will make it possible to reproduce materials such as tests quickly and economically. Teachers sometimes do not make and use the new-type tests because they do not have the facilities for making copies of tests in sufficient numbers for class use. However, much may be done without mechanical devices. A teacher may have prepared a test consisting of 40 items. The pupils can be given sheets of paper on which they will write the numbers 1 through 40 in a vertical column. The teacher can then tell the pupils how they are to respond to each question by number when he writes the question on the blackboard or presents it orally. This method or similar methods may be devised and used by ingenious teachers.

Frequency of Testing

The cost and other administrative factors prevent the use of general survey tests more often than once or twice a year. Even so, they will yield sufficient data regarding the status of a school system or an individual school. The individual classes require much more frequent testing. Diagnostic tests are appropriate when any major topic of instruction is being taught. Teacher-made tests may be given at any time as an integral and essential part of classroom work, and also as aids in establishing ratings. Pupils usually enjoy taking these tests, but they may lose interest in them if they are given too frequently.

Pupils who take the new-type tests regularly become to some extent "test-wise," for they gain facility in handling them. Pupils who have had less experience in taking these tests than others in a class should receive some special attention and practice in being tested, so that they will not be handicapped on this account.

Use of Tests in Teacher Research

Educational research, which has made possible the marked advancement in the knowledge of children's behavior and needs as well as methods of instruction in recent years, has been developed largely through the use of standardized tests. All such research has been and is being carried on by experts.

Teachers frequently find it enjoyable and profitable to conduct simple investigations of their own. For example, a departmental teacher in a junior high school may give a standardized intelligence test to sixty pupils in a certain subject and on a certain grade level. The group will now be divided into two classes that have approximately the same range and level of mental abilities, as determined by the test. A preliminary test of subject matter is given to each class. One class then receives the regular course of instruction for a certain length of time, possibly three months, while the other class, covering the same ground, receives some special motivation from the use of frequent diagnostic analysis and remedial work. At the end of the period specified, both groups again take the same standardized subject test, or another form of it, and the differences in the scores of the two groups are analyzed in some detail to determine which class made the greater advancement. Such a project would not make a great contribution to educational research, but it could prove to be quite beneficial to the pupils.

Teachers who would like to carry on a project such as the one here suggested or who undertake any detailed interpretation of test scores must have an acquaintance with some of the basic statistical techniques presented in Chapter 11. But simple diagnostic tests could be used in some experimental research without the application of statistical procedures, since the mere counting of errors and their identification might be all that is needed to reach desired conclusions.

Chapter 11
Elements of Statistical Techniques

Measurements are of little value unless they are properly interpreted. Statistical techniques, simple or complex, supply the tools by which masses of data may be analyzed and studied in such a way as to lead to definite conclusions. By their use, groups may be compared with each other and with established norms, and the status of individuals in relation to other individuals, groups, and norms may be determined. A teacher who does not have a practical understanding of these techniques can neither comprehend test manuals nor follow their recommended procedures intelligently or accurately.

Only a few of the statistical procedures can be presented in this short chapter, but the topics treated here will be adequate for most classroom teachers and supervisors, and the mastery of these techniques will be of great benefit to them in their testing work and in the reading of educational literature. A thorough knowledge of the subject, such as is needed by specialists in research, requires a great deal of study and involves a mastery of some topics of higher mathematics.

Interpretation of the Measure

The interpretation of statistical information requires an understanding of the manner in which data are arranged, as in series, unit-intervals, and group-intervals.

The Series. Any item of data, even if not obtained by the use of a measuring instrument, is considered a *measure*. Every compilation of measures of a similar type that are accumulated from the same source is called a *series*. The mass of scores made by a class group on Test A would be a series, and the scores made by the same class on Test B, or the scores made by another class on Test A, would be another series. When the measures in a series are arranged according to some systematic plan, they are called an *ordered series*. The plan may be an alphabetical order, by pupil name or number, an order of size of measures, a chronological order, or any other convenient arrangement. If the measures are organized according to size from high to low or the reverse, the series is *ranked*. The measures may be given the form of a *scaled series* by distributing them along a scale, with all possible measures from the low through the high measure included, whether or not any actual cases fall at any of the places on the scale.

The Unit-Interval. Every measure is thought of as falling at the lower limit *or* the midpoint of a *unit-interval*. All test scores are treated according to the latter of these plans. Thus, the score of 28 on a test is understood to be the midpoint of the interval 27.5 *to* 28.5, or 27.50–28.49+, which is usually written 27.5–28.4. Even when the interval is not recorded in this form, the measure is treated statistically in this manner.

Special care must be taken in the interpretation and treatment of certain measures, such as stated ages. It is customary to consider a person as being of the age he had reached upon his last birthday, but a child who is thus eight years old is really somewhere between eight and nine years of age, and his approximate age is the midpoint of the interval 8.0–8.9 or 8.5 years. If, following the practice of insurance companies, his age were taken to the nearest birthday, the interval would be either 7.5–8.4, or 8.5–9.4, depending on whether his age were nearer eight or nine, the midpoints of the two intervals. School administrators sometimes set the age entrance to school at five or six years without defining just what they mean. The ages and grade levels of pupils should not be recorded by one method and then compared with age and grade norms or averages computed on another basis.

The Group-Interval. Measures are frequently grouped, so that *group-intervals* replace the unit-intervals. Grouping is used for condensation of wide ranges of measures in order to make the handling of the measures less unwieldy. In a group-interval, two or more adjacent unit-intervals are taken together and treated as a unit. Thus, the scores 5, 6, and 7 may be grouped in one interval, 4.5–7.4, with a midpoint value of 6. The size or height of the interval (h) is simply the number of adjacent units in the interval, in this case three.

In this illustration, all individuals who are five, six, or seven years of age are considered to be six years old. It is evident that this assumption is not true. All grouped data and all computations from grouped data are less accurate than would be the case if the data were left ungrouped. However, when, and only when, there is a relatively large number of cases, the errors will tend to be adequately neutralized.

The Frequency Distribution—Ungrouped

From this point on throughout our presentation of statistical techniques, it would be well for the reader not only to seek to understand the procedures but also actually to do the work on the problems used in connection with every topic.

The symbols here used for the various statistical values may, in some instances, differ from those used in other treatments, but you will readily learn to recognize them and their functions. Mathematical statistics employs specialized technical symbols, while those presented here are somewhat simpler and more widely used.

The Frequency Table. As usually collected, measures are in *mixed order* as to size. In looking them over, we gain only the impression that there are some large measures and some small ones as well as many middle values. They need to be arranged in order of size so that we can see at a glance how they are distributed. This is done by making a *frequency table*. Given in Figure 7 a series made up of scores of the pupils of a class in a spelling test, we can organize the measures according to size, preferably in a scaled series rather than a ranked series, since the scaled series will clearly show the range of measures and their distribution along a scale.

A frequency table is constructed in the manner shown in Figure 8. The highest score (43) and the lowest score (29) are found by looking carefully through the scores. A scale is now prepared

Pupil	Score	Pupil	Score	Pupil	Score	Pupil	Score
1	37	9	39	17	34	25	37
2	42	10	37	18	37	26	39
3	33	11	38	19	32	27	36
4	36	12	36	20	38	28	37
5	38	13	37	21	40	29	38
6	34	14	43	22	34	30	33
7	39	15	38	23	42	31	35
8	30	16	36	24	29	32	37

Fig. 7. Scores made by a class on a spelling test.

(1)	(2)	(3)	(4)	(5)	(6)	(7)	(8)
X	Tally	f	Ident.	f	f_p	cf	cf_p
43	/	1	14	1	3.1	32	100.0
2	//	2	2,23	2	6.3	31	96.9
1						29	90.6
40	/	1	21	1	3.1	29	90.6
9	///	3	7,9,26	3	9.4	28	87.5
8	ℳ	5	5,11,15,20,29	5	15.6	25	78.1
7	ℳ //	7	1,10,13,18,25,28,32	7	21.9	20	62.5
6	////	4	4,12,16,27	4	12.5	13	40.6
35	/	1	31	1	3.1	9	28.1
4	///	3	6,17,22	3	9.4	8	25.0
3	//	2	3,30	2	6.3	5	15.6
2	/	1	19	1	3.1	3	9.4
1						2	6.3
30	/	1	8	1	3.1	2	6.3
29	/	1	24	1	3.1	1	3.1
	N	32		N	32	100.0	

Fig. 8. Frequency distribution table—ungrouped.

extending from 43 at the top to and including 29 at the bottom, as in column (1) of Figure 8. This column is headed by the letter X, as it is customary to designate the measures of a series with a capital. Another series might bear the heading "Y," "Z," "A," or "B," and so on. Now note the score made by pupil No. 1, which is 37, and place a tally in column (2) opposite the scaled score of 37. Next, place a tally opposite the measure 42, the score made by pupil No. 2, and continue in order through the series until all of the measures have thus been tallied. Note the grouping of five tallies. Add the tallies in each row and record the sums in the column (3) with the heading f, for frequency. This column of frequencies is added to give the total number of cases or N, here 32. N = the sum of the frequencies or Σf. The Greek capital letter Σ is used always in statistical procedures to designate "the sum of."

It is sometimes desirable, especially in diagnostic analysis, to indicate which pupil received which score, and to this end some method of identifying the pupils may be used instead of making tallies. This is done here in column (4) by using the pupil numbers. Initials might do, but would require more space. A frequency column—column (5)—is added as before. The three columns (1), (2), and (3), *or* the three columns (1), (4), and (5), constitute a frequency table.

Per Cent Frequency. Given the f values, we can readily see how many individuals have the same measure, but if we wish to compare groups of different size, the f values of the two distributions must be reduced to a common base. It is preferable to use the base of 100, and thus the f values may be expressed as per cents. In Figure 8, $\frac{100}{N} = \frac{100}{32} = 3.125$. Each frequency is then 3.125 per cent of the N value. Note that the division is carried here to three decimals, so that later computations will be correct to one decimal. Now each f is multiplied by the reciprocal or quotient 3.125 and the product is recorded in column (6) headed by the symbol f_p. These figures state the proportion of the total cases that fall at any given measure. Approximately 22 per cent of the class received the same score of 37.

Cumulative Frequency. In the analysis of distributions it is sometimes helpful or necessary to compute the *cumulative fre-*

quencies, as shown in column (7) of Figure 8 with the heading *cf*. These values may be computed from the bottom of the table to the top, or from the top to the bottom, but the former is generally preferred. If the former method is used, as in Figure 8, the value in any interval shows how many cases fall below the upper limit of that interval which is the same as the lower limit of the next higher interval. In this illustration, there are 20 cases falling below 37.5. If accumulated from the top down, we would find there were 12 cases falling above the lower limit of this interval or above 37.5.

The *cf* values, like the *f* values, may be expressed in terms of per cent values, as is here done in column (8) headed by the symbol cf_p. In Figure 8, it can readily be seen that 25 per cent of the cases fall below the score of 34.5. These values may be computed by multiplying the reciprocal $\frac{100}{N}$ by *cf*, or by accumulating the f_p values, taking care that no error accumulates in the decimals. The cf_p columns will be found useful, not only in comparing groups of different size, but also in arriving at other computations, as will be demonstrated later in this chapter.

The Frequency Distribution—Grouped

For the sake of simplicity, in discussing this topic, the data given in Figure 7 will be used.

The Grouped Frequency Table. It is not customary practice to group measures when there are so few cases distributed over so narrow a range as is the case with these data. However, this series will serve to demonstrate the processes dealt with here. As the first step, the size of the interval (*h*) must be determined. It is an advantage to have intervals where the height of the interval is an odd number, for in data such as these, the midpoint would then be integral. It is also well to provide for enough intervals to minimize the errors due to grouping, and yet not so many as to be unnecessarily unwieldy. In this case an *h* of 2 is selected, which provides 8 intervals, since the range of measures is from 29 through 43, or 15. In general practice, the number of intervals ranges from 12 to 20.

The grouped frequency table is shown in Figure 9.

(1)	(2)	(3)	(4)	(5)	(6)	(7)
X	m	Tally	f	f_p	cf	cf_p
42.5–44.4	43.5	/	1	3.1	32	100.0
40.5–42.4	41.5	//	2	6.3	31	96.9
38.5–40.4	39.5	////	4	12.5	29	90.6
36.5–38.4	37.5	𝍬 𝍬 //	12	37.5	25	78.1
34.5–36.4	35.5	𝍬	5	15.7	13	40.6
32.5–34.4	33.5	𝍬	5	15.7	8	25.0
30.5–32.4	31.5	/	1	3.1	3	9.4
28.5–30.4	29.5	//	2	6.3	2	6.3
		N	32			

Fig. 9. Grouped frequency table.

Procedure. After the value of h is decided, the next step is to lay out the scale of measures in column (1) with the symbol X. The subsequent step taken here, the recording in column (2) of midpoint values of the intervals, is not required but is a helpful reminder to the beginner. Now, as was done in Figure 8, note the score of pupil No. 1 (37) and place a tally opposite the interval 36.5–38.4 in which the score falls, and so continue. It would be difficult to use any system of identification here because of lack of space. Again the f column is added to find the N.

The f_p, cf, and cf_p values have also been computed and entered in Figure 9, following the procedures used in Figure 8. It can readily be seen what per cent of the class had scores falling in any given interval (e.g., 37.5 per cent in the interval 36.5–38.4) and what proportion of the class received a score less than any given lower limit of an interval.

The Ranking of Measures

Rank is a general term indicating the relative position any measure in a series holds in terms of scale placement, as compared with other measures in the series. The rank of an individual may be expressed in terms of the actual number of cases or in terms of per cent values.

Ordinary Rank. This type of ranking is in general use. The concepts involved are evident in published results of golf tournaments and other sporting events, even though other terms may be employed. This type of ranking may be computed from the bottom, or low measure, upward, as in golf scores. As a rule the high-valued measure, large or small, receives the rank of 1.

There are as many ranks to be considered as there are cases. If two or more individuals have the same measure, each will receive the same rank, which will be the average of the ranks achieved by these individuals. Referring to Figure 10, which treats the same data as Figure 9, note that the top interval with one frequency has a rank (R) of 1 in column (4). The next lower interval has a frequency of 2. These individuals are competing for ranks 2 and 3; therefore each receives the same rank of 2½. In column (3) the cf_d (or cumulative frequencies down) values are given because these figures will be helpful in the procedure. Column (3) tells how many cases have been accumulated down to the lower limit of any interval. A quick and accurate method of finding ordinary rank is by first finding the rank (R_1) of the first interval, then adding the number of cases in that interval (f_1) to the number of cases in the next lower interval (f_2), and dividing the sum by 2. Now R_2, the rank of the next lower interval, will be this average added to R_1. The formula

$$R_2 = R_1 + \frac{f_1 + f_2}{2}$$

looks complex, but the process is simple. Thus, the rank of cases in interval 36.5–38.4 would be $5½ + \frac{4+12}{2} = 13½$.

Percentile Rank. Ordinary rank has no significance unless the N is known. A person might boast that he won third prize, but the picture changes when it is discovered that there were only three contestants. Therefore, this type of rank cannot be used to compare the placement of individuals in series of different size. The *percentile rank* (R_p, or *P.R.*) avoids this difficulty. Although percentile rank may be computed from the top of the series or the high value down, it is customary to place the low percentile values at the bottom. While ordinary rank is counted through the individual, percentile rank is counted to the middle of the case. In the former, one person standing alone at the top of the series would have a rank of 1, but one individual standing alone at the bottom of a series would receive a rank of .5 if N were 100.

(1)	(2)	(3)	(4)	(5)	(6)	(7)	(8)
X	f	cf_d	R	cf	cf_p	cf_m	R_p
42.5–44.4	1	1	1	32	100.0	31½	98.4
40.5–42.4	2	3	2½	31	96.9	30	93.8
38.5–40.4	4	7	5½	29	90.6	27	84.4
36.5–38.4	12	19	13½	25	78.1	19	59.4
34.5–36.4	5	24	22	13	40.6	10½	32.8
32.5–34.4	5	29	27	8	25.0	5½	17.2
30.5–32.4	1	30	30	3	9.4	2½	7.8
28.5–30.4	2	32	31½	2	6.3	1	3.1

Fig. 10. Ranking procedures—grouped table.

In Figure 10, notice column (5), cf. This column is an aid in finding each value in column (7), the cumulative frequency to the midpoint (cf_m), for the cf values plus one-half the f in the next higher interval give the cf_m values of that interval. Taking the product of the reciprocal $\dfrac{100}{N}$ and the cf_m amounts yields the R_p values of column (8). Another method of computation would be to average the cf_p values in adjacent intervals to find the R_p of the higher interval, taking care to carry decimals far enough to avoid an error. Thus, $\dfrac{6.250 + 9.375}{2} = 7.8$.

Interpolation Procedures

By interpolation is meant the process of finding intermediate values in a series of stated measures and frequencies. Standardized test norms commonly state, or provide tables which show, the scores below which a certain proportion of the cases fall, *or* the per cent of the cases falling below a certain score. Therefore, anyone who is involved in testing work should be able to make corresponding analyses of test data. Problems of this type arise in comparing two or more groups as to their standing on a test. Thus far, the midpoints of intervals and their lower limits have been under consideration. Interpolation procedures lead *to* or *from* any point or value in an interval.

Interpolation in the Interval. Test manuals frequently present the decile scores of the universe or of the group used to establish norms. Decile points are those positions on the base scale of measures that divide a distribution into ten equal parts in terms of the number of cases. $D_1 = 10$ per cent, $D_2 = 20$ per cent, and so on up to D_{10} which equals 100 per cent. In order to compare the status of a group that has taken a standard test with the norms, it is necessary to find the approximate scores below which 10 per cent, 20 per cent, and so on, of the group falls.

X	A			B		
	f	cf	cf_p	f	cf	cf_p
113.5-				4	62	100.0
106.5-	2	56	100.0	2	58	93.5
99.5-	1	54	96.4	5	56	90.3
92.5-	6	53	94.6	7	51	82.3
85.5-	7	47	83.9	13	44	71.0
78.5-	12	40	71.4	10	31	50.0
71.5-	10	28	50.0	9	21	33.9
64.5-	8	18	32.1	8	12	19.4
57.5-	6	10	17.9	3	4	6.5
50.5-		4	7.1		1	1.6
43.5-	3	4	7.1	1	1	1.6
36.5-	1	1	1.8			

Fig. 11. Distributions of two groups on a test.

Given the distributions of the scores of two groups of pupils, Groups A and B, as a result of a test, as shown in Figure 11,

we can find a decile by the following steps:
1. In Group A, $N = 56$.
2. 10% of 56 = 5.6.
3. The cf to 57.5 = 4.
4. $5.6 - 4 =$ number of cases to go to reach $D_1 = 1.6$.
5. Then, 1.6 divided by 6 = the fraction of the interval to go to reach D_1.
6. Since there are 7 units in the interval, then $\frac{1.6}{6} \times 7 = 1.9$ units to go above 57.5.
7. Therefore, $D_1 = 57.5 + 1.9 = 59.4$.

Applying the same procedure, but putting it into condensed form, we find the D_1 (decile score) of Group B:

$$D_1 = 64.5 + \frac{6.2 - 4}{8} \times 7 = 64.5 + \frac{15.4}{8} = 64.5 + 1.9 = 66.4$$

If we let a be any decile, 1.1 equal the lower limit of the interval in which the given D_a stands, and cf_{-1} equal the cumulative frequency in the interval below, the general formula would be

$$D_a = 1.1 + \frac{10_a N - cf_{-1}}{f} \times h$$

The diagram given in Figure 12 may help to explain the procedure involved. Here a portion of the scale and the two intervals cited above are indicated in the first two columns. In the f columns for Groups A and B, space is allotted for each case in each interval. The cf columns are included as an aid to understanding. Note in the cf column for Group A, four cases lie below the 1.1 of 57.5. Follow line "a" up to a point below which 1.6 cases fall in the interval. Then follow the intersecting line as the arrow points and take the reading of D_1 on the scale, or 59.4. Also trace line "c" up until it reaches a point below which 6.2 cases fall and follow the intersecting line "d" to the scale and read the value of 66.4 for D_1.

It would be well for the reader to familiarize himself with this procedure by computing the other decile points for these data, checking the computations with those given here:

Decile	Group A	Group B
2	65.6	71.8
3	70.5	76.6
4	74.6	81.2
5	78.5	85.5
6	81.8	88.8
7	85.0	92.2
8	90.3	98.1
9	98.5	106.2

The decile points could be found by working through the f_p and cf_p values: for example, D_1 for distribution A would be

$$57.5 + \frac{10 - 7.1}{10.8} \times 7 = 59.4$$

Quartile points are also frequently used as norms and in other procedures. These are the points on the scale that partition a distribution into four equal parts in terms of the number of cases. Q_1 equals the twenty-fifth percentile point, P_{25}. The procedure in finding the quartile points is the same as for the deciles.

Interpolation in the Frequencies. If the distributions in Figure 11 were the results of a standardized test given to the two groups of pupils, and the test manual showed that the score of 70 was the fiftieth percentile, or D_5 of the norm group, a comparison of the groups with each other and with the norm would be in order. Therefore, the question as to what proportion of each of these groups falls below the score of 70 must be answered. The procedure is as follows:

70 is 5.5 units above the lower limit of the interval.

$\frac{5.5}{7}$ = the fraction of the interval between 64.5 and 70.

Since there happen to be 8 cases in the interval for both distributions, the number of cases falling between 64.5 and 70 is $\frac{5.5}{7} \times 8 = 6.3$ for Groups A and B.

In Group A, cf to 70 is $10 + 6.3$ or 16.3 which is 29 per cent.
In Group B, cf to 70 is $4 + 6.3$ or 10.4 which is 17 per cent.

This procedure is graphically illustrated in Figure 12. The line "e" traced to the right cuts off about 6.3 cases from the bottom

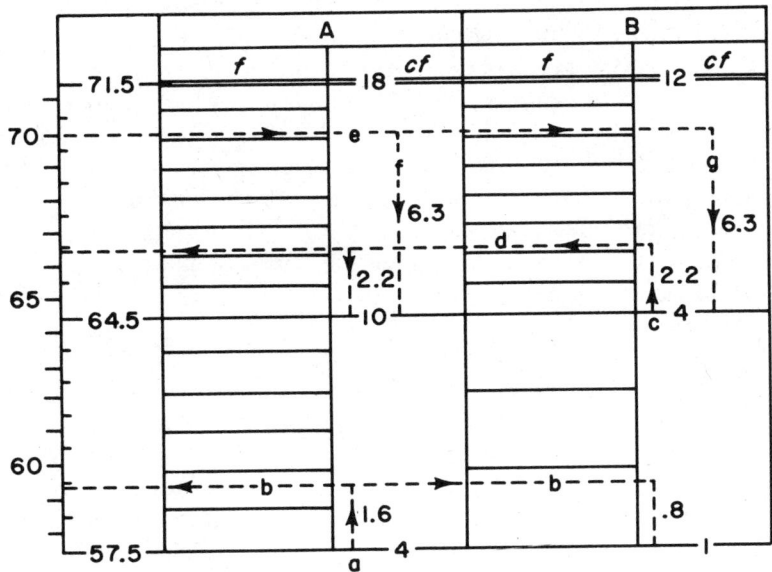

Fig. 12. Graphic illustration of interpolation procedures.

of the interval in both Groups A and B. Also in the diagram may be noted how many cases in Group B fall below the D_1 of Group A (line "b" to the right) and also how many cases in Group A fall below the D_1 of Group B (line "d" to the left).

In all of the procedures presented above, it can be readily seen that Group B is superior to Group A in their standing on the test, and that both groups are well above the norm.

In the computation of the values given above for decile points, and in the interpolation processes, the assumption is made that the cases in an interval are evenly distributed throughout the interval. This assumption is made for all distributions.

Measures of Central Tendency

In the process of treating and analyzing data, especially when groups are being compared with each other, there is a need for a single measure which will give information as to the general trend of the series taken as a whole. The three measures of *central tendency* that are in common use are the mode, the median, and the mean. (Others, such as the harmonic mean and geometric mean, are highly specialized and are treated in advanced statistics.)

The Mode. The midpoint of the measure or interval having the highest frequency in a distribution is called the *mode* (*Mo*). If two or more adjacent measures have the same high frequency, the mode is the average of these measures. Sometimes the distributions are bimodal, with intervals of low frequency between two modes. Sometimes, distributions have primary and secondary modes, and this variation may indicate a significant fact about the composition of a group. For example, a class group made up of children of low I.Q.'s and of high I.Q.'s would probably be thus distributed.

In most situations, the mode is not taken seriously as an accurate measure of central tendency. However, it does have value as a descriptive term. It is usually subject to marked fluctuations, depending on the method of grouping and other factors. In Figure 11 (p. 190), the mode of Group A is 82 and the mode of Group B is 89. However, in both of these distributions, adjacent intervals have frequencies that are almost as large. Had the grouping plan been different as to limits or size of intervals, the modes might have been quite different.

In general, the mode is trustworthy as a measure only if there are many frequencies distributed over a relatively fine and extensive scale. It is sometimes used as an effective aid in describing data, especially when there is a strong modal tendency well removed from the other measures of central tendency.

The Median. The median (*Md*) has already been encountered and computed under the name of D_5, Q_2, or the fiftieth percentile P_{50}. It is that point on the scale below which and above which 50 per cent of the cases fall. It does not take into account the size of the measures, but is simply the midmeasure, or the point of balance of the individual frequencies in an ordered series, ranked or scaled. If the median falls between two measures, the average of these measures is taken as the median. The principle involved in the median is shown in Part A of Figure 13.

The Mean. The measure of central tendency called the *mean*

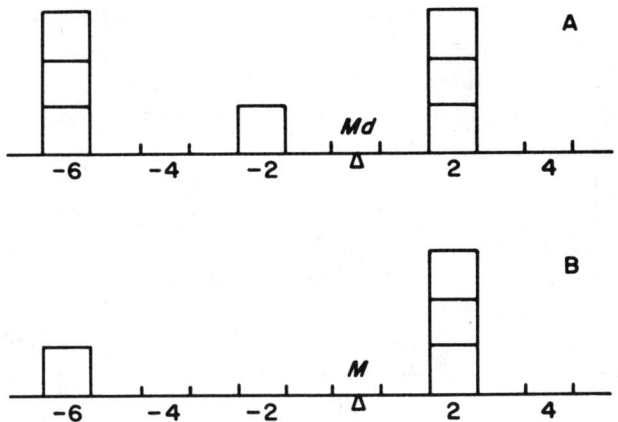

Fig. 13. Comparison of the concepts underlying the median and the mean.

(M) is also popularly known as the *average*. A more accurate name for it is *arithmetical mean*. In contrast to the median which is a balancing of cases, the mean is a true balancing of measures, as shown in Part B of Figure 13. It represents the value which each of the measures would have if, with the same total of measures, each measure were the same as every other measure. The measures above the mean have the same total positive deviation from the mean as the measures below the mean have in the form of negative deviations. Referring to Figure 13, we can readily see that the one frequency with a −6 unit of deviation balances the three frequencies with a +2 units of deviation each.

The procedure used in finding the mean by the *long method* with *ungrouped data* is really long, especially if there are many cases distributed over a wide range of large measures. The basic formula is

$$M = \frac{\Sigma X}{N}$$

or the sum of the measures divided by the number of cases. For example, we may add the scores of Figure 7 (p. 184), using an adding machine, to find the sum of 1171. This sum divided by 32 yields the M of 36.6.

The *short method* provides a simpler process of computing the mean. The first step is to assume a mean (M') preferably somewhere near the midmost measure in terms of size. Then, unit deviations (x') are found about the M' by the formula

$$x' = X - M'$$

using ungrouped data as before. This step produces x' values which are much smaller than the X values, and thus reduces the labor of the calculation. For example, if there were three measures, 154, 149, and 141, and the M' were 150, the x' numbers in order would be 4, -1, and -9. The next step is to find the amount of the "correction" that must be made by adding it algebraically to the M' to yield the M. This is simply the average of the deviations about the assumed mean. The basic formula here is

$$M = M' + \frac{\Sigma x'}{N}$$

Applying it to the three measures cited above,

$$M = 150 + \frac{4 - 1 - 9}{3} = 150 - 2 = 148$$

If we apply the procedure to the data of Figure 8 (p. 184), Figure 14 shows the method used to find the mean for the scaled series. Since some of the measures have more than one frequency, each x' must be multiplied by the f for that measure, as in column (5). If the original data of Figure 7, which are in mixed order, were being used, it would be well to provide one column for positive deviations and another for negative deviations. In this instance, the positive and negative values are summed in column (6), giving an algebraic sum of 19. The mean of this distribution then is $36 + \frac{19}{32} = 36 + .59 = 36.6$. The M' is placed rather arbitrarily, but with a view to having small deviations to deal with. The lowest measure of 29 might have been taken as M'. The deviations would then have been all positive, but larger. As a check, the mean has here been computed by the

(1)	(2)	(3)	(4)	(5)	(6)
X	f	fX	x'	fx'	$\Sigma fx'$
43	1	43	7	7	
2	2	84	6	12	
1			5	0	
40	1	40	4	4	
9	3	117	3	9	
8	5	190	2	10	
7	7	259	1	7	+49
6	4	144	0	0	
35	1	35	-1	-1	
4	3	102	-2	-6	
3	2	66	-3	-6	
2	1	32	-4	-4	
1			-5	0	
30	1	30	-6	-6	
29	1	29	-7	-7	-30
	32	1171			19

Fig. 14. Computation of the mean for an ungrouped distribution.

long method, using the formula $M = \dfrac{\Sigma X}{N} = \dfrac{1171}{32} = 36.6$, see column (3).

In case *grouped distributions* are being analyzed, one might use the *long method*, using the formula $M = \dfrac{\Sigma fm}{N}$ in which m is the midpoint of the interval. The *short method* is much easier with grouped data than is the long method, as can be readily seen in Figure 15, using the distributions given in Figure 11 (p. 190). In the procedure involved here, a new symbol d' appears, which is simply the deviation about the M' expressed in terms of

Score	f	fm	A d'	fd'	Σfd'	f	fm	B d'	fd'	Σfd'
113.5-						4	468	4	16	
106.5-	2	220	5	10		2	220	3	6	
99.5-	1	103	4	4		5	515	2	10	
92.5-	6	576	3	18		7	672	1	7	39
85.5-	7	623	2	14		13	1157	0		
78.5-	12	984	1	12	58	10	820	−1	−10	
71.5-	10	750	0			9	675	−2	−18	
64.5-	8	544	−1	−8		8	544	−3	−24	
57.5-	6	366	−2	−12		3	183	−4	−12	
50.5-			−3	0				−5		
43.5-	3	141	−4	−12		1	47	−6	−6	−70
36.5-	1	4340	−5	−5	−37					
	56	4347			21	62	5301			−31

Fig. 15. Computation of the mean for grouped distributions.

intervals. Since the deviations are in terms of intervals, not units, the correction derived from them must be changed back into units by multiplying it by h, the number of units in the interval. The basic formula used in this procedure is

$$M = M' + h\frac{\Sigma fd'}{N}$$

Applying this formula to the two distributions:

$$M_A = 75 + 7\frac{21}{56} = 75.0 + \frac{147}{56} = 75.0 + 2.6 = 77.6$$

$$M_B = 89 + 7\frac{-31}{62} = 89.0 + \frac{-217}{62} = 89.0 - 3.5 = 85.5$$

The long method used with these data yields the same values for the means, but the process is much more cumbersome.

Of the three measures here considered, the mean is the most accurate, as it takes into account the scale placement of every measure. Therefore, it is generally preferred. However, it sometimes occurs that some individual measures that are not at all typical of the group as a whole are clustered at the upper or lower end of the scale and tend to affect the mean unduly by pulling it toward that end. When an analysis of the distributions and individuals of the group reveals such a situation, these atypical measures may be dropped from the series, or the median may be used, since it is not affected by the scale placement of measures. However, statisticians are aware of the fact that some distributions are normally skewed, with the mode being placed well toward one end of the distribution. Distributions of population, financial income, and golf scores would be of this type. The extremely large or small measures are fewer in number but have a marked effect in pulling the mean in their direction.

The Construction of Diagrams

Diagrams, or graphs, provide another means of analyzing distributions. They present a vivid picture of numerical data in such a way that their relative sizes may be visually apprehended and mentally grasped. There are many types of graphic representations, composed of many variations of dots, lines, and bars, as well as colors. A few of the types that are commonly used in educational measurement are here presented.

With a little training and care, almost anyone can make good diagrams. It is not necessary to be a skilled artist to do so. The required equipment is simple, namely, sharp pencils, a good straightedge, and several kinds of coordinate paper having 5, 8, 10, or 12 spaces to the inch, or providing a millimetric scale. Graphs should be kept simple, and care should be taken not to exaggerate any trend.

The Dot or Block Diagram. In the dot or block diagram, there is one dot or block for each case or frequency. The dot diagram is readily made on the typewriter, as shown in Figure 16.

Score	0	1	2	3	f 4	5	6	7
15		○						
14		○	○	○				
13		○	○					
12		○	○	○	○	○	○	

Fig. 16. Dot diagram.

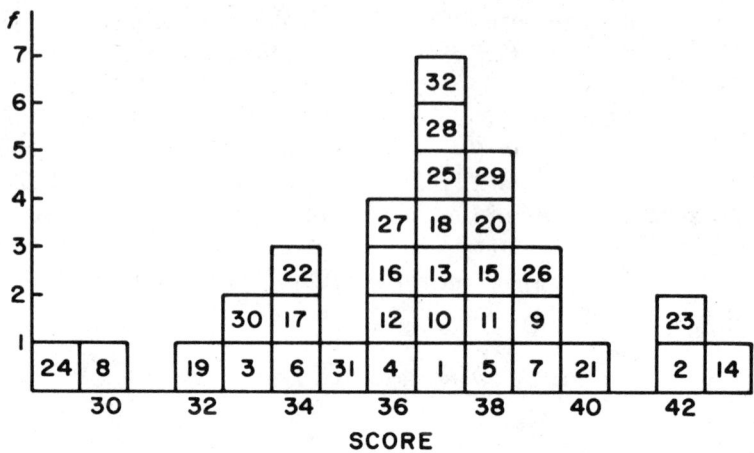

Fig. 17. Block diagram of distribution, with identification.

The block diagram permits ready identification of items of the distribution and is a very useful device for recording the testing of pupils in a class, for it shows clearly which ones made high or low scores. This is done in Figure 17 which portrays the data of Figure 8 (p. 184). This type of diagram is usually made with the measures placed on the base scale (X axis) and the frequencies on the vertical scale (Y axis), but this step is not obligatory. It is not necessary to place all measures or frequencies; some may be omitted to avoid crowding. Here, as usual, the indices for the frequencies are placed at the top of the unit on the scale, while the measures are located at the midpoints of the unit interval. The scales should always be titled by name or symbol. Care should be taken not to make the diagram too tall and narrow, or too flat and wide. The proportions here shown are about right.

The Histogram, or Bar Diagram. When the individual blocks are not depicted, but the frequency of each measure is represented by a bar, the graph is called a *histogram*. Any distribution may be thus represented. Here, in Figure 18, which pictures the distributions of Figure 15 (p. 198), two groups are compared. Sometimes the two histograms may be superimposed, using the same scales, but as a rule this method introduces an element of confusion. Attempts to overcome this difficulty may result in placing the frequency of one group in the lower half of an interval and that for the other group in the upper half of the interval, but this arrangement will not be true to fact. The best procedure is the one here presented with the two histograms placed on the same base scale but with different frequency scales, one being placed above the other.

Alternate lower limits of intervals are here properly placed along the base scale. The midpoints of the intervals might be given if rightly located at the midpoint of the bars. To add a

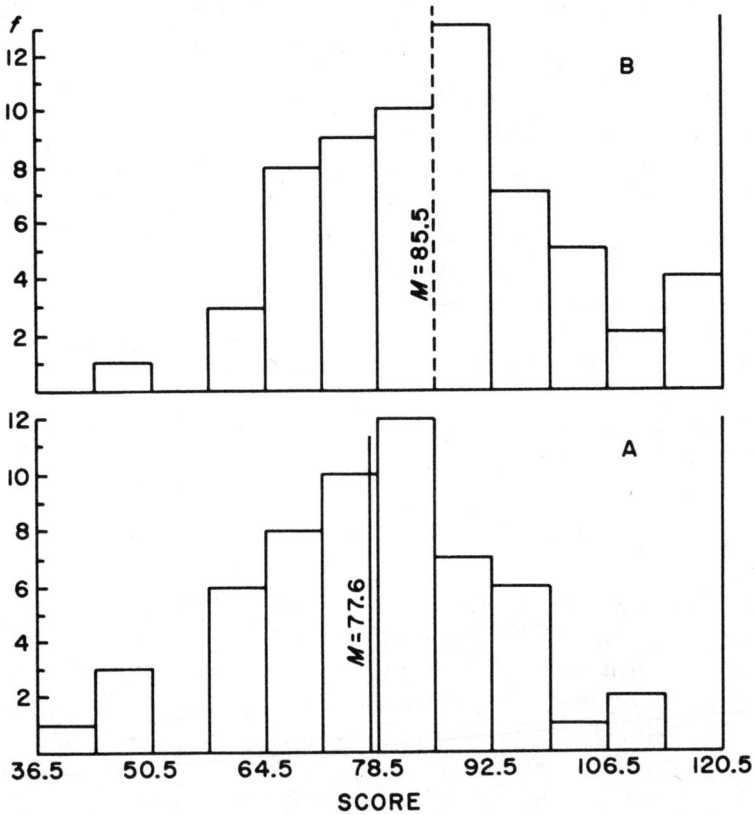

Fig. 18. Histograms used for comparing distributions.

significant feature to the diagram, the mean of each distribution is indicated by a vertical line erected at the correct location on the base scale.

The Frequency Polygon. Serving the same purpose as the histogram, the polygon differs from it in that bars are not used. Instead, lines are passed between points located at the midpoints of the measures at the correct height to show the number of cases falling at each measure. The points are really located at the midpoints and tops of the bars of the histogram that might have been made for these data.

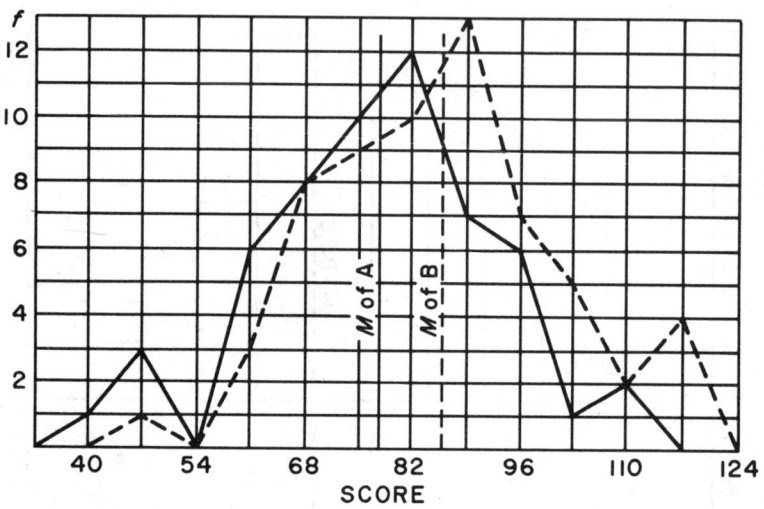

Fig. 19. Polygons used for comparing distributions.

As demonstrated in Figure 19, which is based on the distributions of Figure 15, the polygon has an advantage over the histogram when comparison of two or more groups is called for, since several may be shown superimposed on one frequency scale, if the lines are clearly differentiated. One polygon may be composed of heavy solid lines, another of light solid lines, another of broken or dotted lines, and so on. The lines would be brought down to zero frequency at the upper and lower ends if it were possible to make a score of that size.

Here again the means of the two distributions are indicated in the diagram.

The Ogive. Another graphic form is the *ogive*, sometimes called the "S-curve." It is prepared by plotting the cumulative frequencies, taking care to place the *cf* values at the lower limits of the next higher interval. It is customary to place the *cf* scale on the Y axis.

The most useful form of the ogive, one that permits the comparison of two or more groups of different sizes, is the *percentile curve*. Here the cf_p values are recorded graphically. The base line, the scale of measures, is usually made about the same length as the Y axis, or cf_p scale. The distributions of Figure 15 are here graphically portrayed in Figure 20. The table containing the data that are graphed is incorporated in the diagram.

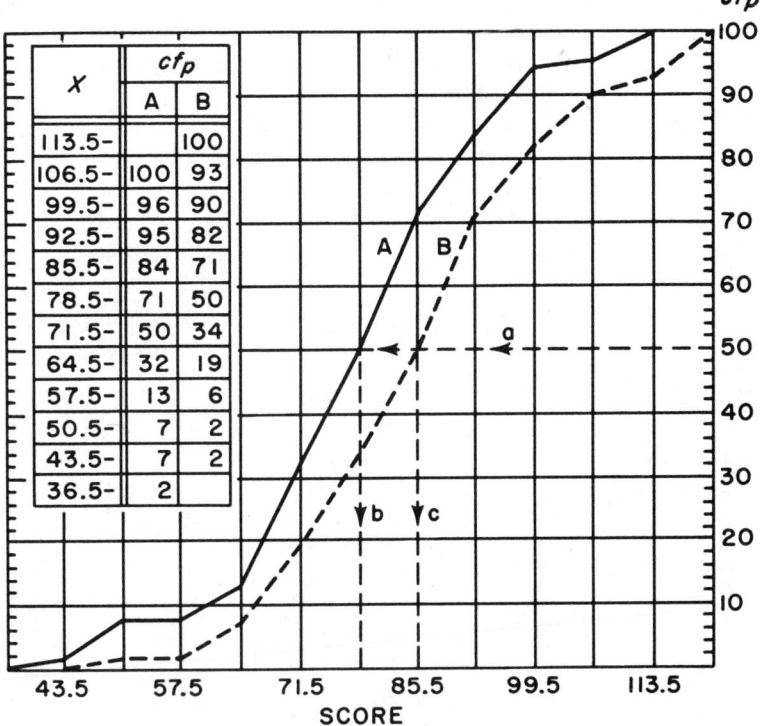

Fig. 20. Percentile curves used for comparing distributions.

It may be noted that the superior group is located at the right. No great violence would be done if the lines for A and B were actually curved instead of being composed of straight line segments. However, as here presented, they are accurate. When a percentile curve (or any ogive) is accurately made on a fine scale, it may be used as a *nomograph*. In this manner the values on either scale may be found with fair accuracy by direct interpolation on the graph. For example, in reading the value of the median from the diagram, extend the horizontal line "a" from cf_p of 50 to its intersection with curve B. From this point drop vertical line "c" to the base line and read the value, $Md_B = 85.5$. Then extend line "a" to curve A to find Md_A. The process may be reversed to find the percentile value of any given score.

The Scatter Diagram. From a practical point of view, one of the most valuable types of graph is the *scatter diagram*, or *correlation chart*. This graph permits a teacher, for example, to analyze the status of the pupils in two sets of measurements which are or may be unrelated. Such occasions arise when an intelligence test and a test of subject matter have been given to a class, or when rate and comprehension of reading have been tested, or when speed and accuracy in arithmetic are being considered. In fact, any two test results for the same group may be treated in this manner. The scatter diagram is a definite aid to diagnosis in the classroom.

Given the data of Figure 21, we can prepare the scatter diagram of the two sets of measures, Figure 22. This shows the rela-

Pupil	Arith.	I.Q.	Pupil	Arith.	I.Q.	Pupil	Arith.	I.Q.
1	30	105	11	26	88	21	15	74
2	38	120	12	24	129	22	36	109
3	16	83	13	13	76	23	43	135
4	36	137	14	41	118	24	25	106
5	32	114	15	26	112	25	22	89
6	25	96	16	48	132	26	27	102
7	19	107	17	32	96	27	35	114
8	45	117	18	21	82	28	21	97
9	33	108	19	28	121	29	11	80
10	39	130	20	40	123	30	18	92

Fig. 21. Scores of pupils in arithmetic test and I.Q.'s.

tive status of each of the pupils in the two categories. Here the pupils are identified by number. This is a decided advantage and can readily be done if the number of cases is not too large.

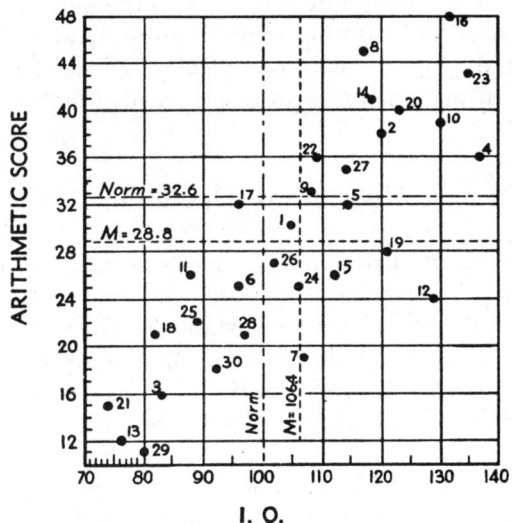

Fig. 22. Scatter diagram of a class showing scores made in arithmetic test and I.Q.'s.

The diagram was planned so that the X and Y scales would be about the same in length. After the scales were planned and drawn, the score made by pupil No. 1 on the arithmetic test was noted and located on the vertical or Y scale and from that point the horizontal line was traced to the right to its intersection with the measure of 105 on the X scale. Here a dot was placed and by it the pupil number "1." Next the measures for pupil No. 2 were located on the graph (38 and 120), and the procedure was continued until all measures were recorded.

Lines indicating the norms in the tests, and also the mean averages, were drawn in as an aid to interpretation. Now it can readily be noted that the class is well above the norm in the I.Q. rating, but definitely below the norm in arithmetic ability as measured by this test. These facts suggest a need for improvement in the teaching of the subject. As might have been expected, those pupils with high I.Q.'s generally made high scores in the arithmetic test, but pupils No. 12, No. 15, and No. 19 received markedly lower scores in the subject than might be expected from their intelligence rating. Pupil No. 17 was the only one below the I.Q. norm who had a rating above the mean average in arithmetic. This diagnostic analysis indicates the need for remedial instruction in arithmetic, including special attention to certain pupils.

Measures of Deviation

Another method of describing a series of data and of comparing distributions is through the use of measures that indicate the extent of the spread, scatter, or deviation of the individual measures along the scale. The distributions may be similar in terms of their central tendencies and number of cases involved, but they may be widely variant with respect to their compactness on the scale of measures. This fact is shown in the hypothetical data of Figure 23. A numerical value is needed to supply an index of the amount of deviation of a series of measures, so that various distri-

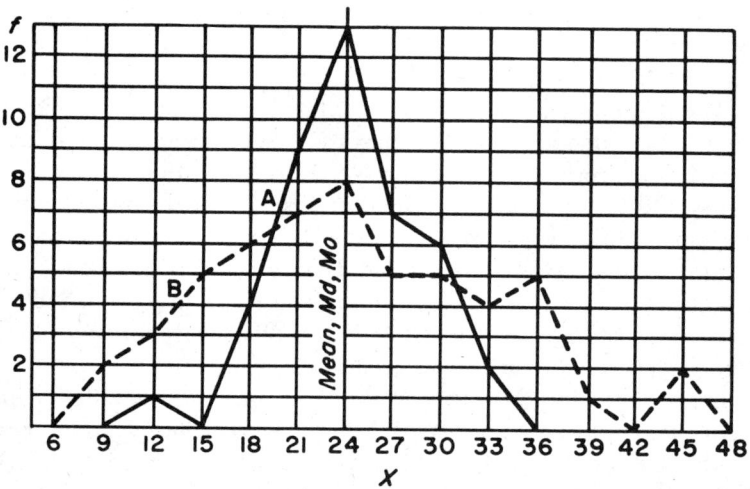

Fig. 23. Distributions with the same means but different measures of deviation.

butions may be compared in this respect. The three common methods of doing this are here presented.

Quartile Deviation. The *quartile deviation* (*QD*) is a relatively rough measure secured by counting cases. It is employed primarily in situations where the median is taken as the measure of central tendency. It is sometimes called the semi-interquartile range because it is found by taking one-half of the distance between the Q_3 and Q_1 points in a distribution. Technically it is the average of the two ranges, $Q_3 - Q_2$ and $Q_2 - Q_1$, but when these two are added, the Q_2 values are cancelled, leaving the formula $\frac{Q_3 - Q_1}{2}$. Applying this formula to the data of Figure 15 (p. 198),

Group A

$$Q_3 = 85.5 + \frac{42 - 40}{7} \times 7 = 87.5$$

$$Q_1 = 64.5 + \frac{14 - 10}{8} \times 7 = 68.0$$

$$QD = \frac{87.5 - 68.0}{2} = 9.8$$

Group B

$$Q_3 = 92.5 + \frac{46.5 - 44}{7} \times 7 = 95.0$$

$$Q_1 = 71.5 + \frac{15.5 - 12}{9} \times 7 = 74.2$$

$$QD = \frac{95.0 - 74.2}{2} = 10.4$$

The results show that Group B has a slightly larger spread than Group A.

The Mean Deviation. In contrast to the quartile deviation, the *mean deviation* (*MD*), sometimes called *average deviation*, is a mathematically accurate measure of deviation. It is the mean of the deviations about the mean of the measures without regarding signs of the deviations. The basic formula is $MD = \frac{\Sigma x}{N}$.

To apply this procedure to the data of Figure 21 (p. 204), dealing with the scores in the arithmetic test, first find the M which is 28.8, then find the deviation of each measure from this mean: 1.2, 9.2, 12.8, 7.2, and so on. Then add these deviations and divide the sum by N which is 30. Actually there would be no significant error if the M were called 29 and the deviations were taken in terms of units.

To find the MD of a distribution by the *long method*, with the data grouped, it would be necessary to find the difference between each interval midpoint and the mean, multiply each of these differences by the frequency in the interval, and then add these products and divide by N, a really long process even if deviations are taken to the nearest unit value. The *short process* is preferred in this situation. If we apply the long process to the distribution A of Figure 15 (p. 198) with $M = 77.6$, the m of the highest interval $= 110$, $m - M = 110 - 77.6 = 32.4$. This figure, multiplied by $f = 2$, gives 64.8. Continue through the distribution and add these products, disregarding signs, and divide by N, or 56.

All of the data needed for the use of the short method are given in Figure 15. The sum of the fd' values is $58 + 37$, or 95. Multiplying this sum by the h of 7 gives a total uncorrected deviation of 665 units. The basic error is the difference between M and M' or $77.6 - 75.0 = 2.6$. The cases in the distribution up to and including the interval 71.5 have been assigned deviations that are too small by 2.6 units, and those above this interval have received deviations that are too large by the same amount. Now if there were 30 in the first group and 26 in the latter, all but 4 cases would balance out and the remainder of 4 would be multiplied by the unit error to yield 10.4 which would be added to the 665 units, and the sum would be divided by N of 56. But in this case, since there are 28 frequencies in each group, the correction is zero, and $MD = \dfrac{665}{56} = 11.9$. The correction must always be added.

The mean deviation has largely fallen into disuse. This fact is unfortunate, as it is a mathematical average and one that is meaningful as well as accurate and stable. It is rather easily computed. The range of measures -1 MD to $+1$ MD generally includes from 55 to 60 per cent of the cases; hence it is larger than the Q_1 to Q_3 range which includes 50 per cent of N.

The Standard Deviation. The deviation measure which has come into general use among statisticians and which is a very accurate, stable mathematical measure is the *standard deviation*. The symbol for it is σ, but *SD* is sometimes used. Since the measure is in such common use in educational research and measurement, it is well for the amateur in statistics to know how to compute and use it.

The standard deviation is an abstract value derived by mathematical formulas. It is sometimes called "the root mean square deviation" since it is the square root of the mean of the deviations about the mean. The basic formula is

$$\sigma = \sqrt{\frac{\Sigma x}{N}}$$

The range -1σ to $+1\sigma$ includes about two-thirds of the number of cases in a distribution.

The *long method* of computing σ, using this formula, is merely mentioned here, as the procedure would be too involved to be of practical value. If the unit deviations are carried to two decimals to insure accuracy in the final results, the process is indeed cumbersome.

At this stage, many students find that they need to relearn the procedure in extracting the square root. This step may be expedited by the use of published tables of square roots, with values carried far enough to insure accuracy.

The *short process*, primarily for use with mixed series, treats deviations in terms of units, and no decimals appear before averages and square roots are taken, so that the procedure is relatively simple, though the formula is longer:

$$\sigma = \sqrt{\frac{\Sigma x'^2}{N} - \left(\frac{\Sigma x'}{N}\right)^2}$$

As the first step, the M' is taken at a convenient number, itself a unit. The formula is expanded because of the necessity of making a correction. When any x' is squared, the error $M - M'$, which is a part of x', is also squared, and the squaring process makes all signs positive. Since these x' values are squared, then added and averaged, in the first term under the radical, the average error must be squared in the second term under the radical, and subtracted from the first term. The numerator of the second term is the algebraic sum of the x's.

The procedure is shown in Figure 24, using the data of Figure

Pupil	Score	x' −	x' +	x'^2	Pupil	Score	x' −	x' +	x'^2
1	30		0	0	16	48		18	324
2	38		8	64	17	32		2	4
3	16	14		196	18	21	9		81
4	36		6	36	19	28	2		4
5	32		2	4	20	40		10	100
6	25	5		25	21	15	15		225
7	19	11		121	22	36		6	36
8	45		15	225	23	43		13	169
9	33		3	9	24	25	5		25
10	39		9	81	25	22	8		64
11	26	4		16	26	27	3		9
12	24	6		36	27	35		5	25
13	13	17		289	28	21	9		81
14	41		11	121	29	11	19		361
15	26	4		16	30	18	12		144
							143	108	2891

Fig. 24. Computation of σ for ungrouped data. Mixed order.

21 (p. 204). The M' was taken as 30. Each unit deviation from M' is squared and these squares are added to yield 2891. The net total of the deviations about M' is 108 −143, or −35. Therefore,

$$\sigma = \sqrt{\frac{2891}{30} - \left(\frac{35}{30}\right)^2} = \sqrt{96.37 - (1.17)^2} = \sqrt{95.01} = 9.7$$

This computed value has little meaning, since there is no related measure of another group with which to compare it. The procedure outlined above would be very lengthy if there were many large measures.

The short method for use with scaled or *grouped* distributions is much easier chiefly because the deviations from M' are expressed in terms of intervals (d') rather than in units (x'). The procedure that follows uses the data of Figure 15 (p. 198). The values required for the computation are already in Figure 15 except for the squares of the deviations. Therefore, only the fd'^2 columns for the two distributions are given here.

fd'^2	
A	B
	64
50	18
16	20
54	7
28	0
12	10
0	36
8	72
28	48
0	0
48	36
25	
265	311

Formula:

$$\sigma = h\sqrt{\frac{\Sigma fd'^2}{N} - \left(\frac{\Sigma fd'}{N}\right)^2}$$

$$\sigma_A = 7\sqrt{\frac{265}{56} - \left(\frac{21}{56}\right)^2} = 7\sqrt{4.73 - .14} = 15.0$$

$$\sigma_B = 7\sqrt{\frac{311}{62} - \left(\frac{31}{62}\right)^2} = 7\sqrt{5.02 - .25} = 15.33$$

Since the computed square root is expressed in terms of intervals, it is of course multiplied by the size of the interval (h) to put f_p into units.

In review, it was noted that Group B was found to have a slightly larger QD and MD than Group A, and the standard deviations tell the same story.

The Standard Score

Now that σ has been presented, another term that is in common usage may be introduced, the *standard score*. Since σ is a distance on the base scale of a distribution, we may transmute any measure in a series into a value which indicates how many standard deviations the measure is from the mean. Therefore, applying the formula

$$\sigma\text{-score} = \frac{X - M}{\sigma}$$

to the data of Figure 15 (p. 198), we find that a pupil with the score of 66 in Group A would have a standard score, or σ-score, of $\frac{66 - 77.6}{15}$, or $-.8$, while a pupil in Group B with the same score would receive a standard score of $\frac{66 - 85.5}{15.3}$, or -1.3.

In order to eliminate negative values and provide apparently integral values, statisticians sometimes provide a base scale extending from 0 to 100, with the limits being placed a certain number of σ-scores from the mean of 50. The most common practice is to fix 0 at -2.5σ and 100 at $+2.5\sigma$, since there is little possibility of any ordinary distribution falling below or above these points. In this instance, each σ value is equal to 20 points. The score of 66 in Group A would be a σ-score of 34 and in Group B a σ-score of 24. These values may be used instead of, or be transmuted into, age scores, grade scores, or other criteria, such as percentiles.

Correlation

In the computations in which central tendency and deviation were treated, interest was centered in single distributions or comparisons of distributions of comparable series. In the area of *correlation*, concern is directed to the discovery of any tendency toward *covariation* between two series of measures, comparable or incomparable, of a group that is the object of study. In other words, do those individuals who have high measures or low measures in one variable tend to have correspondingly high or low measures in the other variable, or is there an opposite tendency, the high measures in one being associated with low measures in the other? In some cases, there may be no ascertainable relationship of these types.

This topic was suggested in connection with the scatter diagram of Figure 22 (p. 205). This graph indicated a positive trend, in the sense that high scores in one variable were found to be associated with high scores in the other, and low scores were similarly associated. If the number of errors had been used instead of scores in arithmetic, a negative relationship would have been found.

The Coefficient of Correlation. A statistical value is needed that will indicate both the type of relationship that exists, if any, and the amount of it. This need is supplied by the *coefficient of correlation*, with the symbol r. This may range anywhere from -1 (perfect negative correlation) through 0 (no correlation) to $+1$ (perfect positive correlation). Referring again to Figure 22 (p. 205), if all of the dots had been placed along a straight line in the lower left and upper right quadrants, there would have been perfect positive correlation. If this straight line had extended through the upper left and lower right quadrants, there would have been perfect negative correlation. If the dots had been uniformly scattered over the diagram, the correlation would have been non-existent or zero.

Methods of Computation. It is not likely that many readers of these pages will have occasion to compute the coefficient of correlation frequently, if at all. However, it is well for those who read educational literature, and who have any contact with measurement work, to know how to use the processes and to interpret the outcomes of investigations in this area.

A relatively simple and easy procedure in finding correlation is by the use of *rank methods*. Although they yield a rather rough estimate of the amount of correlation, they are suitable for some situations where there are not many cases. The Spearman Rank Method is presented at the left side of Figure 25 (p. 215), columns (4) through (7), and the computation with formula is shown at the bottom. D here represents the difference in rank without regard to signs. The rho (ρ) here used is technically an intermediate figure which may be transposed to r by the use of tables, but it is a close approximation to r. The obtained value of .81 indicates a fairly high positive correlation.

Rank methods of finding the correlation do not take into account the scale displacement of the measures, but this factor is fully considered in using the *Pearson Product-Moment Method*. The term "product-moment" means simply the product of the deviations of the measures of the two variables from their respective means. The signs are taken into account.

The basic product-moment formula is:

$$r_{xy} = \frac{\Sigma xy}{\sigma_x \sigma_y}$$

This simple-appearing formula is never used because the process would be too complex, since decimal values would be involved throughout. Instead, the *short process* is used. The formula, adapted to mixed or ungrouped data, indicating the detailed steps in computation, is:

$$r_{xy} = \frac{\frac{\Sigma x'y'}{N} - \frac{\Sigma x'}{N}\frac{\Sigma y'}{N}}{\sqrt{\frac{\Sigma x'^2}{N} - \left(\frac{\Sigma x'}{N}\right)^2} \sqrt{\frac{\Sigma y'^2}{N} - \left(\frac{\Sigma y'}{N}\right)^2}}$$

The coefficient of correlation is computed by this method on the right side of Figure 25. The algebraic signs are kept for the deviations, the sums of deviations, and the products of deviations, as well as the sums of the products. The deviations about M' are in terms of units, so that decimal values do not appear in the deviations themselves, but only in the quotients. Since the errors $(M - M')$ have been multiplied and averaged in the product of the deviations, the product of the average error in the two variables is the correction, which is always subtracted. However, the signs must be watched carefully, for if the correction is a minus value, it will be added.

The *short method* is also always used with scaled or *grouped data*. In fact, the procedure is easier than with unordered data, because the deviations from the assumed mean are expressed in intervals. There is no need to change any of the values back into terms of units by multiplying by h, unless it is in order to know the standard deviations.

$$r = \frac{\dfrac{4014}{30} - \dfrac{-35}{30} \cdot \dfrac{192}{30}}{\sqrt{\dfrac{2891}{30} - \left(\dfrac{35}{30}\right)^2} \sqrt{\dfrac{10772}{30} - \left(\dfrac{192}{30}\right)^2}}$$

$$= \frac{133.8000 + 7.4667}{\sqrt{96.0661 - 1.3611} \sqrt{359.0667 - 40.9600}}$$

$$= \frac{141.2667}{\sqrt{95.0056} \sqrt{318.1067}}$$

$$= \frac{141.2667}{173.8134} = .81$$

r is approximately equal to ρ, but may be found more accurately by transposing with the aid of tables found in textbooks.

Fig. 25. Computation of r by rank and product-moment methods.

	Test			Test			Test			Test	
Pupil	A	B	Pupil	A	B	Pupil	A	B	Pupil	A	B
1	47	33	15	48	27	29	32	26	43	49	31
2	38	30	16	62	38	30	45	33	44	43	30
3	29	20	17	24	25	31	40	34	45	41	36
4	51	37	18	33	24	32	49	30	46	32	25
5	60	38	19	35	36	33	35	29	47	43	33
6	35	26	20	40	29	34	30	32	48	34	31
7	59	42	21	41	32	35	52	38	49	60	38
8	46	31	22	60	45	36	50	35	50	35	24
9	41	35	23	27	19	37	36	28	51	37	33
10	45	28	24	36	26	38	39	26	52	42	32
11	39	23	25	53	32	39	38	36	53	39	28
12	42	39	26	29	22	40	47	35	54	42	35
13	53	35	27	53	41	41	43	33			
14	45	30	28	37	30	42	25	20			

Fig. 26. Scores of a group on two tests.

The data of Figure 26 consists of the scores made by a group of pupils on two tests. To find the correlation coefficient, the first step is to form a correlation tabulation, which is really a scatter diagram with both distributions grouped. Looking over the scores in Test A, we see that the range of measures is 39, or 24 through 62. This indicates that 8 groups of 5 units each would be appropriate. In Test B, the range is 26 units, suggesting 9 groups of 3 units each. Therefore, the scale is planned as: 23.5–, 28.5–, etc., for A; and 18.5–, 21.5–, etc., for B. Since most people prefer to locate the measures in the first column on the Y axis, then move horizontally to locate the others, the A scale is thus planned and the table made accordingly. (See Fig. 27.) Now, as was done in making the scatter diagram (p. 205), the score (47) made by the first individual in Test A is located in the interval 43.5–. This row is now traced to the right to the interval with midpoint of 32, which contains the score 33 made by this person in Test B. A tally is made in this cell of the table, and the procedure is continued in order until all tallies have been recorded.

If the tallies are placed in the lower left corner of the cells, then the frequency in each compartment (f_{xy}) may be noted in the center, as is done here. The f_x row and f_y column are now filled in and added as a check.

Elements of Statistical Techniques — 217

	Test B											f_y	d'_y	$f_y d'_y$	$\Sigma f_y d'_y$	$\Sigma f_y d'_y{}^2$	$\Sigma f_{xy} d'_x d'_y$
	20	23	26	29	32	35	38	41	44								
58.5–									16 / 1 /	5	4	20		80	58
53.5–								12 / 1 /								
48.5–						4 / 2 / 2 //	8 / 2 //	6 / 1 /		8	2	16	43	32	16
43.5–			3 / 1 /	−2 / 1 / 2 //	2 // 3 ///	1 /				7	1	7		7	−3
38.5–				−2 / 2 //	4 ///	4 ///	1 /			14	0	0			
33.5–	8 / 1 /		4 / 2 //	3 /// 4 ////	4 /// 2 //	−2 / 2 //				11	−1	−11		11	9
28.5–	24 / 2 //	12 / 2 //	8 / 2 //		2 /					6	−2	−12	32	24	28
23.5–			6 / 1 /		1 /					3	−3	−9	11	27	30
f_y	3	4	7	10	12	9	6	2	1	54				181	138
d'_x	−4	−3	−2	−1	0	1	2	3	4						
$f_x d'_x$	−12	−12	−14	−10	0	9	12	6	4			−17			
$\Sigma f_x d'_x$				−48					31						
$\Sigma f_x d'_x{}^2$	48	36	28	10	0	9	24	18	16	183					

Fig. 27. Correlation table for scores of a group on two tests.

(left side: Test A)

The detailed formula used here appears long, but the procedure for computing r is relatively easy.

$$r_{xy} = \frac{\frac{\Sigma f_{xy}d'_x d'_y}{N} - \frac{\Sigma f_x d'_x}{N} \cdot \frac{\Sigma f_y d'_y}{N}}{\sqrt{\frac{\Sigma f_x d'_x{}^2}{N} - \left(\frac{\Sigma f_x d'_x}{N}\right)^2} \sqrt{\frac{\Sigma f_y d'_y{}^2}{N} - \left(\frac{\Sigma f_y d'_y}{N}\right)^2}}$$

The lines of the table are extended vertically and horizontally so that all items called for in the formula may be found, and heads are placed for these rows and columns.

The actual solution of the formula is as follows:

$$r_{xy} = \frac{\frac{138}{54} - \frac{17}{54} \cdot \frac{11}{54}}{\sqrt{\frac{183}{54} - \left(\frac{17}{54}\right)^2} \sqrt{\frac{181}{54} - \left(\frac{11}{54}\right)^2}}$$

$$= \frac{2.5556 + (.3148)(.2037)}{\sqrt{3.3889 - .0990} \sqrt{3.3518 - 1.0415}}$$

$$= \frac{2.62}{(1.91)(1.81)}$$

$$= .80$$

Special attention is called to the small figures in the upper right corner of the cells of the table that show a frequency. These are the $f_{xy}d'_x d'_y$ values, keeping signs. In other words, they are the product of the deviations in X and Y for that cell multiplied by the number of cases in the cell. Also it is well to note that the minus sign in the second term of the numerator leads to the addition of the correction instead of its subtraction. Here again we find a fair amount of correlation between the tests in this situation.

Applications of Correlation

Whenever there are two sets or series of measures for the same individuals so that the measures may be paired, it is possible to apply some of the correlation techniques. In some instances, it is urgent that the nature and extent of the relationship be known. For example, it is generally recognized that the speed and quality of work should progress together in most if not all learning situations. In other words, there should be a fairly high correlation between the accuracy and rate of work. But, although a class may be up to or above the norm in both rate and quality, there may be no relationship between the two. In fact it sometimes happens that there is a negative relationship, for speed is attained at the expense of quality, or the reverse.

Correlation problems arise in many situations such as the relation of teachers' marks to the results of standard tests, and the relation between intelligence test scores and mastery of a subject matter such as reading.

Prediction may be the matter of chief concern. Here there are many questions to be answered. To what extent can a certain test be relied upon as a criterion of success in school work at any specific level? Is it advisable to use one test as a substitute for another test? Are the results of diagnostic tests more dependable than standard tests relative to the ratings and grades in particular subjects?

The *validity* of a test can be established if the scores made on it can be shown to have a rather marked correlation with an objective, infallible criterion. Such a criterion is sometimes very difficult to single out and establish, but a high correlation between the scores made on an achievement test and marks received in class work would indicate some validity of the test.

In the study of *reliability*, the investigator may repeat a testing procedure of a group after an intermission and correlate the test results to find to what extent the two series of scores agree. Or, instead of repeating with the same test, another form of the test may be used. A test may be split into two halves by taking odd-numbered items for one test and even-numbered items for the other after the test has been administered, or by some other method that would insure chance selection, and finding the correlation between these two parts.

Other Correlation Techniques

Four fold methods of correlation which consider only the number and proportion of cases in each quadrant of the correlation table are used where only simple alternatives are used for both the X and Y scales. These methods provide a rough indication of the extent of correlation.

In the correlation procedures that have been dealt with here, a "straight-line" relationship has been assumed. This means that the lines of best fit to the means of the rows in a correlation table, and the means of the columns, are straight lines. In the case of certain types of data, these lines of best fit are curved, and *curvilinear* correlation techniques are employed.

Multiple correlation techniques are used to discover the relationship that exists, at least theoretically, between a certain variable and two or more other variables taken together. This procedure is used, for example, in finding the relationship between grades made by pupils on a standard achievement test in arithmetic and the results of a test battery consisting of an intelligence test, a reading test, and a reasoning test.

Partial correlation procedures are used to discover the theoretical relationship between two tests, such as arithmetic and reading tests, when the results of an intelligence test are ruled out. Any number of such test results may thus be eliminated.

The techniques mentioned in this section are not developed here, since they fall in the area of advanced statistics.

Probability

About a century ago it was discovered that many types of measurements of natural phenomena, such as sizes of sea shells, and heights and weights of people, are distributed in the form of a *normal curve*. This was known in mathematics as the normal probability curve. Of course, in establishing such a distribution, enough cases must be involved and the population must be a true random sample of the universe. This bell-shaped curve, having the mode, mean, and median at the center, and being well balanced in form below and above the center, is shown in Figure 28. Here the standard deviation lengths or units are measured off on the base line on either side of the mean ordinate (y_o). The limits of the curve are infinitely extended, always approaching but never reaching the base line. However, in practical situations, the curve is cut off at certain points since the frequency beyond them is negligible.

The few distributions that have been shown here, as in Figure 19 (p. 202) and Figure 27 (p. 217), suggest the normal curve in their forms, with the accumulation of frequencies at the center and diminishing frequencies at the extremes. A good deal of evidence supports the assumption that measurements of mental ability and achievement are normally so distributed. There are, of course, distributions of certain types of data that are normally skewed to the right or left.

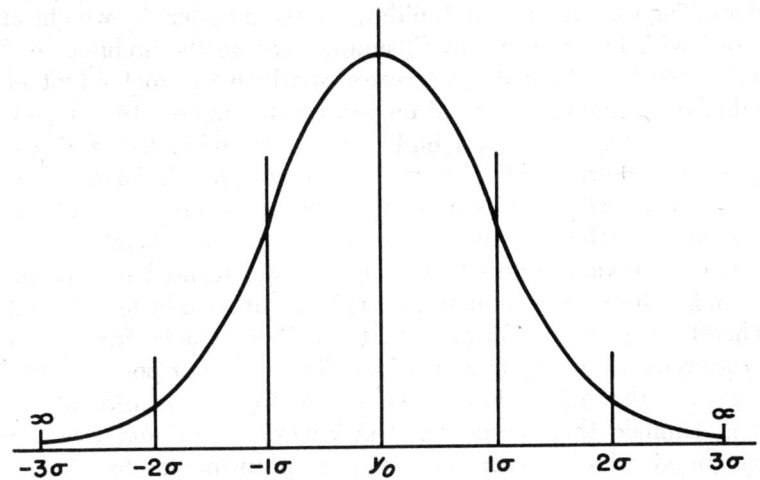

Fig. 28. The normal probability curve.

A prominent use of the normal curve is in the distribution of ratings of pupils. So, various schemata have been used for this purpose. For example, cutting the normal curve off at 2.5σ and -2.5σ provides a range of 5σ. Then the Grade A would extend from 1.5σ up, Grade B from $.5\sigma$ to 1.5σ, Grade C from $-.5\sigma$ to $.5\sigma$, and so on. Suggested distributions for grades, based on the proportion of cases falling within certain ranges of the normal curve, are proposed. One schema provides for 7% A's, 24% B's, 38% C's, 24% D's, and 7% E's. Different results would be forthcoming if the normal curve were cut off at $\pm 3\sigma$. Such plans are more or less arbitrary and highly formalized, and therefore should be used with caution.

A chief use of the normal curve of probability is in establishing the relationship between standard scores made on a standardized test and percentile scores, and transmuting one of these into the other. It is sometimes the practice to use the normal curve to determine an individual's chances of falling above or below certain points on the base of a distribution or within certain areas of the distribution.

Another area of application of normal probability is in the computation of the *standard error* (σ_e) of statistical computations. The roof of a school building caved in under the weight of snow, with loss of some lives, simply because the architect had not properly estimated the stresses to which the roof might be subjected. A good structural engineer will compute the average of the stresses to which a building may be subjected, and also the standard error of the averages, and will provide for sufficient strength in the roof trusses so that there will be practically no possibility of their giving way under any possible weight.

It was previously noted that any measure secured is only one of an infinite number of measures that might have been obtained. Therefore, any computation that has been made from these measurements is only one of an infinite number of possible computations that might have been made. In such considerations, it is assumed that there is a "true" computation, and that any computed value is a more or less close approximation to this true measure. The standard error of the computation is used to give an estimate of the chances there are that the computed value will fall within such and such distances from the *true* value.

In Figure 28, a section of the base scale used in Figure 15 (p. 198) is given with the M_A being placed at the mean ordinate (y_o) of a normal curve. This curve represents all of the possible means that might have been found. It is assumed here that the mean 77.6 is at the midpoint. (See Fig. 29.) The question now arises as to the chances there are that the true mean will fall within certain distances from the obtained mean.

$$\sigma_M = \frac{\sigma}{\sqrt{N}} \text{ or } \frac{15.0}{\sqrt{56}} = \frac{15.0}{7.48} = 2.0$$

This value subtracted from the mean (77.6) gives 75.6, and added to 77.6 gives 79.6. Now the conclusion may be made that the chances are about 2 to 1 or 2 out of 3 that the true mean will fall between 75.6 and 79.6. We can be practically certain that the true mean will fall within the range $\pm 2.5\sigma$, or between 72.6 and 82.6. The *probable error* (P.E.) may be used instead of the standard error (σ_e) (P.E. $= .6745\sigma_e$). The chances are even that a measure will fall within the range of ± 1 P.E. Anyone conducting researches involving such values will use tables giving the

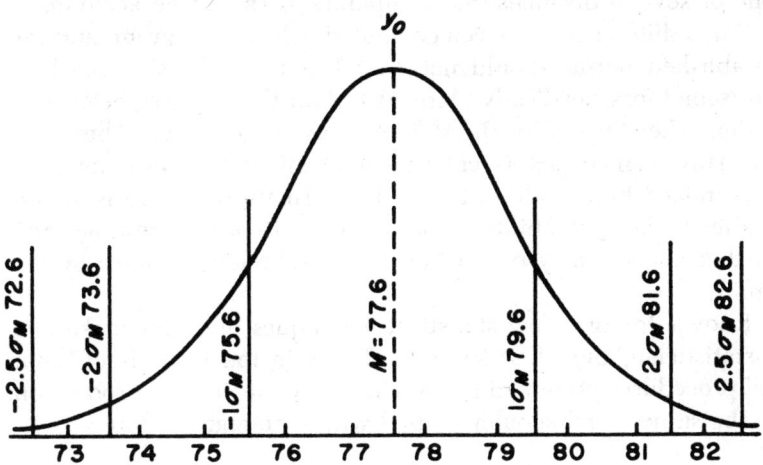

Fig. 29. The meaning of the standard error of the mean.

probable error or standard error values for the proportions under the normal curve. Every computed value may be given its corresponding standard or probable error. Some of these standard errors are $\sigma_{(M_x - M_y)}$, σ_r, σ_σ, or the corresponding P.E. values.

In recent years there has been a marked increase in the emphasis placed on probability, especially in the area of measurement. In earlier days, there was a tendency to take any computed value very seriously as fact and as a basis for sweeping conclusions. The practice now prevails of estimating probabilities, in recognition of the fact that the computations are not precise representatives of the sample being dealt with or of the universe.

A Word of Caution

Special attention and care must be given to accuracy in all statistical work. Computations and transfers of data should be critically checked. Small errors may lead to major inaccuracies in the final results.

Ordinarily, data are rather rough approximations, and there is seldom any great need for refinement in calculations. However, whether such values as quotients and square roots are taken to one or several decimals, the computations should be accurate.

Small differences between computed values for a group and the established norms should not be taken too seriously. Teachers are sometimes needlessly alarmed to find their classes below the norm, when in reality the difference is insignificant. There are so many chance factors entering into any testing situation that it is indeed impossible to assert that a small difference is attributable to lack of ability or knowledge. Repeated testings and further analysis may reveal the cause of the lower values by the group.

Knowledge of a few statistical techniques does not make one a statistician, though it should aid him in the analysis of data. All procedures presented in this chapter are a simple introduction to the subject and should be used with care and caution.

PART FOUR

Mental Health and Character Education

by Adolph W. Aleck

Chapter 12
Mental Health

The mentally healthy individual can adjust his thoughts and feelings to the changes he perceives occurring in the world about him, and in this way he learns to live and work satisfactorily and happily with others. Obstacles to mental health arise when excessive fears or other causes, organic or cultural, impair the person's ability to adjust to other people and to problems encountered in everyday experience.

Individuals vary widely in their reactions to life situations, in their attitudes and objectives, and therefore in the opportunities and experiences they need in order to achieve and maintain the universal goal of a healthy mind in a healthy body. Some are lacking in self-esteem; they feel inadequate, and put their need for security first, equating any change with danger or threat. Others are self-confident persons attracted by the new, the unexplored, the adventurous experience. The security-minded apply their energy to building defenses to consolidate present gains. The adventure-minded, on the contrary, are impelled by their enthusiasm to explore new means of solving their problems, and for them change is not a warning but an inspiration. Experienced teachers have learned to recognize these differences among individuals, and have also learned how to encourage moderation in their pupils instead of emotional extremes of pessimism and overoptimism.

Elements of Personal Adjustment

The teacher should be alert to detect mental and emotional difficulties of pupils in the light of four basic elements of personal adjustment: reaction to stress; self-acceptance; ability to meet commitments; and ability to face reality. If he bears these factors in mind as he guides pupils, the teacher will be able to encourage his students to apply the principle of moderation to their problems, and thus help them to make satisfactory adjustments. The mentally healthy person reacts successfully to the unavoidable stresses and strains of modern living. He demonstrates his achievement of self-discipline and self-acceptance; he meets his responsibilities with confidence and courage; and he faces the reality of his circumstances, ready to cope with the consequences of his purposive behavior. It is the teacher's function, by means of instruction and guidance, to assist every pupil in developing these basic characteristics of the well-adjusted person.

Methods of Adjustment

The principal ways in which individuals attempt to deal with their inner anxieties and conflicts are aggression, compensation, rationalization, fantasy, projection, identification, repression, sublimation, and regression. These methods of adjustment may impede the mental health of pupils if they are carried to an extreme, but they are not all necessarily injurious. Teachers can do much to communicate and work cooperatively with pupils so that extremes will be avoided as far as possible, while beneficial modes of adjustment will be encouraged.

Aggression. A moderate degree of aggression based upon rational and realistic thinking is usually approved in our society. To say of a man that he is intelligent, capable, and aggressive is to pay him a compliment, to praise him as a competent person endowed with commendable initiative. Carried to an extreme, however, aggressive tendencies can become more emotional than rational, the difference between the two being one of degree, not of kind.

The teacher should encourage pupil initiative and a reasonable amount of mentally aggressive behavior which exhibits certain approved characteristics: (1) It may be reality-oriented aggression used only for self-defense, free from sadism or antagonistic relationships. (2) It may well be used as a means of defense, but against a genuine, not an imaginary, enemy or evil. (3) It has a positive value, as in the defense of right and justice, and it is not a reaction associated with feelings of guilt or shame—indeed, in a worthy cause, it is respected as evidence of candor and courage. (4) It is not continued, as a means of merely relieving emotional tension, beyond the point where its justifiable goal is achieved. (5) It is well-timed and carefully directed to attain maximum results at reasonable cost in time and effort. (6) It is used for carefully selected, constructive purposes after meticulous consideration of alternatives and a realistic estimate of the probability of success. (7) It is accompanied by adequate self-restraint in the face of provocative behavior of others, even though such self-restraint is readily mistaken by adversaries for weakness or cowardice.

Compensation. Compensation is a defense reaction whereby the individual attempts to escape confrontation with reality. He compensates for a real or imaginary weakness by concealing it or by diverting attention to his strength and competency in a different area of activity. In this way he tries to defend himself from a lowering of status and from attacks on his self-esteem. Thus, a boy may have his heart set on being the pitcher on a baseball team but, despite hard work, he loses too many games because his pitching is not good enough. But when reassigned to the outfield, he displays speed, a strong throwing arm, skill in judging the ball, and strong motivation to improve his performance. The failure as a pitcher becomes a fine outfielder, saving his own self-esteem and gaining in status within his group. In this situation, compensation can be a valuable aid to healthy adjustment. However, experienced teachers know that not all modes of compensation are constructive and healthy, for uncontrolled compensatory behavior can often make matters worse if a child experiences repeated failure and augmented feelings of inadequacy.

Rationalization. Rationalization is a means of building self-esteem through attempts to justify one's shortcomings, by finding excuses for them and directing attention away from them toward one's attainments or skills admired by others. The teacher must be on the alert to encourage pupils to practice objective self-evaluation, self-discipline, and self-correction instead of self-display. He should, of course, set an example for the pupils by sympathetic, yet firm and impartial communication with them, facing the facts of each classroom situation or problem frankly and with a calm and reasonable attitude, and stimulating healthy skepticism about rumors, dubious information, excessive guessing, and careless interpretation of events.

Fantasy. The substitution of dreams and fantasy for the reality of one's circumstances, abilities, and problems often becomes an obstacle to self-direction and achievement. While the teacher must not discourage the pupil's free play of imagination and creative expression, he should note any excessive dependence by the pupils upon mythical or miraculous possibilities instead of probabilities of accomplishment in the light of actualities and limitations. Fairy tales and hero worship, for example, have a role to play in the creative imagination of young children; but certainly in the upper grades and high school, fantasy should be discouraged and emphasis placed on careful judgment and evaluation of facts.

Projection. When a pupil attempts to excuse his failures repeatedly by blaming only the circumstances or the actions of others, his real aim is to gain the respect of people whom he holds in high esteem. He seeks to be admired and to be looked up to, and therefore he attributes his difficulties or failures to external causes instead of to his own errors or deficiencies. The teacher's effort to correct or counteract this tendency toward projection needs to be well-considered, sympathetic, and tactful in the realization that the pupil's basic motives may be more positive and constructive than his apparent disregard of the facts may imply. Projection as a means of self-defense will then gradually be replaced by a more realistic and considerate attitude. The pupil may really be in need of greater self-confidence to counteract a feeling of inferiority.

Identification. Children have always been inspired by the attainments of adults whom they admire; they accept the adults as models to emulate and often identify their own personalities and ideals with such models. To some extent identification of this kind can be beneficial, where the models represent high ideals and worthwhile achievements. But identification should not be permitted to form a basis for feelings of superiority in a child when these feelings are not justified by the facts. Sincere admiration of adult models can be encouraged as a basis for emulation, but subsequent boasting and airs of superiority must be frowned upon; the pupil will then come to realize that he is not about to equal the genius of his model, yet he will not be so discouraged that he will think of himself as a failure.

Repression. Repression is the deliberate attempt to forget and to prevent recall of an unpleasant experience. However, the experience then remains buried in the mind without being brought to the surface for discussion or expression. Such repressed ideas, memories, and feelings can often create mounting tension and interfere with the normal growth and wholesome development of the individual. Excessive supervision of everything the child does in school and at home, forbidding him to engage in interests and activities even when they are customary in his group or constructive in his own judgment, may inhibit self-expression and growth, just as the other extreme of lack of supervision may convince the child that he is not being given attention and affection. Experienced teachers apply the Golden Mean to the problems of discipline, to avoid creating in the pupil either extreme tension or frustration and despair. The pupil must be helped to grow up emotionally. An optimal level of tension, one that is neither too weak nor too strong, is most favorable to healthy growth toward emotional maturity.

Sublimation. Sublimation is a method of adjustment whereby the individual who is unable to fulfill his intense urges or desires diverts his own interest and energy into alternative channels of satisfying activity. As in the case of the sex drive, or immediate impulses in some other area of interest, the individual disciplines himself to abandon these drives and finds substitute satisfaction in other forms of self-expression, such as music, art, creative literature, and recreation.

Sublimation reminds us of the displacement of aggression, a

Freudian term denoting a common reaction to frustration. An angry man comes home, storms at his wife, kicks the door, then calms down and finds relief of tension in social games or other socially approved activities. It is said of Confucius that he never displaced his anger; however, most people undoubtedly displace their aggressive impulses much oftener than they would like to believe or would care to admit. In the classroom, an abundance of opportunities for creative self-expression will help the pupils to achieve the constructive goals of personal satisfaction and wholesome adjustment.

Regression. Regression is a form of withdrawal in which the individual reverts to a previous stage of his behavior. Children coming to school for the first time often miss the familiar relationships of family life, for example, and may tend to withdraw from the actual classroom situation into a dream world of their own in which they relive the warm and tender care and comforting experiences of the home. They may become confused and helpless and demand attention as if they were still infants. An understanding and sympathetic teacher can easily note and correct such instances of regression. This type of regression also may find expression outwardly in extreme shyness or in negativism at any level of school experience, as when a high school girl accustomed to a sheltered life at home is afraid to attend a school dance or when a boy rebels against school discipline as a reversion to childish behavior in the home.

Personality Adjustment in School

The school can do much to promote the mental health of students. It can provide a wholesome environment conducive to emotional stability. It can stimulate and guide students to form the habits of thought and activity necessary for self-appraisal and realistic self-understanding. It can suggest goals and provide models for students so that they will work toward constructive, socially approved objectives. It can advise and guide students who must cope with situations causing conflict and frustration. It can practice the highest ideals of the community and help students to live up to the best ethical standards. Finally, it can take remedial action based upon prompt recognition of the symptoms of maladjustment when these occur.

Play activities in the school provide an excellent illustration of the ways in which our schools can promote the mental health of children. The same or similar techniques of guidance used in this field of experience can be applied to many other school programs. Teachers should consider what is involved in each such area of experience, how children are helped to grow thereby, and the principal psychological factors which must be taken into account.

The meaning of play, one of the most effective influences upon a child's development, is too often misconstrued. Adults tend to regard play as a means of entertainment, escape from routine, relaxation, or rest. But to the young child, play is a serious business of discovery, communication, expression, and an aid to understanding himself and others. Since the world in which the child grows up is controlled by adults, he is constantly subject to their influence. Play is something real in the mind of a child and it is taken seriously just as an adult takes his work seriously.

Child play differs from adult play in several important respects. It follows a developmental pattern. As Gesell has shown, the play of very young children progresses from simple motor activities with toys to socialized play and later to dramatic and constructional play. Late childhood is characteristically the "play age," for at that time the number of play activities reaches its highest point. Some of these play activities continue into the period of adolescence. Although the older child will devote less of his total time to play, he will tend to concentrate on specific activities and to one or more of these he will devote more time than he did at an earlier age.

Child play is informal and spontaneous. The child plays when, where, and with whatever materials he chooses at the moment. Adolescents tend to play in a more formal, less spontaneous manner and with less gusto than younger children. Teachers and parents who take these differences into account will understand the differential play requirements of children at the various age levels and will know how to cope with any difficulties or personality problems which may arise.

Young children gain in strength, endurance, speed of movement, coordination, and balance as they learn to run, throw, catch, dodge, or gauge moving objects with increasing confidence, control, and safety. These activities form the experiential background for teamwork, self-discipline, and competitive sportsmanship regulated by strictly observed rules of games. In supervising a child's play activity, adults should understand the child's play history, his attitudes, and the details of the game itself. Some games, for instance, stimulate aggressive reactions more than others do. Commenting on the supervision of children's games, Dr. Redl has pointed out that "the adults must sense the approach of the point where the game is no longer fun," [1] if trouble is to be avoided. Playground emotions often run high. It is essential that leaders supervising the activities choose games most appropriate for the participants—games to build confidence in a timid child and other games to impel well-matched players to exert their all-out efforts.

As in other competitive school enterprises, the losers and winners in games display varying reactions. Some young children are "hard losers," while others take their setbacks rather philosophically and make up their minds to win the next time. The adult supervisor, observing these diverse reactions, usually confines himself wisely to the assurance of fair play and an equal chance for all participants. He notes with satisfaction the way in which a thrill-seeking anxiety-filled boy, perhaps repressing deep feelings of guilt, anger, or fear, finds a healthful outlet in lively, wholesome, exciting sports and games which channel his energy into experiences testing his strength and competence. Such a boy will probably improve in academic achievement as well, inasmuch as physical activity and physical health relieve tension and facilitate concentration. Superior physical performance is usually associated with superior mental ability and accomplishment.

---

[1] Morton Edwards (ed.), *Your Child from Two to Five* (New York: Perma Books, 1955), p. 339.

Chapter 13
Psychology of Character

Character may be defined as the sum total of personality traits exhibited by the individual in his relationships to other people. His habitual ways of responding to social situations reflect the type of moral standards in which he genuinely believes and by which he lives. As Socrates stated the matter in Plato's *Republic*, ethics is "no chance topic, but a question of the fashion in which a man should live."

Character Traits

Among the basic components of character are such traits as readiness to conform (or conversely, readiness to show hostility), spontaneity, friendliness, honesty (or dishonesty), conscientiousness (and flexibility or cooperativeness), altruism, and moral stability (reflected especially in habits of self-discipline). Such traits are developed gradually in the child through guided experience in homes, schools, and communities, from their beginnings in infancy when the individual is quite amoral and has had little or no practice in self-direction. Teachers should be aware that some children develop desirable behavior traits more rapidly than others, and some retain infantile lack of self-control throughout the early years of childhood. In the majority of cases, however, by the age of ten years the child is likely to have built the foundations of his character.

Conformity. No person is completely immune to the influence of custom and public opinion. Group opinion may pressure the individual to behave on a level below his own sense of propriety or against his own preference. Children in school tend to follow the group mores, avoiding deviations from the pattern in order to win respect and approval. Those who deviate markedly from the folkways might be regarded as eccentric. However, children eager to conform may do so at too great a cost, by their failure to develop their own creativity and self-expression. Teachers can do much to encourage such children to act more spontaneously and to express their individuality more freely.

Spontaneity. An objective of the school should be to help the child achieve a healthy balance between submissiveness and self-assertiveness. The teacher should always take the child's wishes into consideration, for the preferences of children often mean as much to them as adult preferences mean to adults. Children like to be consulted about ways to do things instead of always being told how to do them. They need the opportunity to make their own decisions and face up to the consequences of their spontaneous activities.

Friendliness. Sympathetic understanding of others can be developed in the child through his experience in trying to establish rapport with schoolmates and through emulation of admired personalities. If the teacher is warm and open-minded, the children will eventually respond with reciprocal friendship toward him and toward each other. Their questions should not be brushed aside or their self-esteem hurt by ridicule or abrupt reproval. An attitude of generosity and friendliness on the teacher's part is especially appreciated by sensitive children, and a teacher who sincerely admits his own mistakes to the class will frequently endear himself to the pupils.

Honesty. Lying takes various forms and occurs under many diverse circumstances. According to Dr. Ben Karpman, types of deception include the following: benign, for the sake of politeness and not intended to hurt; hysterical, to attract attention or sympathy; defensive, to escape from a difficult situation; compensatory, to cover up for inferiority feelings; malicious, to deceive for profit; gossipy, to hurt a specific person and derive satisfaction thereby; implied, using silence as a substitute for truth-telling; love-intoxicated, to express "sweet nothings"; and pathological, to express fantasies and delusions.[1] From another point of view, Hartshorne and May in their classic *Studies in Deceit* reported the following conclusions: honesty and dishonesty are learned, not inherited, traits; mere exhortation by teachers and preaching of ideals of honesty do not influence conduct control; the social situation is the important factor in the value of suggestion or the use of behavior controls; the personal relationships of the child should be carefully studied; and individual children should not be judged on the basis of inadequate information about their specific dishonest practices.

Conscientiousness and Flexibility. Some overconscientious children tend to persist in a course of action even though conditions may have been altered so that change would be desirable. Such children find it difficult to listen to criticism or to admit that they may be mistaken when the group or the teacher disapproves of their course of action. On the other hand, flexibility can also be carried too far. Nursery educators, for example, recommend a technique for teaching children to make their own rational decisions when alternative behavior choices present themselves. Thus, if the owner of a toy is in possession of his prize and another child casts covetous eyes on it, let the rightful owner decide whether or not to hand the toy over. If the decision is in the negative, it must be respected without scolding, for the will to defend what one loves is, at crucial times in life, just as important as the willingness to sacrifice for others.

Altruism. The attitudes of adults help to shape the child's attitudes. If the teacher and parents show sincere enthusiasm when they help the child, he will tend to emulate them. Allow the child to be unselfish in his own way, without dominating his actions. Encourage him to see the other person's point of view and to anticipate the other person's feelings and reactions—for example, to a gift. Do not allow him to be imposed upon by others who take undue advantage of his generosity. The child needs to learn to stand up for his own rights with due consideration for the rights and well-being of his peers.

Moral Stability. The necessity to obey the rules, the social code, is not easily realized by young children. Most people enjoy the

---

[1] *Science Digest*, XXVI, No. 4 (October, 1949), p. 8.

experience of doing good deeds consistent with the social code, although they do not always agree on what the "good" really is. But the teacher should not waste time on merely deploring or worrying about children's habits of lying, stealing, cheating; the need is to seek out and to understand the causes of these reactions and to take positive action to encourage more rational and socially approved behavior patterns. Moral stability in children is influenced by the sympathetic conduct of adults such as acceptance of children as persons worthy of attention and respect, encouragement of individuality with a minimum of requisite conformity, guidance of the individual child's interests, discipline which is neither too rigid nor too lax or submissive, prompt approval of constructive tendencies, and moderation and restraint in adult relationships to children. Teachers need to consider the individual differences among children. Some children are fact-minded, and have "a basic temperament for accepting the teachings of others."[2] They are likely to put much emphasis on manners and formal situations. At the opposite pole are the extremely creative and imaginative children who in their early years find it difficult to distinguish between fact and fiction and shift from one to the other, sometimes deceiving even themselves.

Character Development

The formation of character traits is a slow process developing out of a person's experiences in thinking, feeling, and acting. Present traits of the individual are the result of all his past attitudes and reactions. Moral development depends upon knowing what is right, wanting to do what is right, and the repetitive experience of actually doing what is right. Motivation, that is, the child's definite aim and desire, connects his knowledge of what is right for him to do and his overt activity.

The school can play a role in promoting all these aspects of character development. Studies by Plant and Telford in the 1960's indicated that formal education can have a favorable effect

---

[2] Frances L. Ilg and Louise B. Ames, *Child Behavior* (New York: Harper & Row, 1966), p. 286.

upon the formation and strengthening of desirable character traits, such as self-reliance and self-discipline, and can help to modify undesirable traits such as authoritarian attitudes, intolerance, and excessive self-assertiveness. But results cannot be achieved overnight; the child's sense of right and wrong develops slowly.

A Rational Basis for Character Development. The frank discussion of problems, issues, and values with children often helps to improve immature or unjustifiable attitudes toward moral standards—for example, in coping with problems of cheating and sportsmanship, social beliefs, and habits of independent thinking. Dr. Robert Lynd [3] cited a number of conflicting social beliefs which exemplify the contradictory pressures which make it difficult for adults as well as children to choose the most acceptable ideals to practice. We are told that individualism is the law of nature and the secret of America's greatness, that restrictions on the individual's freedom are un-American and destroy initiative, but on the contrary, that no man should live for himself alone, that people ought to be loyal and stand together and work for common purposes. We are told that everyone should try to be successful, and yet that the kind of person one is is more important than being a success. Our society often faces a hard choice between competing aims. Is the family our basic institution and the sacred core of national life, or is business our most important institution because the national well-being depends upon business and other institutions must conform to its needs? Are religious values and the "finer things of life" the things we are really working for, despite the socially approved principle that a man owes it to himself and to his family to earn as much money as he can? Other contradictory appeals are those of change and tradition, thrift and risk-taking, honesty and concealment of information, idealism and practicality. The teacher endeavors to help children make choices of their own among these conflicting standards in formal and informal individual and group activities.

Children's Activities and Character Education. The school pro-

---

[3] Robert Lynd, *Knowledge for What?* (Princeton: Princeton University Press, 1939), p. 268.

vides social situations in which pupils are most likely to develop desirable character traits. Group enterprises offer an opportunity for them to form habitual attitudes of cooperation, honesty, fair play, courage, spontaneity, and self-discipline. In fact, to some extent all educational experiences affect these character traits. The teacher is in a position to encourage them through his approval (or disapproval), advice, and guidance, and the use of reasonable direction and supervision; his rapport with the children is the most significant factor. Children see and hear much more than one might suppose. They like to have adults talk directly to them instead of talking about them in their presence. They like to ask questions, often interminably, and the adult strategy of shrugging them off will not work, as in offering the lame excuse: "You wouldn't understand if I told you." If the child asks his question in good faith, he deserves an honest answer given in good faith.

Games, camping, athletics, and club activities provide opportunities for character education in a social setting. They give the child a chance to learn how others think and feel about situations and people. The child can, if properly guided, contribute to the interests of the entire group and develop good character traits from the experience. Unfortunately, some community influences, such as certain poorer types of radio and television programs and motion pictures, have not presented the most desirable values for children to admire and accept. It becomes all the more important for teachers to encourage the practice of desirable values in school activities, to discourage instances of exaggerated self-importance or excessive shyness, to approve of behavior showing consideration for the rights and feelings of others, to show appreciation of the child's efforts to do the right thing, to suggest ways of sharing and cooperation, to consider the child's wishes, to encourage a Golden Mean between self-sacrifice and overaggressiveness. The lack of discipline is just as inadequate and undesirable as autocratic or rigid discipline. The alert teacher knows that rational, consistent discipline and warm affection go together as contributions to mental health and character development.

PART FIVE

The Psychology of School Subjects
by Lester D. Crow

PART II

Chapter 14
Psychology of Elementary School Subjects

Teaching no longer can be defined as merely the process of helping a child acquire knowledge; it has the more difficult function of guiding the learner in the best development of his capacities for efficient living in an ever-changing society. In the learning of a school subject, a child is concerned with (1) the acquisition of new information, (2) the manipulation of this information to make it usable in new situations, and (3) self-evaluation whereby he discovers how much he has learned and what he still needs to learn.

Basic Considerations

The processes of learning become functional as the child brings adequate experiences to the teaching-learning situation. For example, the child who lives in a disadvantaged area prior to entering school is handicapped as compared to children who have experienced enriched environments and can profit from school instruction that assumes these early basic experiences. This difference in learning readiness persists and sometimes widens as the respective children continue in school.

The extent to which the child adequately adapts and utilizes acquired information in the solution of the problems of living is a measure of his mental progress. In order to help the learner to attain the greatest mental development the teacher must be able not only to understand and apply the psychological principles underlying individual differences and group similarities, but also to utilize the accepted laws involved in the learning process. The child begins with little or no mental power but adds to it gradually as he lives, develops, and continues his learning both in and out of school.

Such inherent factors as sex, age, mental ability, original drives to behavior, emotional equipment, and special abilities or defects of the child should be taken into account in any program of education. The teacher should understand and know how to apply the principles of economic learning: repetition and reinforcement in learning, laws of association, satisfaction versus dissatisfaction, and incidental versus intentional learning. He should note carefully individual differences as well as group similarities and adjust his procedures to them. He should know the facts concerning transfer of learning and should be alert to the conditions which make transfer of power or skill possible.

The study of school subjects should ideally be based upon their intrinsic interest to the pupils as challenging tasks which the pupils themselves are eager to perform. The efficient teacher stimulates such interest and purposive effort. There should be little or no need for the imposition of external controls or extrinsic rewards; children should develop the ability to discipline themselves and habitually direct their own behavior toward socially acceptable goals. Thus, in applying psychological principles to the teaching of school subjects, the teacher contributes greatly to the wholesome attitudes and environment essential to success in all aspects of the school program.

Psychology of Language Arts

Language is the tool through which human beings communicate with one another. The better each individual understands the symbols of communication, the better will be the transfer of ideas among the individuals directly involved. Influences in the social setting exert an impact on what is listened to and what is spoken, or what is interpreted in written form. Hence various environmental factors, other than language itself, affect an individual's interpretation of oral or written expression.

Both the formal and informal language work of the elementary school have for their purpose the development in the pupil of the ability to express himself adequately, either orally or in writing, in the symbols of communication used by the members of his social group. It is important that the pupil be aware of fineness of distinctions among the language symbols used so that he will think clearly and will understand what is being communicated.

Factors Affecting Language Ability. The learning of language is greatly influenced by inherited and environmental factors. For example, the impulse to express oneself is inherent in the individual. At an early age the child tends toward oral expression; as he attempts to speak a specific language he begins to develop facility in it. If exposed to a particular language environment, a child will acquire facility to express himself in that language.

The young child tends to satisfy his wants by bodily movements, largely uncontrolled, and by sounds and cries. Satisfaction shows itself in gurgles, coos, and cessation of arm, leg, and body movements. Slowly, through imitation of his elders, he develops associations between certain objects and impulses to behavior, and more conventional language sounds. His first attempts at articulation may be no more than an approximation of the intended word or phrase symbol, for his vocal mechanism is not yet under complete control and his perceptual powers are not yet mature. Adults sometimes mistakenly assume that the young child can understand only this so-called "baby talk." They stimulate him with this jargon and thus interfere with the child's mastery of adult symbols of expression. Adults should endeavor to provide a model of language worthy of imitation by the child.

The language habits that a child brings to his school life are very important for him. He establishes these habits through the experiences of living with people in his home and in his expanding social environment, for he gradually acquires the habits, attitudes, behavior, and language of those near him. The teacher accepts the child with his language potential as he enters the school and attempts to provide him with a basis for the development of desirable interaction with his peers and with his elders. The teacher is especially concerned with giving the child the kind of help that will enable him to communicate adequately with others, to understand them and to be understood by them.

A rich background of reading, travel, and social intercourse leads to enriched language expression. The children of any cosmopolitan school group vary greatly in experiential background. One function of the school is to ameliorate, insofar as possible, deficiencies in experiences by encouraging children to take part in all types of social activities. Meager experiences give rise to inadequate self-concepts. Deficiencies in a child's self-concept make it difficult for him to develop a proper attitude toward school or the teachers, or to acquire adequate perceptions and wholesome cultural values.

A child who finds the task of maturing physically an energy-sapping experience often does not have enough surplus energy to allow him to develop with any degree of success in oral expression. He is likely to be reticent in the classroom and slow in formulating his thoughts, and other children who have greater facility in speaking will respond before he has had an opportunity to organize his thinking. The reticent child is therefore apt to be timid and lacking in self-confidence and needs to be encouraged by the teacher to become an articulate member of the group.

Readiness to learn differs among children. Some children are slow learners and others are rapid learners. These differences show themselves in language learning as well as in other learning situations. The teacher needs to discover as much as possible about the mental capacity of each child and the learning habits that he has acquired in order to utilize the proper approaches which will motivate him to learn. With good motivation, all children can be helped to improve their language skills.

Educational Approaches. The teaching of language in the elementary school includes giving specific attention to language form, grammatical construction, vocabulary, and precise meanings of words. In general, careful attention should also be directed toward encouraging clearness in thinking, fluency of expression, and logical organization in both oral and written communication. Power in language ability can then develop as the child progresses through school.

Language skills may be developed either incidentally or in formally-organized language periods. For practice in fixing good habits, attention should be given to language in every lesson, on whatever subject. In the early grades, the teacher should focus on language usage, for the child needs to be helped to widen his experiences and to think clearly about them so that he can communicate many of them in a simple, direct way to others. In the upper grades, however, even if the lesson may be science or mathematics, the use of correct oral and written expression should be required. Proper language usage is important for success in any learning, and it should be a responsibility accepted by all teachers to help students develop this ability.

The study of formal grammar seems to have little effect on the development of language skill. In the elementary school, the work in formal grammar should probably be limited to the explanation of correct grammatical usage. Major emphasis should be given to contextual practice in correct form rather than to lengthy explanations of the reasons for using the particular form.

The child should be stimulated to do his best; he should be encouraged to compete with his own past performance, and by so doing, to improve his learning. He should be made aware of his progress, as in spelling or vocabulary, and should be commended for achievement. The too often neglected art of careful listening before speaking can be made a central emphasis in conversation. Interest in language can be developed through games, storytelling, recitations, dramatizations, oral and written reports, class discussions, creative writing, assembly programs, and written work contests. Since children in any grade or age group differ widely in their language ability, opportunities should be provided for individual progress through specific assignments. Supervised study can aid the less able pupil to attain normal achievement. Committee work in which the more able pupil may give help to his less able classmate is a valuable experience for both participants.

Psychology of Reading

The main purpose in reading is to obtain thoughts or ideas from the printed or written page. However, this purpose can be achieved only when the individual concerned puts his own thoughts into the symbols to which he is responding. In the past, excessive failures have accrued in the upper elementary grades, high school, and college because of students' failure to develop proper reading habits in earlier years, and it is essential that proper techniques of reading quickly and easily, and of comprehending what is read, be learned during the first years of schooling.

There are three types of reading: (1) oral reading in an audience situation, (2) silent vocalized reading, and (3) silent eye reading in which there is little or no vocalization. Since the child generally comes to the first grade with a vocabulary in which auditory images predominate, reading in school begins as oral reading and associations are made between sound and sight images and between sight and motor images. The child's perception develops gradually out of the mental images he obtains from the printed page. The printed word symbols are constantly transformed into mental responses and as the child's perceptual power increases, vocalization becomes unnecessary and is uneconomical in silent reading for information and enjoyment. To increase the speed of silent reading, the child should be encouraged to decrease and control his habit of vocalizing as soon as possible.

Factors Involved in Reading. Reading is not a simple function but is a complex of many coordinated skills. Among these must be included sound-sight associations, word meanings, eye-muscle control, voice-muscle control, recognition, recall, retention, judgment, use of material, and physiological factors. The child who has learned to speak correctly has a great advantage in learning to read. Oral expression and reading complement and reinforce each other.

Reading as Visual Exploration. Reading may be described as visual exploration. Photographic studies of eye movements show that during reading the eye moves along the line of reading material in jumps; the words are seen during the pauses, or fixations, between jumps. The eye then swings back and down to the next line. With less able readers, or in the reading of difficult material, there may be a backward swing of the eye or a regressive movement. The more skilled the reader the fewer pauses the eye must make and the fewer are the regressive movements. Both the difficulty of the material being read and the purpose of the reading influence the number of eye fixations in a line; a skilled reader may have only three fixations across the line on an average page.

Measurements have been made of the eye-voice span in oral reading, or the number of letters intervening between the letter which the eye is seeing and the letter which the voice is producing. The span is usually larger at the beginning of a line than at the end of the line. There is a wider recognition span in silent reading than in oral reading, but with correct practice the speed of oral reading can be improved. As ability to read increases, entire words and phrases are recognized as easily as letters.

Comprehension and Speed. Comprehension of reading material depends upon such factors as the extent of the child's vocabulary, his experiential background, the relative difficulty of the material, and the type of material. Boys tend to respond successfully to stories of adventure, science, and easy mechanics. Girls seem to prefer romantic types of reading material, although there is a growing interest in more diversified types of reading among girls in the upper grades.

In general, speed of reading is no deterrent to comprehension. Readers can be grouped, according to speed and comprehension, as high rate, good comprehension; slow rate, good comprehension; slow rate, poor comprehension, and so on. Where comprehension is good, speed can be improved through practice. On the other hand, excessive speed may encourage careless reading habits, especially in the reading of subject-matter requiring attention to details and thinking about what is being read.

Competence in reading increases with advances in age and grade. Generally, the rate of improvement is rapid in the early grades and then decelerates. Girls usually read more rapidly than do boys, but boys tend to comprehend and retain what they read better than do girls. There is a high positive correlation between intelligence and success in learning to read.

Educational Approaches. The child should be trained to skim, to read for details, to anticipate outcomes, and to critically evaluate reading material. His rate of silent reading should be flexible, depending upon the reading purpose and the content of the text. Skimming, for example, provides an overview of a complete story or topic, facilitating appreciation of the work as a whole. Reading for information requires close attention to details. Anticipation of outcomes enriches understanding as the child continues to read an assignment. Comment, discussion, and written reactions often contribute to fuller understanding.

At one time, training in oral reading was considered a "must," for it was mistakenly believed that proficiency in oral reading would insure skill in silent reading. Now it is believed that children require training to be able to learn to read silently. However, although the greater part of an individual's reading is silent, occasionally there is a need to do some oral reading. The needs of present-day culture, arising from radio and television, renewed interest in amateur theatricals, and the like, are creating new demands for competence in oral reading to insure good oral expression.

The teacher must be able to analyze the needs of each pupil so that he can give each one the remedial help that may be necessary. Poor reading may be caused by such factors as visual and auditory defects, congenital word blindness, limited vocabulary, improperly developed reading habits, too difficult material, or a lack of interest or motivation. Difficulties which may arise in oral reading include mispronunciation, repetition, and substitution.

Improvement in reading can best be achieved by providing many opportunities for practice in reading. The pupil should be encouraged to make his reading functional, that is, to use it in following directions for construction work, for games, in plays, and the like. Since a rich vocabulary enables a child to read more efficiently, all unfamiliar words should be learned as they are encountered. Where possible, the meaning of these words should be discovered through the context of the reading material, but when this is not feasible, the child should be encouraged to use the dictionary. A tendency in pupils to "slide over" difficult words or phrases in a reading assignment may be overcome by having them state the thought of the material in their own words.

Children ordinarily like to read. The teacher can help to make learning a satisfying experience for the child by not emphasizing the mechanics of reading but rather by allowing him a reasonable freedom of choice in the selection of reading material; by encouraging an interest in the better forms of literature without being unduly "preachy" or overstressing the content; and by appealing to the child's imitativeness, mastery, curiosity, and the desire for approval. The child should be introduced to individualized reading as soon as he is able to read independently. When adequate reading material is available, he is likely to be motivated to read for understanding and enjoyment.

Psychology of Spelling

The aim of the teaching of spelling in the elementary school is to make automatic the reproduction of the letters in about five thousand word units which constitute the writing vocabulary of the average eighth grade pupil. Ideally, correct spelling should be so spontaneous that the pupil, under normal conditions, is free to give his attention to the organization of his thoughts without having to stop to reason concerning the correct spelling of the words which he is using to express those thoughts.

Each child should be encouraged to develop a sense of responsibility for accurate spelling, and correct spelling habits should become as well established as are proper eating habits and desirable group manners. Competence in spelling increases generally with age, grade, and intelligence. Girls tend to excel boys in spelling, and this superiority may be the result of habits of attention to details emphasized in the early training of girls.

Factors Affecting Spelling Ability. Individuals differ in their ability to spell because of different interests, unequal social background, and varying earlier habits of learning. For example, the voracious reader tends to be a better speller than a child who spends a great deal of time on the playground. Poor spelling may result from certain physical defects, such as faulty visual perception, hearing difficulties, improper pronunciation of words, poor motor coordination, or poor handwriting. Social factors such as the home environment, poor speech habits in the family, or emotional disturbances may have an adverse effect upon a child's spelling, as may ineffective methods of study, lack of interest, and inadequate methods of teaching.

The most common spelling errors involve the transposition of letters, the omission of a letter or a syllable of a word, or the "tacking on" of a part of a word as one writes. The long word is not necessarily the most difficult one to spell, and common errors in spelling lie in the often used one and two syllable words.

Jones's list of "one hundred spelling demons" is made up of simple words such as *there, which, said, any,* and so forth.

Educational Approaches. The learning of spelling can be made interesting through correct presentation of spelling materials, the encouragement of successful achievement, sufficient and varied opportunities for practice, and constant checking for the fixing of proper habits. Children usually respond to the practical value of spelling and can be stimulated to serious and productive accomplishment.

Since correct spelling depends upon adequate response to an adequate stimulation, poor perception often is a cause of poor spelling. The student should be able to recognize the various elements in the word which he is to reproduce so that his response will be accurate in each detail. As many types of imagery as possible should be employed to help the student fix his response; appeals to visual, auditory, and muscular imagery are made by having the pupil see the word, form a mental image of it, hear it, pronounce it, and write it.

Some investigators claim that words presented in context so that their meaning is clear have a greater chance of being spelled correctly than have words presented in unrelated lists. This may be the case with words which the child has seen so frequently in context that he readily recalls their spelling. However, a certain amount of classroom drill on word lists is necessary and helpful. Before the teacher presents a group of words to a class for study, it is desirable to administer a pretest to determine the ability of each member of the class to spell the words on the list. Each pupil should be required to note and list correctly in his notebook the word or words he missed on the pretest.

Since the objectives of the teaching of spelling are practical, great care needs to be exercised in the choice of words to be studied. These must be within the pupil's possible and consistently developing use. Many standard word lists, organized in graded form, are available for classroom use and drill. The pupil also should be encouraged to develop his own spelling list of words with which he has particular difficulty, and to use this in conjunction with the standard lists.

Difficulties Within Words. When words are presented to the pupils, their attention should be called to difficulties within the words, especially to those syllables that are other than the first or last in the word. The memory process seems to function better for the syllables at the beginning or the end of the word than it does for those in the middle.

Discovery and Correction of Errors. Teachers should be constantly on the alert to discover spelling errors. An experienced teacher comes to note spelling errors in all written work and should train the pupil to do the same as he develops habits of correct spelling. Errors in spelling should be discovered, studied for the purpose of determining the type of error made, and corrected in a definite program of remedial teaching.

Spelling rules, once considered indispensable, are no longer popular. Time spent in memorizing the rule in spelling can be spent to better advantage in making automatic the correct letter sequence in words. For example, pupils might devote hours to studying the rule that *i* precedes *e* except after *c*, but there are so many exceptions that teachers might well decide to spend most of that time upon the practice of both the applications of and the exceptions to the rule. However, a few of the more generally applied rules can be presented to the pupils as interesting generalizations of word formation.

Psychology of Handwriting

The purpose of training in handwriting is to assist a student to develop sufficient skill in controlled hand movements that he may correctly produce those symbols that are required for written expression and communication. He is thus able to focus his attention on the organization of his thoughts as he attempts to express them in written form.

Psychological Factors. Handwriting is a sensory-motor skill, for it is a form of motor response to perceptual or ideational stimulation. It requires a complex set of reactions including in its successful performance the factors of external conditions, muscular adjustments of arm, hand, wrist, and fingers, and intelligent perception and memory of details.

The child's first muscular movements are uncontrolled; his perceptions are unrefined. The teacher of handwriting has a double duty of developing control of the finer movements of the hand

and fingers, and of guiding the pupil in increasing ability to perceive relations of size, space, slant, etc., of the letters to be formed. In handwriting, attention should be given to both quality and speed, but of the two, quality is the more important. However, the two usually go together, although various combinations may be found such as quick legible writers, slow legible writers, quick illegible and slow illegible penmen.

Developmental Patterns. There appears to be a steady rate of growth in handwriting ability through the elementary grades starting with the second year. In general, girls tend to perform better than boys, possibly because girls have superior abilities in making fine coordinations. Even though there seem to be distinct differences between the handwriting of men and women, any claims to accurate character reading by handwriting analysis have been discredited.

Handwriting should become automatic, and it can be made so only through attentive practice of the desirable motor reactions. Practice is best done with writing units that may be organized rhythmically, but time spent on rhythmic practice or drill as such can be used to better advantage in the rhythmic practice of the word or phrase units. With young children, in writing on the chalkboard or in the sand pile, the whole arm movement is employed; but as the handwriting becomes smaller and more controlled, forearm and finger exercises are needed.

Importance of Perception. In the development of handwriting habits, attention should be directed to the accurate perception and imitation of uniform slant of letters, proper alignment, careful and uniform letter formation, spacing and quality of line. The child must simultaneously perceive those relationships and translate his perceptions into written letters or combinations of letters. At first he sees and reproduces, then he may hear and reproduce; finally the process becomes mechanical to the point that continuous thought automatically is reduced to legible written symbols. In the beginning, this reaction process will be slow; but it is best to develop speed and quality together. In the early stages of learning, counting helps to direct the child's attention to the various parts of the letter and at the same time tends to accustom him to a speed of writing proper to his age and grade.

Lefthandedness. Lefthandedness presents something of a problem. If a child is slightly lefthanded, especially in the early grades, it is usually desirable to help him change to righthandedness in handwriting. However, if this change does not come easily it should not be forced and the child should be allowed to continue his handwriting training for his left hand, since the possible connection between handedness and speech difficulty is still being investigated.

Educational Approaches. The child should be encouraged to develop handwriting skill as a part of his fundamental equipment for successful living. Standardized handwriting scales are available and the child should be taught to rate his own handwriting in terms of a scale and to be interested in his own improvement. Analysis of his handwriting difficulties should begin early for the child so that his practice may be intelligent. The goal should be the achievement of the norm for his age or grade.

Practice periods should not be too long, especially in the lower grades. Ten to fifteen minutes daily is sufficient. By the end of the sixth year the child should have developed a satisfactory and legible handwriting with adequate speed. In general, except for those cases where specialized handwriting is needed, adult performance does not exceed 70 on the Ayres Scale. It is doubtful whether time devoted by the school to the development of quality beyond that point is well spent unless the individual has no other subject weakness.

Handwriting instruction often begins (in kindergarten or first grade) with the manuscript form, which resembles printed letters already known to many pupils. But some schools begin with cursive writing, while others change from manuscript to cursive forms during the first two or three grades. Although many school systems devote less time to the teaching of handsome cursive forms, probably because of the wider use of the typewriter and the increasing popularity of manuscript writing, this change in emphasis should not excuse careless or illegible penmanship in school or out of school.

Psychology of Mathematics

The purpose of the study of mathematics in elementary grades is to help the child organize those mathematical ideas which he has already acquired from perceptual experience and to introduce new concepts which he will need in the course of everyday living in our current science-and-technology-oriented society. The subject should be studied as an orderly arrangement of knowledge that is gained through scientific inquiry. Although concrete material may act as a stimulus, the child's mathematical response to this material is a mental one of organizing the relationships of experiences gained through the process of observation, selection, generalization, and abstraction. This process is valuable to the extent that it is exact, precise, and understood.

The classroom work in mathematics should be balanced among such factors as concepts, computational procedures, and problem solving. In order to attain precision in mathematical organization the pupil must have amassed adequate experiences and formulated basic concepts. However, the new mathematics in the elementary school strives to encourage the child to learn by discovery rather than by drill, to encourage creativity rather than the memorizing of rules. Its aim is to assist the child to discover relationships and to establish mathematical concepts that are fundamental to his gradually increasing ability to understand and to react to the higher mathematical concepts.

Psychological Factors. The child inherits from the race an entire system of number relations. Primitive man is said to have depended upon indefinite concepts of size and quantity (e.g., ideas of "muchness," "moreness," and "lessness"), and similarly a child's early experiences are indefinite except in terms of wanting "moreness"—of cake, for instance. Gradually this "moreness" gives way to a more definite "handful" and finally he discovers that *two* pieces of cake are preferable to only *one* piece. At first the child's number concepts must be tied up with concrete objects; then he develops the ability to make a connection between words as symbols of relationship; and the ultimate mathematical process is reached when he is able to complete the abstraction.

The learning of mathematics is a complex process embodying mental responses of perception, imagery, memory, and judgment. Even counting, the earliest experience in learning number relations, is difficult. Mathematics is essentially abstract, and the child shows mastery of the function when he is able to generalize abstractions. Mathematics is primarily a thinking process, and the teacher should encourage the pupil to do the thinking. Here, as in other fields of learning, the pupil must be given an opportunity to practice a function as he will be expected to use it, and there should be in the mathematics instruction a balance among such factors as discussion of basic concepts, learning of computational procedures, and practice in problem solving.

It is desirable that the child understand what he is doing, rather than merely follow a process learned by rote memory. It is now believed that the basic principles that underlie the fundamental mathematical operations can be understood by young children and should be taught to them. To do this, of course, requires much skill on the part of the teacher. Thus, children can be shown how to compare objects in a group or set, so that the same sum will be counted as 4 plus 1, 3 plus 2, etc. The meaning of number relationships can readily be developed in this way. Once the child understands the principles involved he is better able to apply them. Failure in complex mathematical computation in higher schooling often can be traced to failure of mastery of preliminary number concepts in elementary grades. If these concepts are not acquired in their proper sequence, the deficiencies accumulate and the learning of mathematics becomes more difficult for the child in each succeeding grade.

Problem solving is a complex process and includes a multiplicity of chances for error. There may be many reasons for a child's difficulty in this area: he may not understand the language in which the problem is presented; he may have difficulty with a computation because of poor grasp of fundamentals; he may not fully understand the operations involved; or he may not be able to evaluate the correctness of his answer.

Mathematical ability increases with age and grade. In general, boys and men show a slight superiority in mathematics over girls and women, but the difference is not enough to warrant separating the sexes in classes. Differences within each sex group far exceed the differences between the sexes. Achievement in mathematics does not show a high correlation with other school subjects such as reading, spelling, and composition. There are wide divergences in mathematical performance in every school grade.

Mathematical performance of children in the fourth grade, as measured by standardized tests of fundamentals and simple problem solving, may exceed the median score of eighth grade students in the same test.

Educational Approaches. The attitude of the teacher toward the mathematics lesson has much to do with the nature and extent of interest and of achievement of the pupil. From the counting stage upward, there should be emphasized at all times the practical application of mathematics in the child's daily activities. Therefore, although some pupils can be encouraged to do creative work for enrichment of understanding and the pure joy of problem solving, the course of study in mathematics should emphasize throughout all those types of computation or problems which have a practical value. The pupil can be stimulated to successful mastery of mathematics by associating classwork with school and home activities, and with worthwhile projects. In this way pupils can be taught the operational techniques of addition, subtraction, multiplication, and division at the same time as they are taught the fundamental principles that are basic to an understanding of these techniques.

Every teacher of mathematics should have a fundamental knowledge of number systems, including elementary number theory of primes, composites and divisibility, the nature of space, and how to apply the principles of arithmetic and geometry to the solution of practical problems. He must be able to adapt his procedures to the maturity and experience levels of his pupils, for children require considerable help to develop an attitude and comprehension of scientific inquiry. The teacher should be able to judge when and how to introduce drill that is essential to the overlearning of habits required in the mental processes in problem solving. While mathematics should not be fundamentally a drill subject, there are certain functions which must become automatic so that the thinking processes are free to concern themselves with the organization of the concepts. The teacher should help the child to automatize skills for combinations in addition, subtraction, multiplication, and division by furnishing him with sample situations that will enable him to carry out the mental activities. Whatever drill is introduced should follow, not precede, understanding.

Such aids or crutches as counting on the fingers, putting down the number carried in addition, and the like, while not detrimental to learning and often helpful in the initial stages, should be discouraged as early as feasible. Economy of performance is improved as the number of mental and motor steps required to speed the response to the stimulation is reduced.

There are many standardized tests in mathematics available for survey and diagnostic purposes, so arranged that the pupils' progress may be tested at regular intervals. The teacher is well advised to make abundant use of diagnostic tests in order to discover specific errors being made by the students. Remedial work should follow. The intelligent use of these tests can assure continuing improvement in classroom work.

Psychology of Social Studies

There have probably been few times when the need of adequate education in the social studies has been felt more keenly than at present. The political, social, economic, and educational problems of the day are being discussed constantly by all news media and shown pictorially on television. Young people are regularly being exposed to all varieties of social and intellectual stimulation. The social studies curriculum in the school aims to help students understand the past history of man and society in order better to understand the current civic, social, and economic conditions surrounding them, and to teach them ways they can make a meaningful contribution to the improvement of these conditions.

Psychological Factors. The attitude of the social science teacher is of great importance. He should have an understanding of present-day problems, the ability to interpret the present in terms of the past with as little bias as possible, and a sympathetic realization of what can be expected in the way of pupil comprehension on the different age and grade levels.

The teaching of social sciences presents several major problems which are now being studied because of their controversial nature. Among them are: (1) Shall the historical, the civic, and the geographical phases be combined and taught in terms of the pupils' living experiences; or shall history, civics, and geography be taught as separate subjects? (2) In either case, what shall be chosen from the great mass of available material as best suited to achieve desired aims? (3) How can the child best be stimulated toward desirable social response?

There is a growing tendency toward an integrated program of social studies in which much of purely factual memorization of military events, locations, and dates is omitted, and only those contributions of the past that have bearing upon present conditions are explored in their geographic setting. (Dates and major events are used as aids to fix and clarify the lessons of history.) Stimulation of the child's imagination through visits to places of historic, civic, and geographic interest, through well chosen magazines and pictures, biographies of famous persons, and the like, help him to become a citizen of a world far larger than his immediate surroundings. He needs to feel himself a necessary and integral part of this larger community and should be given training toward that end.

The child should be so guided in his development of social concepts that he will be able, with confidence, to do his own thinking. Although bright children may have this competence, the average child is probably unable, at least before he has reached the sixth year of the school course, to appreciate logical and chronological social development. It is the duty of the teacher to attempt to arouse his imagination and stimulate him to use a proper questioning attitude, to encourage a desire for further study, to develop an appreciation of social behavior suitable to his age and grade, and to arouse in the child a desire to perform his social responsibilities.

Educational Approaches. All children need not be trained in the same pattern. Within their respective capacities, desirable social attitudes of tolerance, civic honesty, understanding of other peoples and countries, respect for the rights of others, and democratic principles of government should be fostered. With the slower children, emphasis should be placed upon the specific duties associated with desirable membership in a community. This training should be accompanied by simple examples taken from their immediate environment. Brighter children may be guided in constructive criticism (within their comprehension limits) of past and existing conditions, and may be stimulated to make simple suggestions for future improvements.

The teaching of the social sciences, or geography and history separately, may be motivated by such incidents as the various national and state holidays, or important news items such as the issues involved in an election. This type of teaching is valuable in the development of ideals. The teaching may be a somewhat formal presentation of certain historic or geographic units in their relation to the pupil's life. Examples of this type are projects dealing with our American Indian or colonial forebears or our South American neighbors.

One of the most successful aids in teaching the social studies to young children is the use of simple biography, for a child's imagination is stirred by tales of heroism, unselfishness, and industry. However, the two extremes of emphasis should be avoided. On the one hand, in an attempt to develop interest in the biographical story so much attention may be centered upon the hero's accomplishments that he is made to appear as a paragon of all virtues, impossible of imitation by the average individual. A counter attempt to show that the hero was quite human may lead to an emphasis on certain petty failings, suggesting to the pupil weak excuses for his own shortcomings.

Active participation in plays, construction projects, and tours of exploration are excellent means of arousing the interest of the pupil in a particular problem under study. Care should be taken, however, that the details of the project do not become so important in themselves that historic or geographic influence is overshadowed. For example, we should not be concerned with training artisans in the craft of wigwam construction, but should attempt to develop an appreciation of the entire culture of the American Indian. Pupils should be encouraged to interrelate and integrate specific information in the social sciences as the basis for general concepts and conclusions.

Psychology of Elementary Science

The average child is innately curious about the physical world in which he lives. In his early years he is constantly asking questions concerning the "whyness" of natural phenomena. Utilizing this natural interest as a starting point, the teacher of science in the elementary school should endeavor to assist the child in discovering general principles and concepts which will help him understand his own immediate environment and develop his interest in the larger physical world in which he lives.

The child should have some knowledge of animals, birds, trees, and plants. Change of season, the stellar world, climate, weather, space travel, and the like should be made to mean more to him than casually observed and passively accepted phenomena. An appreciation of nature should be developed and an attitude of scientific inquiry should be acquired.

Psychological Factors. The child is not naturally cruel with other forms of life. Ordinarily, he does not deliberately destroy flowers or shrubbery, or tease animals. Such behavior is a matter of habit formation beginning with curiosity. It is possible to develop in him, through correct teaching, an attitude of affection and care rather than of destruction.

Boys tend to be interested in the manipulative and experimental aspects of science; girls are inclined toward the personal and aesthetic aspects of the subject. Both boys and girls are interested in animals but their interests vary according to their age groups: children in the middle grades respond to the appearance, food, and habits of animals; older children are interested in their geographical location and their life history.

Educational Approaches. In the study of science, the child in a rural area has some advantages over the urban child. He is able to experience directly what the urban child must acquire vicariously. However, as methods of travel and communication are improved, the child who has never seen a cow, for example, is becoming less common. To stimulate his pupils to become interested in and understand science the teacher needs (1) to discover the experiential strengths and lacks of each child, (2) to provide experiences to enable each child to obtain an enriched background of knowledge, and (3) to motivate each child in such a way as to help him increase his interest in science.

The teacher should organize the science classwork into continuing units based upon the interest of the pupils and the difficulty of the material. Pupils can be encouraged to share in the planning of the classes so that their special interests can be explored. The information thus gained about pupils' interests can also aid the teacher in selecting new areas to be investigated by the students.

A minimum of emphasis should be given to the mastery of purely technical material. Concepts are best retained when they are acquired by functional learning, by seeing and doing; and therefore, when possible, it is desirable for children to devote more time to observing concrete objects and handling them than to reading about them. Where technical apparatus is involved, demonstrations by the teacher can help make concrete objects become more meaningful for children. Above-average students can be encouraged to pursue their interests beyond general class level by additional reading and developing special projects. Television programs and motion pictures are often useful for motivation and integration of data, as supplementary aids to instruction.

The teacher should encourage students to discover things for themselves, and both within and without the schoolroom there should be as much contact with the learning material as possible. Teacher and class should together keep abreast of new developments in science. Well planned field trips should become an important part of the teaching-learning program. Parks, botanical gardens, zoological gardens, beaches, and similar areas can be used to give first-hand experiences in science to children. Seasonal activities and opportunities should be taken into account in the planning for a variety of experiences.

Psychology of Health Education

The aims of health education in the elementary school are practical. These aims include (1) correct body development, increase in motor skills, and growth in recreational and social values through physical activities such as games, corrective exercises, and dances; (2) strengthening of the physical constitution by developing good sanitary and health habits, especially those related to personal cleanliness, proper diet, and basic care of the body and mind, with sufficient appropriate exercise, rest, recreation, suitable clothing, etc., and prevention or remedial action in regard to illness and accidents; and (3) prevention of physical disturbances (or correction of defects disclosed) through periodic examination of the teeth, eyes, ears, heart, and the like.

Psychological Factors. The young child has an active imagination and tends to imitate, and is relatively uncontrolled in his movements. The work in health education should center around the setting up of simple health habits. Through organized games, dances, and the like, there should be developed muscular control and social consciousness, as well as cultural and artistic appreciation.

As the child matures, there is an increasing awareness of himself as an individual who possesses a strong desire to excel in something. Competition is a strong incentive to the improvement of skills. The child also responds to the approval of his schoolmates, and admires one who excels in baseball, football, and dancing. All of these qualities influence the individual in his physical and health activities.

Educational Approaches. Explanations for desirable health habits should be simple but correct; systematic practice of health habits should be encouraged. Care should be taken lest so much approval be given to the reported following of health rules that children either try to do the impossible or, failing in this, develop habits of dishonesty. Development of habits of good sportsmanship, honesty, accuracy, and obedience should be outgrowths of the health program. To the elementary school child the health education activities should be a joy and a satisfaction. The teacher should provide an example of self-discipline, emotional stability, and physical efficiency worthy of emulation by the children.

Psychology of Music

Music and art merit a place of distinction in the elementary school curriculum. In our complex modern society, there is an increasing need for children to be given opportunities for desirable emotional experiences. The individual is not only a more or less adequately functioning series of muscular skills, or a more or less organized set of mental connections; he is also a highly complex combination of emotional reactions. In the past, the schools have probably given too little attention to the development of healthy emotional behavior and its direction into creative and rewarding channels.

The aim of music teaching is two-fold: (1) to improve musical performance, which should include singing, instrumental music, composition, conducting, and the dance, with individual and group participation, (2) to develop musical appreciation, emphasizing sensitivity and discriminating taste, enthusiasm for music, and enduring interest in music as an emotional outlet, a source of relaxation and inspiration, and an important aspect of personal equipment and community culture.

Psychological Factors. Children enjoy listening to music and engaging in its production. They tend to express themselves rhythmically. In school they look forward to the music period unless great emphasis is placed on the understanding of the techniques of performance or on the memorization of musical facts. Children delight in creating their own simple melodies. There are few children who cannot be encouraged to participate in some form of musical activity. If they are not interested the fault is usually not in their lack of musical ability but is due to acquired inhibitions resulting from previous unsatisfying experiences.

Coordinate with the beginning of competence in music should come the ability to appreciate musical selections and to be able to discriminate between types of music. The musical tastes of children are easily influenced by environmental factors. Children respond in emotionally desirable ways to good music whether it is current or not.

Educational Approaches. Songs selected for children should reflect their own personal interests. The words and meanings should not go beyond their power of comprehension. It is much more desirable to have simple songs produced correctly and with understanding than to have more difficult selections rendered badly.

The elementary school child needs to know a minimum concerning the meaning of such terms as pitch, intensity, and duration of tone. The child needs to develop accuracy of production in simple and suitable musical selections and should be able to appreciate the music that he experiences.

There is available a great mass of good musical material. This includes songs sung by the children themselves, musical performances of gifted schoolmates, radio and television programs, and recitals given in the school by artists. Care needs to be taken to make sure that the child's appreciation is real rather than mere verbal responses. Oral or written statements of music appreciation may be little more than attempts at pleasing the teacher. Better measures of appreciation include the attitude displayed by the pupil as a listener (influenced by external factors), growing competence in music, and a desire to select good music. Throughout the curriculum adequate attention must be given to folk music of contemporary cultures and the music of past societies.

Standardized tests have been devised to determine music abilities and knowledges, whether native or acquired. There has not yet been devised an adequate method to determine objectively the extent to which music may stimulate pleasurable activity, provide healthful enjoyment, or achieve significant appreciative values.

Psychology of Art

One of the early modes of expression of the young child is that of pictorial presentation. The individual needs systematic training in careful observation and technical skill as a means of communicating his thoughts through drawing. In the elementary school the aims of art study should be to acquire facility in (1) the accurate and pleasing reproduction of simple objects, both from observation and from memory, (2) creative expression in simple design and other art forms, and (3) appreciation of art in its various forms on different age and grade levels, emphasizing design and beauty, proportion, color, perspective, etc., in buildings, sculpture, paintings, objects in museums, and common objects of everyday life, including personal belongings.

Psychological Factors. The young child scribbles pictures of his home, his daddy, his pussy, as means of expression. As he grows older he begins to recognize the extent to which meaning can be put into or obtained from drawing. If properly encouraged, he will tend to gain control of the media of art as a means of expression and communication.

Drawing is a complex function. To draw, a child must see, remember, have a sense of space relation; recognize line, rhythm, and proportion; and perhaps be able to discriminate color. Verbal intelligence, as measured by tests, beyond the early development period is not highly correlated with drawing ability. Competence in drawing needs to be considered in terms of certain factors of drawing which may or may not be the result of learning, or which may or may not be innate apart from intelligence. As the child develops skill, his work reflects increasingly his own personality and individual experience.

Educational Approaches. In creative work in drawing and related fields, attention should be placed upon the need of the pupil to continue his creative work until he has produced his best. There may be undesirable psychological effects if the child is permitted to attempt many expressions in drawing, but leaves each in a crude and unfinished state without the satisfaction which comes from fulfillment. The teacher has the responsibility to provide sufficient guidance to facilitate reasonable, successful achievement without undue sacrifice of creativity and self-direction by the pupils. But adult or professional standards of accomplishment should not be imposed or expected.

Deep appreciation should not be expected of the young child. Elementary school children should be stimulated to understand simple beauty of line, rhythm, color, form, and composition so that their appreciation may be influenced both by their emotions and by their intelligence.

The young child is afforded opportunities for artistic expression without regard for refined detail through such activities as clay modeling, finger painting, and easel painting. Children can give and exchange free expression during these activities, and the teacher can encourage, commend, and perhaps offer suggestions for improvement. There should be gradual development in terms of the child's emotional and intellectual maturation.

Chapter 15
Psychology of Subject Areas in the Secondary School

The entering secondary school student, as an individual, has had, in common with his fellow students, certain basic experiences of elementary school training. However, individual differences recognizable during the earlier years are still present. The individual's day-by-day habits were developed in his past, but continue to determine the trend of his present behavior. The wise teacher makes use of these behavior influences in his attempt to reach the student.

Psychological Needs of the Adolescent

The emotional life of the adolescent is greatly enriched during these secondary school years because during this stage of his development he experiences an increasing number of stimuli that did not arouse him a few years earlier. The maturing of his physical, intellectual, emotional, and spiritual life provides a challenge to the secondary school teacher. This challenge is being met by the application of psychological principles in the teaching-learning situation.

Adolescent Drives. Every adolescent has potent dynamic drives that serve as strong motivating forces. They influence his thoughts, his attitudes, his emotions, and his overt behavior. Some of these drives grow out of physical, life-sustaining needs; others are acquired through experience. The adolescent has inner desires for social recognition and approval. Whether his overt behavior is motivated by inner drives or by social factors, there always is an impulse toward action. His overt behavior usually reflects the impact of all of the influences that affect him at one time. In general, the adolescent strives to satisfy organic needs, to achieve a constructive goal or purpose, or to gain social prestige.

The teacher needs to recognize the nature and strength of drives and direct the energy of the adolescent in such a way as not to injure him or the society in which he lives. The adolescent needs help to control the sex urge which is one of the strongest and most important influences in his psychic life. Conflicts arise between expression of this urge and the restrictions and inhibitions of social conventions and moral codes. The persistency of the sex drive makes necessary a psychological development of the individual for the good of himself and of society.

Psychological Considerations. The learning process functions in the individual's life from the cradle to the grave. The teacher in the secondary school should teach in such a way that orientation, integration, and assimilation of learning will occur. The insightful teacher who is willing to apply the principles of teaching to the learning needs of each of his students is making use of psychological approaches in his teaching.

The teacher should not lose sight of the fact that education is essentially interested in producing a socially useful person. This does not mean that conflict should always be avoided since, through it, a developing person arrives at adjustments which better enable him to do whatever a changing social order requires. An adolescent with a trained intellect is able to make these adjustments provided he experiences those influences that have been found helpful to citizens in the social order.

Psychology of Mathematics

Mathematics is concerned with the development of adequate concepts of number and symbols and their quantitative relationships. Since these are difficult concepts to learn, the day-by-day experiences of the individual should be utilized to put meaning into them. It is important to develop the concept of measurable quantity.

Psychological Factors. The secondary school student should, perhaps, be introduced to geometry before algebra because he already has had much experience with the data of geometry. He has experienced space since early infancy. He has made many simple measurements involving space relationships through his early years of life, even though he may not be skilled in space perception. Geometry is the specialized subject that helps the student understand space and spatial relations. The advance of scientific knowledge requires that the individual be kept informed on what is happening in the field of space exploration. Man has been able to extend his knowledge in outer space largely because of his interest in doing so and because he has developed instruments which enable him to explore and measure space.

Space can be experienced by everyone. It is experienced as a blend of sensations such as color-muscle, sound-muscle, and touch-muscle sensations. Space is always present, is uniform in its qualities, and is material upon which the child's mind is constantly reacting. Of course, a trained scientist experiences space differently from a casual observer and eventually fits the materials of space into an orderly system.

As an individual experiences space, the perceptions that he forms are at first of the *whole setting*. The details are brought into his consciousness only as his attention is directed to them as separate experiences. Since the development of the scientific attitude toward space has usually been neglected in the elementary school, the student in the secondary school may have difficulty in bridging the gap between his earlier mathematics experiences and the highly formalized and symbolized space structure to which he is subjected in geometry. Unless he has an understanding teacher, he will then proceed to memorize this elaborate system of abstractions and generalizations, often without comprehension. Unfortunately, mere rote learning does not insure a solid grasp of the basic principles and propositions in geometry. To help the student generalize, the teacher should direct the learner's attention to the proper logical and spatial order of the essentials in space. This will guide the student in correct thinking as well as in formulating correct conclusions.

The abstractions involved in learning algebra present even more difficult problems to the student than are encountered in geometry. It is true that the student has already been introduced to number symbols; however, they were more or less attached to something concrete. In arithmetic he could perceive that *four* apples stood for something concrete, thereby making the symbol 4 mean something to him.

Algebra involves most of the ideas found in arithmetic and, in addition, many more abstractions. Even though many of the thinking processes are similar to those in arithmetic, the student may become bewildered when he is called upon to learn a new number language. This new and abstract language requires that mathematical combinations rather than particular numbers command the concentrated attention of the students. Then, too, the symbols used in algebra are constantly taking on a different value in terms of arithmetic particular-number systems. It is this working with symbols with no assigned values and the use of them in evolving particular values that is especially difficult for the student to comprehend. It also is difficult for the student to discover that algebra is largely concerned with combinations of indefinite quantities.

In a general mathematics course, the student should be helped, at as many points as possible, to make practical application of the principles involved. With the changing college entrance requirements, all mathematics courses are already adopting a better approach by drawing attention to the fact that the mathematical sciences present many common reasoning procedures. In generalizing, the facts that hold in one science are equally true in all. It is this attitude of mind—the emphasis on logic, decision making, and importance of underlying principles—rather than the learning of a stipulated number of symbols, that needs to be cultivated. Where students have had the benefit of learning through the new mathematics, they have found many valuable elements which serve them well in other sciences.

Educational Approaches. The adolescent needs help in developing the ability to do reflective thinking. He needs to learn to interpret the examples given in his textbooks and to solve original examples. He thus can learn to be resourceful. He soon discovers that his success in mathematics is dependent both upon his knowledge of the subject and his ability to use this knowledge in dealing with available data.

It is not easy to measure progress or extent of achievement in mathematics. This is true of both the mental processes involved and the accomplishment in terms of results obtained by the students. Among the factors to be weighed in measuring progress are the nature of the abstractions being studied, the degree of difficulty of the problems or exercises, the amount of time available to the student, the mathematical background of the individual student, and the extent of the student's reliance on memory and/or reasoning during the solving of exercises or problems.

The teacher of mathematics should strive primarily to give the students an understanding of the mathematical symbols and their meanings and of the operational relationships among the symbols. Mere memorization of the symbols should be avoided. The desired understanding can be achieved through the use of appropriate teaching techniques and by a careful study of the learning capacity of each student. In order to stimulate all students it will be necessary for the teacher to utilize a variety of procedures: the visual, the auditory, the motor, the association of ideas, and so forth.

Individuals differ in the nature and extent of their difficulties in the learning of mathematics. The teacher should give attention to each of these difficulties, taking care that his assistance will help rather than hurt the learning process of the student. The student should be permitted and encouraged to think for himself.

Psychology of Language Arts

More time is devoted to the study of language in the secondary school than to any other subject, for as a means of intercommunication, as an instrument in the thought process, language is indispensable. Included in the language arts are speech, literature, grammar, and composition.

Psychological Factors of Language. Language involves a series of abstractions that must be understood. In order to use these symbols (words) intelligently, we must not only know the meaning of the respective symbols but must know the relationships that exist among the various combinations of symbols.

To the person who first has learned another language, the English language seems to lack any logical sequence; it is irregular and confusing. If the listener does not have the experiential background, a series of words (a sentence) may sound like a drawn out hum when uttered in rapid fashion, but a person who understands the symbols can interpret the sounds. For example, in a restaurant a customer mumbles his lunch order to a waitress. Although she may not hear it distinctly, she gets the order correct because the combinations of sounds used have come to mean but one thing to her.

Language is a means of socially useful communication which originated in the efforts of human beings to respond to their mutual needs. It is essential to all the mental processes. If an individual is conscious he is conscious of something which, if expressed, must be made known through some form of language. The functioning of language and the thought processes cannot be separated. Human beings are rhythmic in nature and the motor processes of language are likewise rhythmical. This rhythm varies among people and accounts for many of our likes and dislikes of expressions, either oral or written, used by others.

Language is a part of our social heritage and has become more and more complicated through the years. Some systematization has taken place. For example, certain word endings—such as mortgagee, teacher, realtor, and the like—tend to suggest a particular person. These forms did not just happen but evolved in definite ways and were refined and adopted through usage. By familiarizing himself with commonly used prefixes and suffixes, the student will be able to understand new words as he encounters them. At one time in the schools an attempt was made to analyze words exhaustively, in minutest detail; that procedure gave way to study of the use of words as expressed through sentences or parts of sentences.

The human being has a tendency toward unit reaction. The entire body mechanism responds to a stimulus and the presence of a unit idea is helpful to performance. Therefore, psychology recognizes that *words* rather than *letters* should be taught, and even sentences rather than words, especially when they serve as a completed unit. If more attention would be given to the usage of language units and more practice given to their correct form, an intensive study of formal grammar might safely be deferred to the college period of study. The adolescent is concerned with expression and formulates his ideas in units. He has no need for the disturbing labels that are given to the parts of the unit which he already has mastered. Just as the adolescent who is learning to drive does not need to know all of the parts of the automobile, so can the student rely on experts to guide him in expression without knowledge of the grammar involved. The teacher should realize that language habits used in a great variety of situations may become habitual modes of expression, difficult to correct or improve; and effective, appropriate forms should be encouraged and expected in all subjects and activities of the curriculum.

Educational Approaches. The teacher, at all times, should plan his procedure so as to promote the proper mental attitude in the student before calling on him to recite. Getting the proper start in oral expression often accounts for the difference between a good and a poor recitation. Clear enunciation and other technical skills should be developed through application in conversation, conferences, recitations, dramatizations, and a variety of audience situations. If a student's voice is satisfying to himself it gives him that confidence which is helpful to continued fluency. It is possible to speak fluently for a long time if there is no undue emotional disturbance; breathing can function normally, thereby assisting rather than inhibiting fluent speech.

Language is one of the instruments through which appreciation is developed. The teacher should not only recognize that appreciation is both intellectual and emotional but he should make it possible for each student to be given an opportunity to experience deep appreciation. To make this most effective the teacher needs to keep in mind the many differences that prevail among students in their respective responses. These differences include such factors as rhythm, experience, emotional behavior, and interest. The depth of appreciation will depend largely upon the number of emotion-arousing elements present as compared with the number of intellectual factors inherent in the situation for any student. Literature, for example, should stimulate the student toward appreciation as well as beauty of expression. Analytical dissection of a story or poem should not be overemphasized, for many students can often keenly appreciate a literary work, and enjoy it immensely, without being expert critics or sometimes even without being able to express or share their reactions. A reasonable amount of analysis and oral or written discussion may, however, be helpful to students seeking greater clarity or fuller appreciation of a literary work.

The teacher of literature has a far-reaching responsibility. The attitude which the student is likely to assume in his adulthood is determined in the secondary school. If the student is compelled to analyze to the point of boredom selections from the masterpieces of literature, he will be driven from the good to the frothy and inconsequential. The literary selections studied in the secondary school should be so treated that they will become the companions of the student, urging him on to further delightful hours with other selections of their kind.

Psychology of Foreign Language

Foreign languages have enjoyed a prominent place in the secondary school curriculum. The advancement in the means of communication during the present century has presented a practical as well as an intellectual need for the mastering of several of the foreign languages. It is perhaps asking too much to hope for the adoption of any one language for universal usage. Even though this were possible, it still would be desirable to preserve, through their language, the rich heritage of the various peoples of the earth.

Psychological Factor. Because of the changing attitude toward the function of secondary education in America it is too much to expect each and every student to pursue the study of a foreign language. If some students have difficulty in mastering the abstractions in their own language, it seems unwise to add to their confusion by expecting such students to learn the abstractions of a second language.

Educational Approaches. Education for international understanding motivates students to an awakened interest in the habits and customs of contemporary people of other countries. More traveling is being done, hence greater practical need is felt for competence in a second language. It is generally agreed that if one is to understand the people of a nation, it is best done through the vernacular of that country. This involves considerably more facility than ability to translate.

Efforts need to be and are being made to help the student master the foreign language in such a way as to enable him to think in that language. It must be recognized by the teacher that various mental functions are involved depending upon whether the student is learning to speak the language, to read it, or to translate it. It should be noted, however, that translation is a specialized skill which may often impede progress in the natural use of a foreign language, by introducing factors that retard development of a "feeling for the language" and the ability to think in the foreign language. The successful student is able to master large units of the language and to use them readily both in speaking and in reading.

Successful methods used for the teaching of a foreign language follow closely the procedures used by the child in mastering the vernacular. Insofar as possible the teaching of a foreign language should embody the practices and expressions as given by the users of that language in order that a more complete appreciation of that people may be realized. There should be more functional teaching and less testing of progress in the foreign language. The student who is taught to use the language is the one who really learns it. Listening to recorded conversation, or to the teacher's speech and his own responses, as in language laboratories, and speaking and writing the language in life situations, are especially helpful procedures.

Psychology of the Social Sciences

Even though the social sciences were brought into the organized curriculum comparatively recently, they are nonetheless gaining a most significant place in the contemporary school, which emphasizes processes of orderly thinking and careful judgment. Civic problems and current events and issues have formed so large a part of our daily experience that too many citizens have taken them more or less for granted, neglecting to bring them actively under the focus of attention and reflecting on them from an objective, critical point of view.

Many of the social problems are so delicate that they cannot be entrusted completely to teachers who are not specifically trained to deal with them. Sex problems are an example. These problems are both individual and social. It is generally recognized that too few teachers have had sufficient training and experience in the handling of these problems to enable them to provide expert guidance in them. However, every teacher should be a good citizen, whom the pupils will seek to emulate, one who will guide them in their constructive group activities, student organizations, methods of study and interpretation in social science, and in their relationships to the home and other institutions, so that the best ideals and practices in the community will be exemplified in the school program.

Psychological Factors. Problems inherent in such matters as unfair use of influence or "pull" in society, the relations between nation states, labor unions, and political and social organizations, are so complex and vital that any attempt to chart their effects on the lives of individuals in a scientific way becomes very difficult. The social sciences are still formulating their hypotheses and collecting their data in a constantly changing world. The ideals of the people, the morals, the customs, the attitude toward the family as a social institution, the place and function of the church, the form of government to be desired, are all in a constant state of flux. These elusive data and changing hypotheses make it difficult to produce an exact science. In a rapidly changing world, it is not easy for the student to understand and practice the ideals to which adults are giving approval but too often are negating in everyday living.

A look at the past reveals that in former times our needs were considerably fewer. The social structure was simpler then, and the means of communication were not as efficient. Time was thought of in terms of large units; a variation of a few minutes or even hours did not matter much. Recently, the precise timing required for train and airplane schedules, the telephone, radio, and television have shown us the importance of a small unit of time. Today, economic and social planning is necessary in the conduct of business and in almost all phases of life. As programs of social planning are perfected, hopefully the social sciences will be put on a more scientific basis.

There is wide disagreement about causes of and solutions for many of our social problems. It is difficult to make satisfactory judgments because we cannot control most of the stimuli which affect our judgments. It is equally difficult to measure mass reactions adequately. What is desirable is a course of training which will assist students in acquiring those attitudes and habits of action which make for desirable leadership in certain social functions and desirable followership in others. Training in both leadership and followership in social settings must be given a prominent place in the educational program.

Educational Approaches. History and geography early found a place in the school curriculum because they were readily formalized and organized in their spatial and time elements. A plot of ground could be identified, labeled, and the name learned; happenings in the life of a nation could be recorded and learned in proper sequence. Such has been the nature of these subjects. It has sometimes been difficult to convince school directors that a new point of view in the teaching of social sciences is necessary. Too often they underestimate the significance of the relationships existing between time and space in the events that happen in the lives of human beings. But the traditional emphasis upon chronological arrangement of facts in history is slowly changing as the challenge of writing functional textbooks is meeting with success.

Much of social studies should be taught as something to be lived rather than something merely to be learned as a store of information. The teaching of geography should go hand-in-hand with the teaching of history and community civics. Thus, integrated programs of instruction will explore historical events and trends starting at the local setting and moving in all directions throughout the world.

Effective advancement in social studies can be made by the student if he learns to formulate scientific abstractions and generalizations based on the data available to him. These conclusions should be based upon all the information and experiential background which the individual can muster, and opportunities for critical analysis and interpretation should be provided repeatedly in the school program.

In human relations, a student too often learns a fact but does not learn it in a setting which will provide him with an adequate understanding of it; consequently his judgments are biased. This bias becomes apparent in observable attitudes toward differing political views, or toward any of a number of controversial social problems. To keep pace with these changes requires the student to be adaptable to new conditions and processes. To this end a highly trained imagination will be helpful.

The student is being trained for an economic world. Heretofore, he entered industry through the apprenticeship procedure. Today, however, with the centralization of industrial activities this privilege is being denied to him. The student should be given guidance and assistance in appraising his own abilities and should be helped to recognize and understand his own vocational interests. Whatever he learns in the area of these vocational interests should be as functional as possible for him; formalization of occupational facts or of social data should be avoided. In the social sphere, the student should experience social leadership through participation in student self-government and other organizations which will provide training for active participation in civic and community life.

Psychology of the Natural Sciences

One of the greatest opportunities in teaching comes to the science teacher. He has many opportunities to help his pupils (1) acquire the spirit of inquiry, (2) cultivate an attitude of independent judgment, (3) develop an attitude of openmindedness, (4) acquire fundamental truths, (5) view broadly the forces that influence their surroundings, (6) acquire appreciation of their environment, and (7) become skilled in scientific problem solving.

Psychological Factors. In all sciences the student should be cognizant of the many problems that confront him. These problems should be clearly defined and their solutions striven for by patient accumulation of facts. The proper generalizations should be made on the basis of such facts. Often the student does not follow a scientific procedure because he has not been convinced that that method is superior to the treatment which he has been giving the data.

Scientific principles have come into being as a result of more than mere observation. They are principles to be used rather than mere facts to be learned. An understanding of the facts involved and of the relationships existing among them, and the ability to use these data correctly, are most valuable steps in the learning procedure.

In the past, some teachers stressed content and information in their courses, approaching science as a field of knowledge to be learned by merely acquiring facts. Fortunately, today the project and problem approach is widely used. This method is both logical and psychological; while the student is acquiring the information, he is learning how to use the scientific method of collecting facts, of organizing them to deal with the problem at hand, and of using systematic methods of experiencing, reasoning, and generalizing.

The student should make daily applications of the knowledge learned to as many life situations as possible. This integrating of knowledge gradually helps him develop the ability to make generalizations, through the use of principles and theories that serve as unifiers for a large series of facts. It should be emphasized, however, that the student is not expected to become expert as a scientist, for he is limited in experience and in the possible range of his attention—factors likely to condition the results even though the best scientific procedures are followed.

Educational Approaches. In the teaching of science, emphasis should center around problems and projects that are common to the experiences of the students. Development of a scientific attitude of mind is encouraged by following the logical order of procedure, using the inductive method of presentation and an analytical attack on the problem that confronts the student.

The science laboratory should be used extensively. Students should be presented with problems and encouraged to work them out, learning by doing. The experiments should be simple and so chosen that an understanding of the scientific principles is attained while new knowledge is acquired. The teacher should be aware that the performance of laboratory exercises is difficult for most students, but it is advisable for him to guide the activities of the students rather than complete the experiments for them. Field trips may serve as a valuable supplement to class and laboratory work.

There is a danger of oversimplification in science. There still is too great a focus on specific sciences rather than on the development of scientific analysis and reflective thinking. General science has been introduced into the curriculum for the purpose of correcting the limitations in attempts to master the several sciences separately, even though some of the sciences included in a general course are usually not offered in the typical secondary school. Nevertheless, the subject matter specialist frequently insists upon the traditional practice of concentrating upon one field of science.

Psychology of the Fine Arts

The fine arts are the sources from which many of our rich experiences are obtained; they provide emotion-arousing situations for the purpose of desirable appreciation. Where they have gained admittance into the curriculum, they have demonstrated that they are more than mere "fads and frills." The casual observer thinks only of the subjective side of the fine arts, but there is a technical side as well. The school should concern itself with both and should not formally separate them.

The attitude of the school toward fine arts is different from that of the public. The difference is partly explained on the basis of requirements for college entrance. Credits obtained in the study of fine arts usually are not recognized by colleges. Since the student is denied this practical value of the subjects, an appeal must be made to his aesthetic and emotional values. Unfortunately, the student is often inadequately trained in these life values.

When it is possible for every child who wishes to do so to learn to play a musical instrument, and when each student is instructed in the techniques of drawing, then outlets will be provided for appreciation in these areas. Students will be afforded an opportunity for expression and be given a sound basis of understanding, for it is through adequate education that the fine arts become appreciated.

Psychology of Music. Music grew out of the interest of people in rhythm. Originally, the dancers and serenaders were more interested in the rhythm than they were in the music (noise) they produced. With the development of modern musical instruments, a high quality of melody could be produced. These tones, varying in pitch and timbre, can be produced in such rhythm that the individual will be stimulated to some degree of emotional appreciation. However, if these rhythmical and harmonious sounds are to be produced effectively, long periods of training in special skills are required.

The appreciation of music depends upon the developed motor responses of the individual. Basic understanding and proper emotional experience are necessary to attain full appreciation of the harmony in music. The individual's mode of reaction should be discovered; then he should be trained in appreciation rather than in artistic production. It must be remembered that an individual's appreciation is a personal matter.

Students differ greatly in their ability to discriminate tone. The ear must be trained not only to hear sounds, but to interpret and discriminate as well. Difficulty in tonal discrimination may be due to lack of sensitivity in the sense organs, or it may be due to lack of attention on the part of the listener.

Courses in the appreciation of music are offered in many secondary schools. Through the use of phonograph records, radio and television programs, and through their own instrumental or vocal performances, teachers have an opportunity to encourage in their pupils an appreciation of the best in music. By combining classroom instruction with visits to concert and operatic performances outside the school, the teacher can awaken students to the value of music and to an understanding of what the great composers have attempted to convey in their compositions.

Psychology of Graphic Art. Instruction in drawing in the secondary school should emphasize appreciation rather than skill of production. Courses in graphic art are offered to help the student acquire better understanding of the use of both form and color.

However, long training is required before a student can hope to develop great skill in form and in the correct use of color.

The school should attempt to train the student in art appreciation even though he may never develop sufficient insight or technical skill for excellent reproduction. Appreciation of art is dependent partly upon the sympathy which an individual manifests toward the objects in his environment. This cultivated feeling is a result of cumulative experiences and is affected by varied social situations.

A combination of productive and appreciative values is being brought about in many secondary schools through well-developed courses in poster design, architectural design, costuming, advertising copy, and illustrative work for school newspapers and magazines. Both the aesthetic and practical bases of this work appeal strongly to the adolescent. The results are sometimes strikingly beautiful and an emotional outlet is afforded in fields which are very close to the lives of the students.

Psychology of the Practical Arts

Training in particular skills of the practical arts is a highly technical matter and differs with each skill. The transfer values are small and any reliance upon them as significant learning aids will, in most instances, prove useless. Specialization in industry forces upon the school a different type of procedure than existed before the currently high degree of specialization developed.

Psychological Factors. Society as a whole is interested in all the practical arts, but actual production of economic goods must always depend upon specialized skills. One of these skills usually has little relation to another; therefore, the secondary school student should be given the opportunity to explore many of them before choosing one or more of the fields for more intensive study. Thus, the specialized technical skills will be mastered only by those students who are interested in a particular industrial function.

Specialization in practical skills also involves social cooperation. The child lives in a world filled with tools and becomes as familiar with them and their use as he does with other natural objects. Changes are constantly being made in instruments and inventions. This necessitates change in the individual's skill if efficiency of performance is to be achieved. Although these changes are small for any one year, over a five- or ten-year period they become sizable. The important consideration is that each change necessitates the development of new skills.

The psychological effect of specialization on an individual has not been determined. There is perhaps no more narrowing effect than are habits formed through the utilization of the same thought processes, or the same expression, used over and over by the individual. Any narrowing effect depends upon the degree of mastery, upon the purpose of the specialization, and whether or not the individual is a user of the mechanism or is engaged in its construction. A superior kind of intelligence is required for the latter. It is much simpler to develop skills which are required to function only in the operation or use of mechanisms.

Educational Approaches. The child observes his elders use tools and as his muscles become developed to the stage of manipulation, he, too, desires to engage in this same procedure. He watches carefully the function performed; he asks questions concerning it; he takes hold of the tools; at first opportunity, he endeavors to imitate the activity which he has just observed. He soon discovers that his efforts are crude, and that a great difference exists between what he has produced by his own efforts and what the adult has created. His muscles are not yet ready to make the precise adjustments. However, as the nervous system develops, the child's muscles do perform the right elements of movement in a gradual process of development. Meager perception also limits his ability to perform at a high level of perfection.

If the student is dissatisfied with his own efforts he may be so motivated that he is inspired to further trial. If he is given guidance in discrimination during this trial procedure, adequate habits and skills will be more easily produced. The process of acquiring skills is a complex series of adjustments in which imitation, imagination, and trial movements eventually cooperate in the development of selected habits.

A skill is more easily developed if there is a desire on the part of the student to acquire that skill. It also is helpful if this interest persists beyond the first stages of mere excitement and early attempts at performance. Dynamic motivating elements are required for effective skill development in the school. The steps in the process should be carefully graded to insure success and to hold the interest of the student sufficiently so that he will continue his practice.

To meet the needs of industrial arts courses requires teachers who are trained in skills and in theory, if the student is to secure the desirable values from the subjects. The student also needs help in learning to appreciate standards of excellence. When the skills are taught in conjunction with good theory, and with the opportunity to develop usable constructions, the student usually makes more satisfactory progress than otherwise.

Psychology of Health and Physical Education

Education in the areas of health and physical education is concerned with preserving the physical and mental health of the individual. It involves prudent exercise, an understanding of body structure and functions, proper diet, and factors of emotional balance. A close relationship exists between a person's physical condition and his habitual attitudes and behavior, and unhygienic living is more likely than not to result in serious maladjustments of an individual.

Nature has provided a form of protection for muscles being used in an activity. When there is overactivity, wastes are accumulated faster than they can be carried away by the body system, and the condition of physical fatigue results. This condition inhibits the transmission of nerve stimulation, and under ordinary circumstances, the individual is obliged to rest the affected muscles. Mental fatigue is produced in the same way as physical fatigue; excessive activity of the nerve cells causes wastes to pile up more rapidly than they are carried away by the blood stream. Speed of reaction and accuracy are affected adversely, and a greater irritability results from a condition of nerve fatigue.

Modern civilization places many demands upon the human body which were not faced by primitive man. High industrial specialization demands that adjustments be made to meet these new conditions. When activity is changed, even for recreational purposes, the body is confronted with the problem of making adjustments and balances. Education can help the individual learn to make adequate adjustments to meet the pressures of daily living. Play is used for the purpose of maintaining an internal harmony, thereby insuring the desired physical competence. The school should help the student achieve a scientific understanding of the laws affecting the body conditions.

Psychology of Home Economics

In the secondary school home economics is an elective course. It may be chosen (1) as an aid to homemaking, (2) as a preparatory course for further study on the college level, (3) as an aid in personal living, and (4) as a recommended prerequisite for nurses' training. Because of these different aims the material and methods of the course must be organized to meet the respective purposes.

Home economics is no longer a glorified course in cooking. In the first year emphasis may be placed on the skill factor when the course includes such practical needs as cooking of the simpler foods, the routine of housekeeping, and the like. The young student usually enjoys doing these things. As the course progresses, greater emphasis is placed upon the why and wherefore of good homemaking, with the major emphasis on such topics as food values, balanced diets, special cooking, and principles of nutrition, along with the household chemistry necessary for an understanding of these principles. The advanced course also will give the growing adolescent an opportunity to develop artistic interests by providing instruction in the fundamentals of home planning and decorating, choosing attractive and economical clothing, and related fields.

In elementary courses, home economics should deal with activities carried on in the student's everyday life, with a view to developing good habits related to the home and society; but in advanced courses, home economics should deal with the more abstract, more scientific, and more artistic phases of the subject. Throughout the course, the aim should be successful doing resulting from intelligent understanding.

Psychology of Commercial Education

As in other subjects, for successful teaching of commercial subjects the methods of instruction must be adapted to the learning capacity and experiencing capacity of the pupils. The lessons should be assigned by topics. Many of these topics may be suggested by the pupils, and this class participation helps keep the instruction within the life experience of the pupils. Trips to factories, offices, and other agencies of the community will provide first-hand observation of commercial skills in use. Businessmen may be called in to acquaint the students with the practical aspects of the business world. Since the commercial field includes many types of activities, it is desirable that the different abilities and interests of the pupils be taken into account and the classwork planned to provide for these differences.

In general, the teacher should use techniques and procedures which have been found valuable in other fields of learning. Too much emphasis upon exact details of procedure without an accompanying understanding of the reasons and values for these procedures must be avoided to prevent an over-dependence of the student upon the teacher. Rather, intelligent initiative on the part of the student should be encouraged.

Although teachers need to help students understand and appreciate the values of items taught, and although effective methods designed to arouse the interest of pupils should be used, it must be remembered that in subjects such as the commercial arts, drill will always be necessary for the acquisition of skill. Such drill, however, should be assigned through the students' desire for improvement rather than as a mere formal requirement. Success in the complex activities of modern business requires not only automatic skills but also initiative and the ability to cope with new and sometimes difficult situations.

Psychology of Bookkeeping. A mastery of bookkeeping requires trained accuracy, mathematical ability, and extreme care and neatness. As the students recognize the range of possibilities in this field and have their interest aroused by pertinent problems, they are likely themselves to recognize the need for the development of these qualities.

It is essential that the student understand each step in the bookkeeping process before he advances further. In this way, he may progress easily and intelligently, and will not be thrown into the kind of hopeless confusion which often is the result when too much is attempted at one time.

Psychology of Stenography. It is now recognized that the learning of stenography is as difficult as the learning of a foreign language. The psychological factors involved in the mastery of this subject have much in common with those involved in the mastery of another tongue. For this reason, stenography should not be taken as a substitute course by a student who has failed in a number of the regular academic subjects.

Aside from the intelligence required for success in stenography, the student needs special eye, ear, and muscle training. Some students will need charts to aid them in visualization, some will need to repeat the sounds aloud when copying, and others will need help with their motor responses.

Such factors as spacing, lining, timing, speed, and understanding of words and symbols are important factors in the mastery of shorthand. The stenographic symbols must be mastered through motivated drill, and these drills must be so planned as to vary the habit-forming repetitions. It is important when learning shorthand to be able to focus on intermediate goals. Well-spaced brief periods of practice, with frequent reviews, are indispensable. Students should be called upon to write, and to read from plates as well as from their notes, with emphasis upon speed and accuracy. The drill should be so thorough that the writing of the outlines becomes automatic, that is, the student should make it a part of his reacting mechanism without taxing his memory for rules. The teacher should gradually progress from easy to more difficult dictation with increasing attention on speed. Correctness of outline of symbols should be required of the students at all times.

In giving dictation, the teacher must be careful to pronounce the words correctly in order to enable the student to obtain a clear image of each word. The student must understand all of the sounds, including inflections, if he is to be successful in the learning of stenography.

Psychology of Typewriting. Typewriting is an excellent example of the idea that the most efficient learning is a combination of thinking and doing. For best results, students should be provided with desks that are suitable in height, and the same make of typewriter should be used by the various beginning classes. Also, the single period of practice is to be preferred over the double period, particularly if the entire class is kept working at maximum capacity during the period. All students should strive to master technical skill in operating the machine, accuracy in its use, and the mechanics of writing the language.

Drill is to be used but care needs to be exercised in setting up drill situations. Usually special drill on a large number of selected words will prove fruitful. Although perfection is the goal, too much emphasis should not be placed upon accuracy at the start of the course, since discouragement and confusion may result. A list of words might well be kept by each student for added practice as needed. In the case of words which are generally missed, however, better results may be obtained by giving these words in context rather than singly. Classes in which accuracy is stressed usually acquire greater speed and accuracy than do those classes in which speed is given the major consideration.

From the beginning, the student should be given sentences or a paragraph to type in order to become familiar with those combinations which he later will need for accurate speed typewriting. As the training progresses, the assignments should include increasingly difficult units and actual business material such as letters and reports.

Psychology of Other Commercial Subjects. Commercial correspondence, commercial geography, commercial law, junior business training, salesmanship, and advertising are important subjects in commercial education and, in general, should be taught on the basis of attention to the individual and his interest. These phases of commercial education should be linked to local and contemporary business problems.

The students should have practical material in their assignments. Hypothetical situations, although more easily constructed, lack the interest-arousing factors which will lead the students to exert their best efforts. Success of instruction in office practice and other business subjects depends largely upon the resourcefulness of the teacher who is planning the course.

BIBLIOGRAPHY

Introduction: The Science of Educational Psychology

American Educational Research Association. *Methodology of Educational Research.* Washington, D. C.: National Education Association, 1966.
Bayles, Ernest E., and Hood, B. L. *Growth of American Educational Thought and Practice.* New York: Harper & Row, 1966.
Gage, N. L., ed. *Handbook of Research on Teaching.* Chicago: Rand McNally & Co., 1963.
Hilgard, E. R., ed. *Theories of Learning.* (Sixty-Third Yearbook of the National Society for the Study of Education, Part I.) Chicago: University of Chicago Press, 1964.
Hillway, Tyrus. *Handbook of Educational Research.* Boston: Houghton Mifflin Co., 1968.
Nielsen, H. *Methods of Natural Science.* Englewood Cliffs, N. J.: Prentice-Hall, 1967.
Sax, G. *Empirical Foundations of Educational Research.* Englewood Cliffs, N. J.: Prentice-Hall, 1967.
Wise, John E., et al. *Methods of Research in Education.* Boston: D. C. Heath & Co., 1967.

Part One: Human Equipment and Behavior

Chapter 1. Heredity and Environment

Darlington, C. D. *Genetics and Man.* New York: Macmillan Co., 1964.
Dobzhansky, Theodosius. *Heredity and the Nature of Man.* New York: Harcourt, Brace & World, 1964.
Flavell, J. H. *The Developmental Psychology of Jean Piaget.* New York: D. Van Nostrand Co., 1963.
Gesell, A. *Studies in Child Development.* New York: Harper and Brothers, 1948.
Mussen, P. H. *Handbook of Research Methods in Child Development.* New York: John Wiley & Sons, 1960.

Scheinfeld, Amram. *Your Heredity and Environment.* Philadelphia: J. B. Lippincott Co., 1965.
Stevenson, H., ed. *Child Psychology.* (Sixty-Second Yearbook of the National Society for the Study of Education, Part I.) Chicago: University of Chicago Press, 1963.
Winchester, A. M. *Heredity: An Introduction to Genetics.* 2nd ed. New York: Barnes & Noble, 1966.

Chapter 2. Physical Structure

Cannon, Walter B. *Wisdom of the Body.* Rev. ed. New York: W. W. Norton & Co., 1963.
Davis, H., and Silverman, S. R., eds. *Hearing and Deafness.* Rev. ed. New York: Holt, Rinehart & Winston, 1960.
Hurlock, E. B. *Developmental Psychology.* 3rd ed. New York: McGraw-Hill Book Co., 1968.
Lashley, K. S. *Neuropsychology of Lashley.* Edited by F. Beach and others. New York: McGraw-Hill Book Co., 1960.
Tokay, Elbert. *Fundamentals of Physiology.* Rev. ed. New York: Barnes & Noble, 1968,.
Turner, C. Donnell. *General Endocrinology.* 4th ed. Philadelphia: W. B. Saunders Co., 1966.

Chapter 3. Human Growth and Development

Cole, L., and Hall, Irma N. *Psychology of Adolescence.* 6th ed. New York: Holt, Rinehart & Winston, 1964.
Flavell, J. H. *The Developmental Psychology of Jean Piaget.* New York: D. Van Nostrand Co., 1963.
Garrison, Karl C., et al. *Psychology of Childhood.* New York: Charles Scribner's Sons, 1967.
Gesell, A., and Ilg, F. L. *Child Development.* New York: Harper & Row, 1949.
Hilgard, E. T., ed. *Theories of Learning.* (Sixty-Third Yearbook of the National Society for the Study of Education, Part I.) Chicago: University of Chicago Press, 1964.
McGraw, M. B. *The Neuromuscular Maturation of the Human Infant.* New York: Hafner Publishing Co., 1945.
Sarason, S., et al. *Anxiety in Elementary School Children.* New York: John Wiley & Sons, 1960.
Stevenson, H., ed. *Child Psychology.* (Sixty-Second Yearbook of the National Society for the Study of Education, Part I.) Chicago: University of Chicago Press, 1963.

Chapter 4. Behavior Processes

Brussel, James A. *The Layman's Guide to Psychiatry.* 2nd ed. New York: Barnes & Noble, 1967.
Coville, Walter J.; Costello, Timothy W.; and Rouke, Fabian L. *Abnormal Psychology.* New York: Barnes & Noble, 1960.
Festinger, L. *Conflict, Decision, and Dissonance.* Stanford: Stanford University Press, 1964.
Freud, S. *Outline of Psychoanalysis.* Translated and edited by James Strachey. New York: W. W. Norton Co., 1949.
Stevenson, H., ed. *Child Psychology.* (Sixty-Second Yearbook of the National Society for the Study of Education, Part I.) Chicago: University of Chicago Press, 1963.
White, R. W. *The Abnormal Personality.* 3rd ed. New York: Ronald Press, 1964.

Part Two: The Learning Process

Chapter 5. Nature and Scope of the Learning Process

Bigge, M., and Hunt, M. P. *Psychological Foundations of Education.* 2nd ed. New York: Harper & Row, 1968.
Bruner, J.; Goodman, J.; and Austin, G. *A Study of Thinking.* New York: John Wiley & Sons, 1962.
Burton, W. H. *Guidance of Learning Activities.* 3rd ed. New York: Appleton-Century-Crofts, 1952.
Crow, L. D., and Crow, A. *Human Development and Learning.* Rev. ed. New York: American Book Co., 1965.
Dewey, John. *How We Think.* Boston: D. C. Heath & Co., 1933.
Hilgard, E. R., ed. *Theories of Learning* (Sixty-Third Yearbook of the National Society for the Study of Education, Part I.) Chicago: University of Chicago Press, 1964.
Hill, W. F. *Learning: A Survey of Psychological Interpretations.* San Francisco: Chandler Publishing Co., 1968.
Hunt, E. B. *Concept Learning: An Information Processing Problem.* New York: John Wiley & Sons, 1962.
Keller, F. S. *Learning: Reinforcement Theory.* New York: Random House, 1954.
Köhler, W. *Gestalt Psychology.* 2nd ed. New York: Liveright Publishing Corp., 1947.
Thorndike, E. L. *Psychology and the Science of Education: Selected Papers of Edward L. Thorndike.* New York: Columbia University Press, 1962.

Wertheimer, Max. *Productive Thinking.* Rev. ed. by Michael Wertheimer. New York: Harper & Row, 1959.

Chapter 6. Factors That Condition Learning

Ausubel, D. P. *The Psychology of Meaningful Verbal Learning.* New York: Grune & Stratton, 1963.
Ellington, Careth. *The Shadow Children.* New York: Taplinger Publishing Co., 1967.
Hilgard, E. R., ed. *Theories of Learning.* (Sixty-Third Yearbook of the National Society for the Study of Education, Part I.) Chicago: University of Chicago Press, 1964.
Hill, W. F. *Learning: A Survey of Psychological Interpretations.* San Francisco: Chandler Publishing Co., 1968.
Keller, F. S. *Learning: Reinforcement Theory.* New York: Random House, 1954.
McGeoch, J. A., and Irion, A. L. *Psychology of Human Learning.* 2nd ed. New York: David McKay Co., 1958.
Skinner, B. F. *Verbal Behavior.* New York: Appleton-Century-Crofts, 1957.
Travers, J. F. *Learning: Analysis and Application.* New York: David McKay Co., 1965.
Weinland, J. D. *How to Improve Your Memory.* New York: Barnes & Noble, 1957.

Chapter 7. Laws and Theories of Learning

Green, E. J. *The Learning Process and Programed Instruction.* New York: Holt, Rinehart & Winston, 1962.
Hilgard, E. R., ed. *Theories of Learning.* (Sixty-Third Yearbook of the National Society for the Study of Education, Part I.) Chicago: University of Chicago Press, 1964.
Hilgard, E. R., and Marquis, D. *Conditioning and Learning.* 2nd ed. Edited by Gregory Kimble. New York: Appleton-Century-Crofts, 1960.
Köhler, W. *Selected Papers of Wolfgang Köhler.* Edited by S. E. Asch and M. Henle. New York: Liveright Publishing Corp., 1968.
Skinner, B. F. *The Technology of Teaching.* New York: Appleton-Century-Crofts, 1968.
Thorndike, E. L. *Psychology and the Science of Education: Selected Papers of Edward L. Thorndike.* Edited by G. Joncich. New York: Columbia University Press, 1962.
Wertheimer, Max. *Productive Thinking.* Rev. ed. by Michael Wertheimer. New York: Harper & Row, 1959.

Chapter 8. Transfer of Training: Subject Matter

Dewey, John. *How We Think*. Boston: D. C. Heath & Co., 1933.
Gagne, R. M. "Learning of Concepts." *School Review*, 73 (Autumn, 1965): 187–96.
Kilpatrick, W. H. *Montessori System Examined*. (Riverside Ed. Monographs.) Boston: Houghton Mifflin Co., 1914.
Köhler, W. *Selected Papers of Wolfgang Köhler*. Edited by S. E. Asch and M. Henle. New York: Liveright Publishing Corp., 1968.
Meierhenny, W. C. "New Significance of Learning Theory." *Educational Screen*, 645 (January, 1966): 22–23.
Montessori, Maria M. *The Montessori Method*. New York: Schocken Books, 1964.
Thorndike, E. L. *Psychology and the Science of Education: Selected Papers of Edward L. Thorndike*. Edited by G. Joncich. New York: Columbia University Press, 1962.
Torrance, E. P. *Mental Health and Constructive Behavior*. Belmont, Calif.: Wadsworth Publishing Co., 1965.
Wertheimer, Max. *Productive Thinking*. Rev. ed. by Michael Wertheimer. New York: Harper & Row, 1959.

Part Three: Tests and Measurements

Chapter 9. Measurement—Basic Definitions and Principles

Chauncey, H., and Dobbin, J. E. *Testing: Its Place in Education Today*. New York: Harper & Row, 1964.
Davis, F. B. *Educational Measurements and their Interpretation*. Belmont, Calif.: Wadsworth Publishing Co., 1964.
Durost, W. N., and Prescott, G. A. *Essentials of Measurement for Teachers*. New York: Harcourt, Brace & World, 1962.
Ebel, R. L. *Measuring Educational Achievement*. Englewood Cliffs, N. J.: Prentice-Hall, 1965.
Freeman, F. S. *Theory and Practice of Psychological Testing*. 3rd ed. New York: Holt, Rinehart & Winston, 1962.
Gerberich, J. R.; Green, H. A.; and Jorgenson, A. N. *Measurement and Evaluation in the Modern School*. New York: David McKay Co., 1962.
Lindeman, R. H. *Educational Measurement*. Chicago: Scott, Foresman & Co., 1967.
Thomas, R. Murray. *Judging Student Progress*. 2nd ed. New York: David McKay Co., 1960.

Chapter 10. Applications of Measurement

Adams, Georgia S., and Torgerson, T. L. *Measurement and Evaluation in Education, Psychology, and Guidance.* New York: Holt, Rinehart & Winston, 1964.

Adkins, Dorothy C. *Test Construction.* Columbus, Ohio: Charles E. Merrill Publishing Co., 1960.

Garrett, Henry E. *Testing for Teachers.* 2nd ed. New York: American Book Co., 1965.

Green, John A., Jr. *Teacher-made Tests.* New York: Harper & Row, 1963.

Lindvall, C. M. *Measuring Pupil Achievement and Aptitude.* New York: Harcourt, Brace & World, 1967.

Mehrens, W. A., and Ebel, R. L. *Principles of Educational and Psychological Measurement: A Book of Selected Readings.* Chicago: Rand McNally & Co., 1967.

Noll, Victor H. *Introduction to Educational Measurement.* 2nd ed. Boston: Houghton Mifflin Co., 1965.

Nunnally, J. C. *Educational Measurement and Evaluation.* New York: McGraw-Hill Book Co., 1964.

Remmers, H. H., et al. *Practical Introduction to Measurement and Evaluation.* 2nd ed. New York: Harper & Row, 1965.

Smith, Fred M., and Adams, S. *Educational Measurement for the Classroom Teacher.* New York: Harper & Row, 1966.

Thorndike, Robert L., and Hagen, Elizabeth. *Measurement and Evaluation in Psychology and Education.* 3rd ed. New York: John Wiley & Sons, 1969.

Tyler, Leona E. *Tests and Measurements.* Englewood Cliffs, N. J.: Prentice-Hall, 1963.

Chapter 11. Elements of Statistical Techniques

Bartz, A. E. *Elementary Statistical Methods for Educational Measurements.* Minneapolis: Burgess Publishing Co., 1963.

Edwards, Allen L. *Statistical Methods.* 2nd ed. New York: Holt, Rinehart & Winston, 1967.

Garrett, H. E. *Statistics in Psychology and Education.* 6th ed. New York: David McKay Co., 1966.

Guilford, J. P. *Fundamental Statistics in Psychology and Education.* 4th ed. New York: McGraw-Hill Book Co., 1965.

Lyman, H. B. *Test Scores and What They Mean.* Englewood Cliffs, N. J.: Prentice-Hall, 1963.

McIntosh, Douglas M. *Statistics for the Teacher.* 2nd ed. New York: Pergamon Press, 1963.

Manuel, H. T. *Elementary Statistics for Teachers*. New York: American Book Co., 1962.
Nelson, M. J.; Denny, E. C.; and Coladarci, A. P. *Statistics for Teachers*. Rev. ed. New York: Holt, Rinehart & Winston, 1956.
Popham, W. James. *Educational Statistics: Use and Interpretation*. New York: Harper & Row, 1967.
Tate, M. W. *Statistics in Education and Psychology*. New York: Macmillan Co., 1965.
Thorndike, Robert L., and Hagen, Elizabeth. *Measurement and Evaluation in Psychology and Education*. 3rd ed. New York: John Wiley & Sons, 1969.

Part Four: Mental Health and Character Education

Chapter 12. Mental Health

Bernard, H. W. *Psychology of Learning and Teaching*. 2nd ed. New York: McGraw-Hill Book Co., 1965.
Brussel, James A. *The Layman's Guide to Psychiatry*. 2nd ed. New York: Barnes & Noble, 1967.
Cattell, R. B. *Psychodynamics and Personality*. Boston: Houghton Mifflin Co., 1969.
Coville, Walter J.; Costello, Timothy W.; and Rouke, Fabian L. *Abnormal Psychology*. New York: Barnes & Noble, 1960.
Dinkmeyer, D. C. *Child Development: The Emerging Self*. Englewood Cliffs, N. J.: Prentice-Hall, 1965.
Hamachek, D. E. *Self in Growth, Teaching, and Learning: Selected Readings*. Englewood Cliffs, N. J.: Prentice-Hall, 1965.
Logan, L. M. *Teaching the Young Child*. Boston: Houghton Mifflin Co., 1960.
McKinney, Fred. *Understanding Personality*. Boston: Houghton Mifflin Co., 1965.
Rogers, C. R. *On Becoming a Person*. Boston: Houghton Mifflin Co., 1961.
Sears, P. S., and Sherman, V. S. *In Pursuit of Self-Esteem*. Belmont, Calif.: Wadsworth Publishing Co., 1964.
Skinner, B. F. *The Technology of Teaching*. New York: Appleton-Century-Crofts, 1968.
Torrance, E. P., and Strom, R. D. *Mental Health and Achievement: Increasing Potential and Reducing School Dropout*. New York: John Wiley & Sons, 1965.
Townsend, E. A., and Burke, P. J. *Learning for Teachers*. New York: Macmillan Co., 1962.
Wallach, M. A., and Kogan, N. *Modes of Thinking in Young Children*. New York: Holt, Rinehart & Winston, 1965.

Chapter 13. Psychology of Character

Davidson, R. F. *Philosophies Men Live By.* New York: Holt, Rinehart & Winston, 1952.
Geoghegan, B., Sr.; Pollard, M. P.; and Kelly, W. A. *Developmental Psychology.* Milwaukee: Bruce Publishing Co., 1963.
Gesell, A., et al. *Youth: The Years from Ten to Sixteen.* New York: Harper & Row, 1956.
Glueck, S., and Glueck, E. *Family Environment and Delinquency.* Boston: Houghton Mifflin Co., 1962.
Gross, C. H.; Wronski, S. P.; and Hanson, J. W. *School and Society: Readings in the Social and Philosophical Foundations of Education.* Boston: D. C. Heath & Co., 1962.
Havighurst, R. J. *Education in Metropolitan Areas.* Boston: Allyn & Bacon, 1967.
Jourard, S. M. *Personal Adjustment.* 2nd ed. New York: Macmillan Co., 1963.
Mays, J. B. *Education and the Urban Child.* New York: Harcourt, Brace & World, 1962.
Piaget, J. *The Moral Judgment of the Child.* New York: Free Press, 1956.
Price, K. *Education and Philosophical Thought.* 2nd ed. Boston: Allyn & Bacon, 1962.
Raths, L. E., et al. *Teaching for Thinking: Theory and Application.* Columbus, Ohio: Charles E. Merrill Publishing Co., 1967.

Part Five: The Psychology of School Subjects

Chapter 14. Psychology of Elementary School Subjects

General

Burton, W. H. *Guidance of Learning Activities.* 3rd ed. New York: Appleton-Century-Crofts, 1963.
Crow, L. D., and Crow, A. *Human Development and Learning.* Rev. ed. New York: American Book Co., 1965.
Crow, L. D., and Crow, A. *Child Development and Adjustment.* New York: Macmillan Co., 1962.
Crow, L. D., and Crow A. *The Student Teacher in the Elementary School.* New York: David McKay Co., 1965.
Husbands, K. L. *Teaching Elementary School Subjects.* New York: Ronald Press, 1961.
Kinder, J. S. *Using Audio-Visual Materials in Education.* New York: American Book Co., 1965.

Klausmeier, H. J., and Dresden, K. *Teaching in the Elementary School.* 2nd ed. New York: Harper & Row, 1962.
McKim, H. G.; Hansen, G. W.; and Carter, W. L. *Learning to Teach in the Elementary School.* New York: Macmillan Co., 1959.
Meeker, A. M. *Teachers at Work in the Elementary School.* Indianapolis: Bobbs-Merrill Co., 1963.
Mehl, Marie A., et al. *Teaching in Elementary School.* 3rd ed. New York: Ronald Press, 1965.
Skinner, B. F. *The Technology of Teaching.* New York: Appleton-Century-Crofts, 1968.

Art
Erdt, M. H. *Teaching Art in the Elementary School.* Rev. ed. New York: Holt, Rinehart & Winston, 1962.
Merritt, H. *Guiding Free Expression in Children's Art.* New York: Holt, Rinehart & Winston, 1965.

Health Education
Vannier, M. *Teaching Health in Elementary Schools.* New York: Harper & Row, 1963.
Vannier, M., and Foster, M. *Teaching Physical Education in Elementary Schools.* 4th ed. Philadelphia: W. B. Saunders Co., 1968.

Language Arts, Reading, Spelling, Handwriting
Anderson, P. S. *Language Skills in Elementary Education.* New York: Macmillan Co., 1964.
Barbe, W. B., ed. *Teaching Reading: Selected Materials.* New York: Oxford University Press, 1965.
Botel, M., et al. *Spelling and Writing Patterns.* Chicago: Follett Publishing Co., 1963.
Brogan, P., and Fox, L. K. *Helping Children Read.* New York: Holt, Rinehart & Winston, 1961.
Crow, L. D.; Murray, W. I.; and Bloom, I. *Teaching Language Arts in the Elementary School.* Dubuque, Iowa: William C. Brown Co., 1968.
Eisenson, J., and Ogilvie, M. *Speech Correction in the Schools.* 2nd ed. New York: Macmillan Co., 1963.
Gans, R. *Common Sense in Teaching Reading.* Indianapolis: Bobbs-Merrill Co., 1963.
Gray, W. S. *On Their Own in Reading: How to Give Children Independence in Attacking New Words.* Rev. ed. Chicago: Scott, Foresman & Co., 1960.
Hildreth, G. *Teaching Spelling.* New York: Holt, Rinehart & Winston, 1955.
McKim, M. *Guiding Growth in Reading in the Modern Elementary School.* 2nd ed. New York: Macmillan Co., 1963.
Petty, W. T. *Improving Your Spelling Program.* San Francisco: Chandler Publishing Co., 1959.

Robinson, K. F., and Kerikas, E. J. *Teaching Speech: Methods and Materials.* New York: David McKay Co., 1963.
Russell, D. H. *Children Learn to Read.* 2nd ed. New York: Blaisdell Publishing Co., 1961.
Shane, H., et al. *Improving Language Arts Instruction in the Elementary School.* Columbus, Ohio: Charles E. Merrill Co., 1962.
Smith, N. B. *Reading Instruction for Today's Children.* Englewood Cliffs, N. J.: Prentice-Hall, 1963.
Stern, Catherine, and Gould, T. S. *Children Discover Reading.* New York: Random House, 1965.
Strickland, R. G. *The Language Arts in the Elementary School.* 2nd ed. Boston: D. C. Heath & Co., 1957.
Trauger, W. K. *Language Arts in Elementary Schools.* New York: McGraw-Hill Book Co., 1963.
Veatch, J. *Reading in the Elementary School.* New York: Ronald Press, 1966.

Mathematics

Corle, C. G. *Teaching Mathematics in the Elementary School.* New York: Ronald Press, 1964.
Dwight, L. A. *Modern Mathematics for the Elementary Teacher.* New York: Holt, Rinehart & Winston, 1966.
Grossnickle, F. E., and Brueckner, L. J. *Discovering Meanings in Elementary School Mathematics.* 4th ed. New York: Holt, Rinehart & Winston, 1963.
Kramer, K. *The Teaching of Elementary School Mathematics.* Boston: Allyn & Bacon, 1966.
Rappaport, D. *Understanding and Teaching Elementary Mathematics.* New York: John Wiley & Sons, 1966.
Spitzer, H. F. *Teaching Elementary School Mathematics.* Boston: Houghton Mifflin Co., 1967.

Music

Hartsell, O. W. *Teaching Music in the Elementary School.* Washington, D. C.: Association for Supervision and Curriculum Development, 1963.
Karolyi, O. *Introducing Music.* New York: Penguin Books, 1965.
Myers, L. K. *Teaching Children Music in the Elementary School.* 3rd ed. Englewood Cliffs, N. J.: Prentice-Hall, 1961.
Pierce, A. E. *Teaching Music in the Elementary School.* New York: Holt, Rinehart & Winston, 1959.
Winslow, R. W., and Dallin, L. *Music Skills for Classroom Teachers.* Dubuque, Iowa: W. C. Brown Co., 1964.

Science

Arey, C. K. *Science Experiences for Elementary Schools.* Rev. ed. New York: Teachers College, 1962.

Hone, E. B., et al. *Teaching Elementary Science.* Edited by Paul F. Brandwein. New York: Harcourt, Brace & World, 1962.
Kambly, P. E., and Suttle, J. E. *Teaching Elementary School Science.* New York: Ronald Press, 1963.

Social Studies

Michaelis, J. U. *Social Studies for Children in a Democracy.* 3rd ed. Englewood Cliffs, N. J.: Prentice-Hall, 1963.
Preston, R. C. *Teaching Social Studies in the Elementary School.* Rev. ed. New York: Holt, Rinehart & Winston, 1968.
Wesley, E. B., and Cartwright, W. H. *Teaching Social Studies in Elementary Schools.* Rev. ed. Boston: D. C. Heath & Co., 1968.

Chapter 15. Psychology of Subject Areas in the Secondary School

Alberty, H. B., and Alberty, E. J. *Reorganizing the High-School Curriculum.* 3rd ed. New York: Macmillan Co., 1962.
Alcorn, M. D., et al. *Better Teaching in the Secondary School.* Rev. ed. New York: Holt, Rinehart & Winston, 1964.
Bent, R. K., and Kronenberg, H. H. *Principles of Secondary Education.* 5th ed. New York: McGraw-Hill Book Co., 1966.
Clark, L. H., and Starr, I. S. *Secondary School Teaching Methods.* 2nd ed. New York: Macmillan Co., 1967.
Cole, L., and Hall, I. N. *Psychology of Adolescence.* 6th ed. New York: Holt, Rinehart & Winston, 1964.
Crow, L. D., and Crow, A. *Adolescent Development and Adjustment.* 2nd ed. New York: McGraw-Hill Book Co., 1965.
Crow, L. D., and Crow, A. *The Student Teacher in the Secondary School.* New York: David McKay Co., 1964.
Douglass, H. R. *The High School Curriculum.* 3rd ed. New York: Ronald Press, 1964.
Drayer, A. M. *Problems and Methods in High School Teaching.* Boston: D. C. Heath & Co., 1963.
Green, E. J. *The Learning Process and Programmed Instruction.* New York: Holt, Rinehart & Winston, 1962.
Hall, O., and Pallucci, B. *Teaching Home Economics.* New York: John Wiley & Sons, 1961.
Huebener, Theodore. *Audio-Visual Techniques in Teaching Foreign Languages.* Rev. ed. New York: New York University Press, 1960.
Hunt, M. P., and Metcalf, L. E. *Teaching High School Social Studies.* 2nd ed. New York: Harper & Row, 1968.
Hurlock, E. B. *Adolescent Development.* 3rd ed. New York: McGraw-Hill Book Co., 1966.
Inlow, G. M. *Maturity in High School Teaching.* Englewood Cliffs, N. J.: Prentice-Hall, 1963.

Jersild, A. T. *Psychology of Adolescence.* 2nd ed. New York: Macmillan Co., 1963.
Joseph, A., *et al. Teaching High School Science.* New York: Harcourt, Brace & World, 1961.
Kenworthy, L. S. *Guide to Social Studies Teaching in Secondary Schools.* 2nd ed. Belmont, Calif.: Wadsworth Publishing Co., 1966.
Lee, J. M. *Principles and Methods of Secondary Education.* New York: McGraw-Hill Book Co., 1963.
McLendon, J. C. *Social Studies in Secondary Education.* New York: Macmillan Co., 1965.
Risk, T. M. *Principles and Practices of Teaching in Secondary Schools.* 3rd ed. New York: American Book Co., 1958.
Rivlin, H. N. *Teaching Adolescents in Secondary Schools.* 2nd ed. New York: Appleton-Century-Crofts, 1962.
Silvius, G. H., and Curry, E. H. *Teaching Successfully the Industrial Arts and Vocational Subjects.* Rev. ed. Bloomington: McKnight and McKnight, 1959.
Tonne, H. A., *et al. Methods of Teaching Business Subjects.* 3rd ed. New York: McGraw-Hill Book Co., 1965.
Traxler, A. E. *Techniques of Guidance.* 3rd ed. New York: Harper & Row, 1966.
Vannier, M., and Fait, H. *Teaching Physical Education in Secondary Schools.* 3rd ed. Philadelphia: W. B. Saunders Co., 1968.

Index

ability grouping, 152-54
abnormal psychology, 11
achievement quotient (A.Q.), 84, 116
achievement tests, 156, 167
activity programs, 79, 83
adjustment, methods of, 232-34
Adler, Alfred, 8, 16
adolescence, 45, 49-51
adolescent drives, 268-69
adrenal glands, 43
afferent nerves, 40
age and learning, 51-53, 91
aggression, 228-29, 231
alcohol, 91
algebra, 271
alternate-response test, 174-76
altruism, 237
ambiverts, 65
Ames, Adelbert, Jr., 9
Anastasi, Anne, 23
anecdotal records, 13
Angell, James R., 7, 15
anxiety, 63, 234
apperception, 74, 89, 114
appreciation, 75, 76, 125
aptitude tests, 157
Aristotle, 3
arithmetical mean, 195
art, elementary school, psychology of, 266-67
 educational approaches, 267
 psychological factors, 266-67
art, secondary school, psychology of, 282-83
assigned values, 142
assimilation, law of, 103
association, laws of, 99-100
associative learning, 75, 81
associative shifting, law of, 103
atmospheric conditions, 91
attitude, law of, 103
attitudes, measurment of, 148-49, 155
attributes, 142
audio-visual aids in learning, 133-34
audition, 37-39
auditory defects, 38
Augustine, Saint, faculty theory of, 3, 5
autoinstruction, 134-36
autonomic nervous system, 40-41
average, 195
average deviation, 207
Ayres handwriting scale, 160, 255

Bacon, Francis, 119

Bagley, W. C., 125, 129
bar diagram, 200-2
behavior adjustment, methods, of, 64-67
behaviorist psychology, 15, 48, 58, 71, 72, 76, 100, 106
behavior processes, 57
belongingness, 72, 102, 106
Binet, Alfred, 7
Binet test, 155, 158, 160, 161
blame, 85
blindness, 36-37
block diagram, 199-200
bond, 102
bookkeeping, psychology of, 287-88
boredom, 90, 91
brain, 40, 41
Bruner, J. S., 84
Bryan and Harter's study of learning curves, 114-15

caffeine, 91
Cannon, W. B., 8, 61
Cannon-Dana theory of emotions, 61
case studies, 13
Cattell, James M., 7, 159
cells, 21
central nervous system, 40-41
cerebellum, 41
cerebrum, 41
character development, 238-40
character traits, 235-38
childhood, 45, 48-49
child psychology, 11
chromosomes, 22
chronological age (C.A.), 166
classification of pupils, 152-54
coefficient of correlation, 213
cognition, 78, 82
color blindness, 35
Comenius, John Amos, 133
commercial education, psychology of, 287-89
compensation, 66, 229
completion test, 173-74
comprehension in reading, 249
conception, 74-75
concepts, 74-75, 78
concomitant learnings, 76, 80-81
conditioned response theory, 71, 72, 100, 108-12
conflict, 228, 231
conformity, 235-36
connectionism, 71, 72, 75-76, 106

connection levels, 41
connectors, 40–42
conscientiousness, 237
contiguity, law of, 99, 100
contrast, law of, 99
controlled-response test, 172
correlation, 25–28, 212–20
correlation chart, 204
cortex, 41–42, 61
co-twin control, 54
cramming, 95–96
creativity, 56, 63–64, 106
Crowder, N. A., 136
cultural deprivation, 55
curves of growth, 48–49
curves of learning, 112–16

Darwin, 6
daydreaming, 65
deafness, 39
deciles, 190–92
dependent variable, 12
deviation, measures of, 206–11
Dewey, John, 7, 10, 15, 79, 130, 131
diagnostic tests, 151, 156–57, 168–71
diagrams, construction of, 199–206
disadvantaged pupils, 17, 55
discipline, 240
dot diagram, 199–200
drill in learning, 80, 82
drive, 84
drugs, 31, 91
Dugdale, R. L., 24

ear, structure of, 37–38
Ebbinghaus, Hermann, 7, 95, 159
educational age (E.A.), 167
educational psychology
    approaches to, 15–16
    contributions of, 16–17
    methods of research in, 11–14
    principles of research in, 14
    scope of, 10–11
    subject matter of, 14–15
educational quotient (E.Q.), 167
effect, law of, 72, 88, 102, 105, 107–8
effectors, 42–44
efferent nerves, 40
electroencephalograph, 61
emotions, 60–64
    effect on behavior, 62
    effect on learning, 63–64
    expressions of, 61–62
    modifications of, 62–63
    theories of, 60–61
emulation, 230–31
endocrine glands, 43
environment and heredity, 21–30
equilibration, 32
essay test, 172–73
evaluation, 141, 152, 156
exercise, law of, 72, 102, 104
exocrine glands, 43
experimentation, 12–13
extrinsic motivation, 85
extroversion, 64–65

eye, 32–36
    color blindness, 35
    defects of, 35–38
    dominance, 35
    evolution of, 33
    focusing of, 33
    movements of, 34–35
    muscle adjustments of, 33–34
    sensations and interpretations, 34–35
    structure of, 32–33

faculty theory of psychology, 3, 5, 117–19
family history method, 24–25
fantasy, 230
Farrand, Livingston, 7, 159
fatigue, 90–91
fear, 43, 61, 62–63, 112, 227, 234
fine arts, psychology of, 281–83
flexibility, 237
foreign language, psychology of, 52, 81–82, 275–76
forgetting, 95
formal discipline, 117, 118, 119–20
fraternal twins, 26–27
Freeman, F. N., 26, 29
free-response test, 172–73
frequency, law of, 99, 107
frequency distribution, grouped, 186–87
frequency distribution, ungrouped, 183–86
frequency polygon, 202–3
frequency table, 183–84
Freud, Sigmund, 9, 16, 23, 47–48, 64
friendliness, 236
Froebel, Friedrich, 5, 131–32
frustration, 231
functionalists, 15–16

Galton, Francis, 6, 24, 25
general intelligence tests, 151
generalization, 74–75, 78–79, 82
generalization of experience theory of transfer, 122, 123–24, 126
genes, 22
geometry, 270–71
Gesell, Arnold, 10, 26, 29, 46–47, 54, 59
Gestalt psychology, 8, 16, 58, 71, 73, 76, 100, 106, 111–12, 115, 125–26
glands, 43–44
Goddard, H. H., 24, 25
grade score, 167
grading, 163, 173
graphic art, psychology of, 282–83
grouped frequency table, 186–87
grouping of pupils, 152–54
group-interval, defined, 182–83
group test, 158
growth, 45–56

habits, 115
Hall, G. Stanley, 6
handwriting, psychology of, 253–55
    developmental patterns in, 254
    educational approaches to, 255
    importance of perception in, 254

Index

lefthandedness, 255
hard of hearing, the, 39
Hartshorne and May, *Studies in Deceit*, 237
health education, elementary school, psychology of, 263-64
health education, secondary school, psychology of, 285-86
hearing defects, 38
Herbart, Johann Friedrich, 5, 74, 82, 97
heredity, 21-30
heterosexuality, 50
hierarchy of habits, 115
histogram, 200-2
Hollingworth, 49, 58
home economics, psychology of, 286
homogeneous grouping, 153
homosexuality, 50
honesty, 236-37
hormic psychology, 9, 16
human growth, 45-56
    effects of retardation in, 56
    motor development in infancy, 46-47
    stages of, 45-46
    training in, 53-55
Hurlock, 85

ideal, definition of, 75
identical elements theory of transfer, 122, 123, 126
identical twins, 26-27, 54
identification, 66, 230-31
imitation, 77, 81, 82
incentive, 84
incidental learning, 80
independent variable, 12
individual differences, 15, 30, 116, 136, 152, 154, 168, 246, 251, 272
individual test, 158
infancy, 46-48
    behavior patterns in, 57-59
    language development in, 47
    motor development in, 46-47
inferiority feeling, 66
inheritance of traits, 23-28, 58
    correlation method of studying, 25-26
    family background in, 28
    family history method of studying, 24-25
insight, 71, 73, 77
intelligence
    definition of, 116
    environmental influences on, 28-29
    family background in, 28
    growth of, 51-53, 55
intelligence quotient (I.Q.), 26, 27, 28, 29, 30, 166-67, 168
intelligence tests, 155-56, 166-67
interest, intrinsic, 84-85
interpolation procedures, 189-93
interval scale, 143
interviews, 13
intrinsic motivation, 84-85
introspection, 11-12
introspectionist psychology, 15
introversion, 65

James, William, 7, 60, 61, 120
James-Lange theory of emotions, 60-61
Janet, Pierre, 8
Jersild, A. T, 54-55
Judd, C. H., 87, 122
Jukes family, 24
Jung, C. G., 8, 16

Kallikak family, 24-25
Karpman, Ben, 236
Kilpatrick, W. H., 79, 80
kinaesthesis, 32
knowledge of progress, 87
Koffka, Kurt, 8, 16
Köhler, Wolfgang, 8, 125
Korsakoff psychosis, 98
Kraepelin, Emil, 7-8

Lange, Carl, 60
language acquisition, 81-82
language arts, elementary school, psychology of, 244-47
    educational approaches, 246-47
    factors affecting ability, 245-46
language arts, secondary school, psychology of, 272-75
    educational approaches, 274-75
    psychological factors of, 272-74
Latin, 123
laws of association, 99-100
laws of learning, 72, 101-16
learning
    defined, 71, 83
    effect of age on, 91-92
    effect of atmospheric conditions on, 91
    effect of drugs on, 91
    effect of organic defects on, 89-90
    effect of time of day on, 91
    environmental factors in, 93
    factors that condition, 83-84
    goals in, 73-74
    laws of, 72, 101-16
    logical method of approach, 129-30
    methods in, 75, 93-97, 129-31
    physiological factor in, 89-92
    physiological limit in, 116
    psychological factor in, 84-89
    psychological method of approach, 129-30
    selection and arrangement of material in, 129-37
    speed of, in relation to retention, 96
    theories of, 71-73, 75-76
    types of, 76-82
learning ability, 51-53, 116
learning curves, 112-16
    limitations of, 112-13
    types of, 113-14
    uses of curves, 114-15
lefthandedness, 254-55
lesson planning, 81
Leuba, 86
Lewin, Kurt, 8
lie detector, 62, 155
Lindsley, D. B., 61

localization in cerebrum, 41-42
Locke, John, 4
logical memory, 99
LSD, 31

McCall, William A., 141
McDougall, William, 9, 16
Maller's studies of rivalry, 86
manipulation, 59, 60
marks, 88, 163, 173
matching test, 177-78
mathematics, elementary school, psychology of, 255-59
  educational approaches, 258-59
  psychological factors in, 256-58
mathematics, secondary school, psychology of, 269-72
  educational approaches, 271-72
  psychological factors, 270-71
maturity, 45-56, 51
mean, 194-99
mean deviation, 207-9
measure
  accuracy of, 142, 145
  approximate, 142
  continuous, 144
  defined, 142
  of deviation, 206-11
  direct, 142
  exact, 142
  indirect, 142
  interpretation of, 181
  precise, 142
  ranking of, 187-89
  reliability of, 144-45
  usability of, 145
  validity of, 145
measurements
  characteristics of good, 144-45
  defined, 141
  standardization of, 149-50
median, 194
mediating method of learning, 94
memory, 97-100
Mendel, Gregor, 22
Mendelian ratio, 22
mental age (M.A.), 166
mental fatigue, 90
mental health, 227-34
mental retardation, 25
mental traits, difficulties of measuring, 146-49
method in learning, 129-31
Meumann, Ernst, 7
minor laws of learning, 102-3
mnemonic devices, 98
mode, 149
models in learning, 77
monocular vision, 34
monohybrid cross, 22
Montessori, Maria, 131-32
moral stability, 237-38
Morgan, Lloyd, 14
motivation, 79, 84-89, 151-52
  extrinsic, 85
  intrinsic, 84-85

psychological basis of, 88
multiple-choice test, 176-77
multiple response, law of, 102-3
multiple sense appeal, 89
muscles, 42-43
music, elementary school, psychology of, 264-66
  educational approaches, 265-66
  psychological factors, 265
music, secondary school, psychology of, 282

natural sciences, psychology of, 279-81
  educational approaches, 280-81
  psychological factors, 279-80
neonatal period, 45
nerves, 40
nervous system, 40-41, 90
neuron, 40, 41, 103
nominal scale, 143
non-verbal test, 158
norm, 150
normal curve, 220-22

observation, 13, 76-77
ogive, 203-4
operant conditioning, 110
oral test, 172
ordered series, 182
ordinal scale, 143
ordinary rank, 188
organismic theory, 111
overlearning, 95

paired-associates test, 177-78
paramnesia, 98
parsimony, law of, 14
partial activity, law of, 103
partial vision, 36
Pavlov, Ivan P., 8, 109, 110
Pearson, Karl, 8, 24, 25
Pearson product-moment method, 214
percentile curve, 203
percentile rank, 188-89
percept, 75
perception, 9, 74, 76-77, 89
performance test, 158
peripheral nervous system, 40
personality, 232-40
Pestalozzi, Johann Heinrich, 5
physical defects, 31, 35, 38, 39, 43, 44, 89, 90
physical education, psychology of, 285-86
physical growth in childhood, 48-49
physical structure, 31
Piaget, Jean, 46
piecemeal research, principle of, 14
pitch, 37-38
plateaus, 114-15
Plato, 2, 118
play activities, 233-34
power test, 159
practical arts, psychology of, 283-85
practice periods, 95
praise, 85

Pressey, S. L., 10, 135
primary learnings, 80–81
probability, principle of, 14, 220–23
probable error, 223
problem solving, 79–80, 81, 82
procedure values, 124, 125
prognostic tests, 157
programed learning, 10, 57, 134–36
Progressive Education Movement, 10
projection, 230
project method, 79, 83
psychoanalysts, 9, 16
psychological atomism, 106
psychology, defined, 10–11
puberty, 45
punishment, 86

quartile deviation, 207
quartiles, 192
questionnaires, 13

race relations, 17
Radosavljevich, Paul R., 7, 95
random samples, 149–50
rank, 187–89, 213–14
ranked series, 182
rationalization, 66–67, 229–30
ratio scale, 143
readiness, law of, 72, 97, 102, 107
reading, psychology of, 247–51
  comprehension and speed, 249
  educational approaches, 249–51
  factors involved in, 248
  types of, 248
  as visual exploration, 248–49
reasoning, 79–80
recall, 98
recency, law of, 99
receptors, 32–39, 40
recitation method of learning, 94–95
recognition, 98
reflex acts, 41
reflexes, 58
regression, 232
reinforcement principle, 88, 105, 135
reliability of measurements, 144–45
religion, 51
repetition (exercise), 72, 102, 104
repression, 231
retarded children, 17, 25, 56
retention, 98
retroactive inhibition, 96–97
rewards, 86
Riessman, F., 55
rivalry, 86
root mean square deviation, 209
Rousseau, 5

samples, 149–50
scaled series, 182
scales, 142–44
scatter diagram, 204–6
science, elementary school, psychology of, 261–63
  educational approaches, 262–63
  psychological factors, 262

science, secondary school, psychology of, 279–81
scientific method, 2–4, 14, 120, 128, 129
senses, 32
series, defined, 181–82
sexual development, 50, 65
short-answer test, 173–74
siblings, 27
similarity, law of, 99
Simon, Theodore, 7
skewed curves, 221
skill, 75
Skinner, B. F., 9, 10, 110, 135
Smith, M. E., 47
social approval, desire for, 87
social distance scale, 148
social psychology, 11
social sciences, secondary school, psychology of, 276–79
  educational approaches, 278–79
  psychological factors, 277–78
social studies, elementary school, psychology of, 259–61
  educational approaches, 260–61
  psychological factors, 259–60
sound sensations, 37–38
Spearman rank method, 213
speech, 47, 59–60, 245–47
speed of learning, 96
spelling, psychology of, 251–53
  difficulties within words, 252–53
  discovery and correction of errors, 253
  educational approaches, 252–53
  factors affecting spelling ability, 251–52
spontaneity, 236
Stacey, C. L, 87
standard deviation, 209–11
standard error, 222
standardized tests, 163, 166–68
standard score, 212
statistics, 13, 14, 181
stenography, psychology of, 288
stimulus-response formula, 72, 108–12
structuralists, 15
study, methods of, 93–97
sublimation, 65, 231–32
synapse, 40
synaptic resistance theory, 104–5

teacher-made tests, 171–79
teaching machines, 134
television, educational, 133
Terman, Lewis, 9, 29, 55, 160
test battery, 159
test development, history of, 159–61
testing
  attitudes toward, 162–64
  frequency of, 179
  preparation for, 164–66
tests
  applications of, 162–80
  purposes of, 150–54
  types of, 154–59
theories of learning, 101–16

Index

Thorndike, Edward L, 8, 26, 52, 71, 72, 100, 106, 122, 160
Thorndike's laws of learning, 101-3, 107-8
thyroid gland, 44
Titchener, Edward B, 7, 15
tobacco, 91
totality theory, 111
trace reflex, 109
transfer of training, 117-37
trial-and-success learning, 76, 77-78
true-false test, 174-76
twins, 26-27, 54
typewriting, psychology of, 288-89

uniformity of nature, principle of, 14
unit-interval, defined, 182
universality, principle of, 14
universe, defined, 149
usability of measurements, 145

validity of measurements, 145
variables, 12, 142
verbal rehearsal, 77
verbal test, 158
visceral sensitivity, 32
vision, 32-37
visual arts in learning, 133-34
visual defects, 35-36
vividness, law of, 99
vocabulary, 47, 245-46
vocalization, 47, 59-60

Watson, John B, 8, 15, 62, 71, 72
Wertheimer, Max, 8, 16
Winchester, 26
whole to part method of learning, 94
whole versus part method of learning, 94
Wundt, Wilhelm, 6, 7